Why the SOUTH
Will Survive

Why the SOUTH

Will Survive

by Fifteen Southerners

THE UNIVERSITY OF GEORGIA PRESS / Athens

© 1981 by the University of Georgia Press
Athens, Georgia 30602
www.ugapress.org
All rights reserved
Designed by Design for Publishing
Set in Trump Mediaeval type
Printed digitally in the United States of America

The Library of Congress has cataloged the hardcover edition
of this book as follows:

Why the South will survive / by fifteen Southerners.
229 p. ; 24 cm.

ISBN 0-8203-0565-0
ISBN 0-8203-0566-9 (pbk.)
I. Title.
Southern States—Civilization—20th century.
F216.2 .W49
975'.043—dc19   81-1313

Paperback reissue 2012
ISBN-13: 978-0-8203-3989-4
ISBN-10: 0-8203-3989-X

Contents

IV. A MIRROR FOR ARTISTS

V. REMARKS ON THE SOUTHERN RELIGION

Acknowledgments

James B. Meriwether, McClintock Distinguished Professor of Southern Letters and founder of the Southern Studies Program at the University of South Carolina, provided indispensable aid and encouragement for this symposium in its early stages, as he has for so many others. Without his help, tangible and intangible, it might not have reached maturity. During a meeting of the contributors in Columbia in August, 1979, Professor Elisabeth S. Muhlenfeld of Florida State University asked questions and made comments that were of great value in the shaping of these essays. Dr. Robert Buffington, General Editor of the University of Georgia Press, took time away from his important work on Allen Tate to give aid and encouragement. Most of all, we thank Cleanth Brooks for his participation and Andrew Lytle for contributing his reflections on the half century anniversary of *I'll Take My Stand* and on the essays herein.

CLYDE N. WILSON

Introduction

Should the South Survive?

CLYDE N. WILSON

OF THE MAKING of books about the South there is no end. This one differs from most in at least one respect—its unembarrassed embrace of the notion that the South is a national asset, a priceless and irreplaceable treasure that must be conserved.

The particular group of people gathered between these covers to support and elucidate this audacious contention is occasional. All are friends, or friends of friends, of the person privileged to compose this prefatory statement. I freely admit that many other writers of equal or superior merit might have been called upon, or even an entirely different group assembled for this purpose. When word got around, informally, that a manifesto of Southern pride was contemplated, to coincide with the fiftieth anniversary of the publication of *I'll Take My Stand*, the outpouring of interest and sympathy was surprisingly large, certainly large enough to indicate that the proposal struck a hidden vein of public feeling. Like the Confederacy in its first year, we had more volunteers than we could well make use of.

We will no doubt be subject to charges of presumption in claiming to speak for the South and to commemorate definitively *I'll Take My Stand*. Our excuse lies in the fact that we undertook to satisfy a widely felt need at a time when it seemed that no one else was prepared to come forward. The contributors include a mixture of established scholars and writers, young scholars and writers, and men from public life. They include persons who disagree on many things and who vote three different ways in any one election, although the majority would not, perhaps, be uncomfortable with the label "conservative." The mixture is deliberate; among other things, it serves to illustrate the breadth of thoughtful allegiance to the South that exists today, a loyalty that nowhere else has been, we feel, adequately described and defended.

Unlike most books about the South, this one is not designed primarily to analyze, to criticize, or to deplore it. While some analysis, some criticism, and some lamentation are contained herein, our primary objective is to affirm. Richard M. Weaver, an apostle of the Nashville Agrarians to the Northern intelligentsia, remarked that *I'll Take My Stand* was controversial—"controversial" being a journalistic label for a book that is concerned with values. If he was correct, then this book is also controversial. The essays that follow affirm values, many of them unfashionable. Indeed, in my opinion, the South has always been primarily a matter of values, a peculiar repository of intangible qualities in a society peculiarly preoccupied with the quantifiable. This description of the South explains to my satisfaction why some have not believed in its reality; why others, though convinced of its existence, have been baffled to define it; and why still others have found it endlessly absorbing and problematic.

The writers herein, widely dispersed and collaborators only for this occasion, lay no collective claim to the distinction, eloquence, and prophetic power of the Agrarians of a half-century ago. Even had we been as gifted as they, we have not enjoyed their opportunities for enrichment and refinement of ideas by regular mutual interchange. Yet the degree to which the individual essays herein converge, often in totally unexpected ways—given the different trainings, temperaments, and perspectives brought to bear—has surprised us all, and has provided additional evidence of the fundamental nature of our identity as Southerners.

In mitigation of our presumption to speak in the tradition of the authors of *I'll Take My Stand*, we present in evidence our willingness to pay them the homage of taking seriously what they had to say—which cannot be said of some who have sought to praise or imitate them. For the social implications of *I'll Take My Stand*, at least by repute and in some circles, have been evaded by rendering them abstract or by dwelling on the subsequent literary fame of the participants. Fortunately, their book is there to read, and its self-evident burden is clear. They declared that they loved the South; that they wanted to keep the South in many respects as it was; that, if it had to change, they wanted that change to be one of preservation and adaptation, rather than an abandonment of historic distinction.

Those writers loved the South because it was theirs. So do we. But, more than this, they valued its differentness and intransigence as exemplary. Southerners, they were also a part of a larger society which seemed to them to be in parlous health. Western civilization in 1929 and 1930 was like a sick man, sinking fast and surrounded by a gaggle of sharpers hawking patented nostrums, some of which were as likely to kill as to cure the patient, and none of which offered much hope of reaching his fundamental malignancy. The task they had undertaken, of revitalizing the Southern tradition, suggested itself to them as having considerable relevance to the larger world's ills.

The Agrarians saw that the choices commonly presented in their times realized neither the best of American traditions nor the best of American opportunities. It was obvious to them, as it certainly was not widely obvious to the "informed" public at the time, that Calvin Coolidge, H. L. Mencken, and Eugene Debs did not subsume all or even the best part of the American heritage. Not only was it important to them to defend and preserve the South; it was equally important that the South had something to say to a troubled nation, a nation that was not talking straight to itself and that had forgotten too much. This interpretation of the import of the Agrarian manifesto of 1930 is borne out by the semi-centennial reflections which have been generously contributed by Andrew Lytle and which are included as an afterword to this volume. Mr. Lytle's concern is still the progressive disintegration of the Western social fabric and the relevance of the Southern inheritance to that problem.

The social fragmentation and demoralization that the Agrarians sought to combat have become much more evident and menacing since their work was published, increasing their status as prophets, heralded if unheeded. American society (all the Western world, perhaps) is in even worse condition today than it was fifty years ago. And the diagnoses that receive the most attention and allegiance are still as destructive, irrelevant, or superficial as they were then.

It may as well be said straight out, though many will greet the statement with hostility, derision, or incomprehension: One of the implications running through this book is that the South is, or ought to be, of compelling interest to that thoughtful minority concerned with conserving what is left of Christianity and Western civilization. The book is full of suggestions and illustrations of why and how we think that in the providential inheritance of the South are embedded certain factors highly relevant to the nourishing of religion, manners, family life, politics in the high sense, the arts, and the whole fabric of humane culture that makes for a satisfactory existence. The writers in this book do not claim, any more than did the Agrarians, that these qualities belong exclusively to the South. But they believe, as the Agrarians did, that in the modern world the South relates to such qualities in a special way; that the South has been uniquely resistant to fragmentation and alienation; that the South, not through virtue but through good fortune, maintains a uniquely primary identification with things American and an unpremeditated and unself-conscious relationship with some of the ancient values of Western civilization that are increasingly attenuated elsewhere.

The writers who follow, each in his own way and in an assigned sphere, attempt to come to honest terms with certain questions. Does that intangible reality, the American South—older than the United States, more extensive in territory and more considerable in historic and cultural import than many of the separate nations of the earth—still enjoy a distinctive existence? Is it likely to continue to do so, given the apparently overwhelming tendency of modern societies toward what our forefathers decried as "consolidation"? Does the South deserve to survive? And the underlying question, which gives this book its title and its relationship to *I'll Take My Stand*: What are the implications of the South's survival or non-survival for the larger American Republic?

The calm and positive tone of the answers given to these questions is remarkable. There is no rancor and defensiveness, no raking over of old controversies, no self-indulgent and evasive nostalgia. Southerners have long known how to be good losers; the writers herein have set an example of being good winners. They have carefully observed M. E. Bradford's admonition, in the concluding essay, that they refrain from giving the Yankees hell for having run the country into the ground and content themselves with doing what they can to save the situation.

In "The Same Old Stand?" John Shelton Reed, a talented writer and social commentator who doubles as professor of sociology at the University of North Carolina at Chapel Hill, investigates the transformation and the persistence of Southernness, particularly as exemplified by the average Southerner—no longer a man in the field, but a man in the street—as he enters the 1980s. Reed's observations are, as always, original, solidly based on objective observations, and optimistic as to the continued refusal of the ordinary Southerner to be "modernized"—at least as "modernization" is experienced in less fortunate lands.

William C. Havard, a distinguished student of Southern political thought and phenomena and chairman of the department of political science at Vanderbilt University, follows Reed with personal re-flections upon the multiple aspects of Southern distinctiveness and how these have been thrown unexpectedly into relief and vitality by developments in the nation at large. He finds this distinctiveness, on the whole, of increasing value.

Fred Hobson, associate professor of English at the University of Alabama, describes himself as a moderate Southern liberal pleased with many of the changes that have overtaken the South in the past few decades. Yet he is no more willing to accept a world minus Southern distinctiveness than are his colleagues. A South leveled to the American norm, a South without its vestiges of aristocratic grace and populist perversity, will be a land more truly impoverished than econometricians are able to measure. Hobson challenges Southerners to prosper and progress without falling into the form-less middle.

Hamilton C. Horton, Jr., an attorney and businessman, is by avo-cation and experience intimately acquainted with the present con-dition of Southern agriculture. He has been the leader of his party in the North Carolina General Assembly, state dairy commissioner, and administrative assistant to a United States senator. Horton ar-gues convincingly that the South has had a considerable degree of success in effecting a humane synthesis of traditional ways and in-dustrialization, in that accepting of industry, but with a bad grace, that John Crowe Ransom recommended in *I'll Take My Stand*. He also warns that we continue to fail to be adequate stewards of the land. Throughout his essay, Horton keeps the focus properly on "The Enduring Soil" and its meaning for the Southerner.

Don Anderson approaches the rural South from another perspec-tive. An attorney and former United States congressional staff mem-ber who is active as a director of self-help programs among the rural black poor, he presents a unique but vivid and perhaps increasingly exemplary view of a black Virginian's return to his roots and his at-tempt to give new life and new context to the time-honored tradi-tions of Jeffersonian democracy.

George C. Rogers, Jr., a noted historian of South Carolina and pro-fessor at the university of that state, also concentrates upon the con-tinued relevance of certain Southern political and constitutional traditions and proclivities. He affirms that not only are these still of value, but their *national* restoration is desperately needed, particu-larly the awareness of the relationship between individual character and sound political institutions.

In "Foreign Policy and the South," Samuel T. Francis, a young Tennessean who works as a national security analyst in Washington, D.C., begins with the famous analysis of C. Vann Woodward in regard to the Southern deviance from the American norm and expands it into some original and startling observations regarding the Southern contribution (sometimes for the worse, possibly for the better) to America's position in the world. His observations were made prior to the Shermanesque offenses to international civility in Iran and Afghanistan, in which light they appear even more original.

Thomas Fleming, a classicist and private school headmaster in South Carolina, reminds us that Southerners of another day foresaw and attempted to forestall the educational debacle that has overtaken American society. Educators closed their minds to the warnings of John Gould Fletcher in *I'll Take My Stand* fifty years ago, just as they had failed to heed his precursors in the nineteenth century. But the alternatives Fletcher proposed are still viable, even at this late date, Fleming asserts. With admirably controlled understatement he reminds us of the rage we should feel at the desecration which has been inflicted upon the ancient calling of learning, and also of the inescapable relation of true learning to the survival of the South.

George Garrett, an accomplished novelist, poet, and teacher of writing, begins a discussion of "Southern Literature Here and Now" by reference to Alexander Solzhenitsyn's strictures on the oppressive conformity of the Western press. His essay is reminiscent of the great Russian himself in preference for truth over fashion, in moral indignation, and in love of homeland. Garrett is righteously outraged at the colonialization of Southern writers, generously complimentary in his tribute to their accomplishments in the face of adverse conditions, and serenely confident that Southern literature remains and will continue to be both Southern and important.

Another branch of Southern literature, the "country music" that has recently taken the world by storm, is examined in its origins and its ultimate appeal by David B. Sentelle. Lawyer, judge, and local official, Sentelle appears here as the purveyor of memory, based upon his own upbringing in the mountains of North Carolina. Taking the Southerner and his music without apology or equivocation, he vividly evokes the experiences out of which that music came and which it celebrates.

In "A Note on the Origin of Southern Ways," Thomas H. Landess, chairman of the department of English at the University of Dallas, throws into arresting and original perspective the interrelatedness of Southern manners, family life, and literature, and the ultimate dependence of all three on the South's purchase upon Christian orthodoxy. His exploration of these matters should be of interest to all students of the South and to all persons concerned with the weakening position of Christianity in American society today.

Marion Montgomery, poet, novelist, and professor of English at the University of Georgia, approaches the peculiarly Southern hold upon ancient ways of feeling and living from another direction. He also sees Southern religion, literature, and common life as a seamless whole, and goes on to show that "regionalist" resistance to modernity in the South is based upon the same "piety toward creation" that informs Alexander Solzhenitsyn's resistance to the totalitarian materialist state.

Cleanth Brooks, Gray Professor of Rhetoric Emeritus at Yale University and one of the most distinguished literary scholars and critics yet produced in America, returns to the subject he took up more than four decades ago in *Who Owns America?*—the condition of religion. While the South's religious stance is flawed by the lack of a sufficient theology, the region has retained an amazing freedom from the Puritan heresies that have decimated Protestantism elsewhere. The South remains, Professor Brooks tells us, the best foundation for Christianity to build upon in this country. Without undue optimism but with the courage to hope, he reminds us that, while the hour is late, all is not yet lost.

Of course, there are many important aspects of the South today, and of its relation to the nation, that these essays have not touched upon at all or have only hinted at. We will be content if we are able to play a part in bringing about the discussion that these issues demand.

Many objections will undoubtedly be raised to this book, a number of which we can anticipate. It will be said that we have made a great to-do about "the South" without bothering to define what we mean by the term. I reply that it is not necessary, for our purposes, to engage in the parlor game of defining the South. The South is all around us. It has arrested the attention of countless observers. Hundreds of presumably rational persons spread around the globe are devoting their lives to studying its history, culture, and current condition. It has provided a compelling means of self-identification for millions of people over many generations. Not only has it been meaningful to Southerners; in addition, it has attracted many sympathizers from outside its borders (wherever they be drawn) and continues to do so at this moment. The South is as real and as amenable to discussion as are France, Hollywood, poetry, capitalism, astronomy, or corn.

It is not necessary for the reader to agree with me in order for us to participate in a useful exchange of ideas, but I would define the South as an inherited way of life, expressed in a number of cultural and personality characteristics that are spontaneously shared, to a greater or lesser degree, by a substantial number of inhabitants of the United States. This way of life correlates with a particular history and geography but has an independent existence.

Nowhere in *I'll Take My Stand* will one find a precisely drawn-up definition of the South. The South was taken in the terms in which I have defined it. Though the Agrarians' discussion was somewhat focused on the economic crisis of their time, at bottom those writers were concerned with ways of life, with how men might live so as to best realize the potential of their existence. The answer, they said, was already given in the South. It did not have to be invented; it had only to be recognized, participated in, and preserved.

Another common objection will be that the South is not really all that different. Perhaps it never was (so the argument runs), but if so, it certainly no longer is, or soon will cease to be. Those who believe this are evidently not looking in the same places as the writers of these essays, which are full of observations tending to disprove the objection. The essays may be full of admissions that the South has changed, but they reject the hidden premise that all change is inevitably toward some presumed American norm. Such an inaccurate expectation of reality is related to the kind of self-deluding expectations that Americans bring to other countries; it also contains a fallacious assumption that there is a stable American norm toward which the Southern people are or should be approximating themselves. The fact is that American society outside the South has changed in recent decades so rapidly and in so many critical ways that the South is becoming more, rather than less, different.

It is even possible that "the South," thought by many to be a myth or a product of peculiar circumstances, doomed eventually to merge into the American mass, may prove in the long run more able to survive change without losing its identity than can America at large. Indeed, the Southerner may be justified in wondering whether there is any *American* culture anymore, whether America is anything other than a collection of people sharing a common territory, government, and standard of living, but otherwise having no identity. This is to overstate the case, but the misgiving is a genuine one.

The most serious charge we anticipate is that of divisiveness. But divisiveness is a matter of perspective, of whose ox is being divided, and for what purpose. The belief that Southerners become more American by becoming less Southern is and always has been both false and imperialistic. Rather, the contrary is true: it is doubtful whether Southerners can be American without first being Southern. The periods during which Southerners have been most American—when they have taken part in national life most positively and with least reservation, have made their greatest contributions to the nation, have indeed often been at the forefront of national life—have been exactly those periods when they have been permitted to be Southern, those times when they were not forced to arrange their fundamental allegiances into hierarchies.

The cry against divisiveness is most likely to be raised by those who profit from the status quo. Many elements have vested interests—economic, political, cultural, psychological—in a subservient South. But why should a society supposedly dedicated to pluralism exclude from respectability and self-determination, as it normally has heretofore, its largest, most important, and oldest minority?

When an American turns to the South, it is often to a South of his own imagining, tailored to his own needs, rather than to the real South. Hard as it may be for many of today's intellectuals to believe, there was a time when the South was considered the natural home and mainstay of American liberalism; more lately the South has been courted by the conservatives. The truth is that the expectations of both have been colonialist. At certain times the various poles of mainstream America have united to execrate the South; at other times each group has based its strategy and hopes upon the South. Each has its Southern heroes and Southern demons. Both have tended to find in the South what they wanted or needed at a particular moment, a convenient ally or a ready-made scapegoat. They have, in other words, felt free to range through the South as though it were a conquered province, and to take what they liked without feeling any obligation to take the whole.

In contradistinction, Southerners have always known and have sometimes successfully maintained that true Union is a process of consent, not of conquest. The true friends of Union are those who willingly collaborate while frankly recognizing and cherishing their differences. It is the effort to wipe out differences that is properly defined as divisiveness. A respect for differences flows naturally from that "piety toward creation" which is explicitly or implicitly a part of all the essays which follow. Its opposite flows from the same sources as does tyranny.

For better or worse, the South's fate is identified with that of the Union. Those mellow Southern voices and slow Southern ways, that unpragmatic and unprogrammed preference for chivalry, personality, and piety, that sense of life as a drama and duty rather than a business—all those characteristics which from time to time have driven other Americans to frenzy and malice—are an inextricable part of American history, and doubtless will continue to be.

"Nobody now proposes for the South," declared the Twelve Southerners in 1930, "or for any other community in this country, an independent political destiny. . . . But how far shall the South surrender its moral, social, and economic autonomy to the victorious principle of Union? That question remains open."

What, then, should Southerners do with that moral, social, and economic autonomy that they are entitled to exercise within the Union? In the final essay, M. E. Bradford of the University of Dallas, one of the most eloquent and energetic disciples of Agrarianism, calls upon Southerners to embark upon calculated resistance to standardization and anonymity, to cherish and cultivate—deliberately, individually, and vigorously—their "obdurate particularity." In so doing, he maintains, they will be serving themselves, America, civilization, and posterity.

Such a program presents a challenge of great magnitude. But I suspect that this challenge is already being met by many in their own places and ways, with or without deliberate recognition of what they are about. At any rate, such a challenge should not be too great for a people who have seen the reduction of a lawless frontier to order and prosperity, who have experienced defeat in war and failure of cherished hopes, who have suffered unstinting scorn, unrelenting poverty and toil, and recalcitrant problems of human relationships without defeat of spirit. Southerners have learned not to depend upon utopian visions of an accommodating future, not to insist upon easy solutions and happy endings.

Our Southern people are still stubbornly themselves in ways that need telling about, in ways that need understanding, in ways that need preserving. Aside from a religious vocation, preserving and enhancing a people's way of life is as worthy an enterprise for civilized men and women as may be imagined. That is the affirmative business of the essays which follow. Their affirmation is a modest one, a cautious one, not made at anyone else's expense. Nevertheless, it *is* an affirmation: The South exists. It ought to exist. If Southerners can be brought to acknowledge that "ought," then it undoubtedly will not only endure but prevail.

I

RECONSTRUCTED BUT

UNREGENERATE

The Same Old Stand?

John Shelton Reed

WHEN THE SOUTHERN AGRARIANS took their stand, they did it stoutly, on two feet. Some emphasized the "Southern," others the "Agrarian," but fifty years ago it seemed that the two loyalties, to the South and to rural life, could (indeed, pretty well had to) go together.

Today that juxtaposition is less self-evidently sensible. If ever a society can be said to have repudiated agrarianism, the South, to all appearances, has done so. Two-thirds of all Southerners now are "urban," by Census Bureau standards; of the rural one-third, only a fraction are employed in agriculture; and of those a good many are proprietors or hands in "agribusiness"—an expression that some of the Agrarians blessedly did not live to encounter.

It is still possible to combine an affection for the South with an appreciation of the virtues and strengths of the family farm and rural life, but someone who is not prepared to exclude most residents of the South from the category "Southerner" must recognize that it is no longer a matter of defending a "Southern way of life" against industrialism. Increasingly, that way of life *is* industrialism.

Many feel, of course, that neither the South nor agrarianism has much to be said for it. To hell with them. But even those who find *I'll Take My Stand* pretty much right-headed on both counts must choose, in a single essay, which leg to stand on.

Whether the Agrarians' ideas on the proper relation between work and leisure, on the importance of humanizing scale, on respect for nature, on autonomy and self-respect—whether those ideas can be translated into an urban and industrial context is an important question, and one, I believe, not yet answered. That side of the

Agrarian argument may be more appealing now than it was fifty years ago. We are hearing versions of it from such unlikely quarters as the governor of California and *Mother Jones* magazine. While it does seem to be better received in Vermont and Colorado than in the South, at least it is alive and well *somewhere*.

It seems to me that those arguments can pretty well take care of themselves. What needs to be reasserted is the other half of the Agrarian position, the case for provincialism—in particular, the case for the South. What is now unusual about *I'll Take My Stand* is less the "small is beautiful" motif than its unshakeable affection for the South; less the insistence that the South has something to offer the rest of the country as an exemplar of an agrarian civilization than the assumption that the South has something to offer Southerners. Some of the Agrarians valued the South because they believed it embodied their social ideals; most, I suspect, cherished it because it was home.

Why do Southerners, most of us, love the South? Why should we? In these times, those questions might be rephrased as: What *good* is it? Is the South any different, anymore, from the rest of the United States? If so, what differences are likely to remain, and what good are *they*?

Let me proceed in the approved Southern manner, with a lengthy anecdote about a particular individual, which, despite appearances, does have a point. This story is set in Cambridge, Massachusetts, in the early 1960s, and concerns a young Tennessean, an undergraduate at the Massachusetts Institute of Technology. At that time, Cambridge was not a comfortable place to be a Southerner. To this young man, it seemed that his Southernness, which he had never thought much about, was often being thrust upon him. After a few months he began to understand that, however unimportant his origins seemed to him, they were an important datum for others, a marker they used to orient themselves to him, at least at first. The more ill mannered of his Northern acquaintances made it clear that they saw him as a curious specimen of some sort; a few, at least, saw his Southernness as *the* salient fact about him, overriding all others. About the seventeenth time he was held personally responsible for Little Rock and Clinton (places he'd only heard of) and for Scottsboro and Gastonia (places he hadn't heard of), the novelty began to wear off.

He found that other Southern boys were going through the same sort of thing, and they used to joke about the bottomless ignorance and boundless credulity of their New York and New England friends.

Many of these folks, whether smugly self-righteous or innocently curious, would apparently believe *anything at all* about the South, provided only that it was weird. (Some years later he discovered that William Faulkner said very much the same thing.) When he ran out of true stories to entertain his Yankee friends, he was not above talking about things he knew of only at second hand—swamps and alligators, foot washing and snake handling, moonshining and stock-car racing. When he found a truly gullible listener, sometimes he really laid it on. (For years he remembered with embarrassment a somewhat drunken account of darkies dancing down Main Street on Robert E. Lee's birthday.) The only excuse for his behavior was that he was eager to please, and he had discovered that a Southerner who denied that there was anything particularly interesting about the South ran into almost palpable disappointment, if not the suspicion that he was hiding something.

Some of his friends were more aggressive. One, an Arkansas boy, took to telling Radcliffe girls (who invariably asked) that race relations back home were just fine, that blacks were now allowed out until ten o'clock at night, midnight on Saturday. His friends from less notorious Southern states made allowances for his exasperation.

The result of all this was that Southerners in Cambridge at that time almost *had* to think about the South. Even the most deracinated began to wonder whether the observation that they were not "typical Southerners" was the compliment it was intended to be, since the speaker's idea of typical Southerners had little to do with the people they had grown up with.

Certainly this young man began to think. What was this Southernness he was apparently stuck with? Why was he moved to defend the South? What was it to him? People assumed that he had things in common with other Southerners, but (aside from being on the receiving end of that assumption) did he? These weren't easy questions for a nineteen-year-old. But since he had plenty of other things to think about (he was no Quentin Compson), they didn't weigh too heavily on him. Nevertheless, he did wonder about them from time to time, and they set him up for his first encounter with *I'll Take My Stand*.

Browsing at the MIT bookstore one day in 1963, he ran across the Harper paperback. The title caught his eye, and the authors, "Twelve Southerners," made the book sound even more interesting. He bought it and started reading Ransom's essay, "Reconstructed but Unregenerate," as he walked back to his room. For a Tennessee boy at the Massachusetts Institute of Technology who was having his doubts about both Massachusetts and technology, the book was a bombshell. For someone who felt moved to defend the South, this fire-eating counterattack was a revelation. It suggested an entirely new line: not "We're as good as you," not (God forgive him) "We're no different from you," but, by God, "We're *better* than you." Hot stuff, in those defensive days.

But after the first enthusiasm wore off, he started having second thoughts. What was all this about agriculture? It was clear to him, thirty years after the Agrarians, that most Southerners had nothing to do with agriculture. Surely the point of the book wasn't that he and most of his friends weren't really Southerners after all. He liked the country people he knew, but *they* weren't "typical Southerners." Moreover, he'd spent possibly the worst summer of his life working tobacco for four dollars a day. Idealizing the agricultural life would take some doing. What really appealed to him was the book's unabashed championship of the South, its forthright assertion that the South was doing *something* right. Now if he could just figure out what that was.

His Northern friends mostly assumed that the heart of the matter was racism. He learned later that they weren't alone in this assumption: Ulrich Bonnell Phillips, a distinguished historian from Georgia, had argued the same thing some decades before. Unflinching support for white supremacy, he had said, was "the central theme of Southern history and the cardinal test of a Southerner." But that just didn't *feel* right. Segregation had no charms for him, or for most of his Southern friends in Cambridge, and they resisted and resented the idea that Jim Crow was the essence of Southern life and culture.

This position on race wasn't ideological; it was based on their experience. They might have felt differently if they had come, like Phillips, from the Black Belt. But they didn't. They came, mostly, from the periphery—East Tennessee, Arkansas, East Texas—or from the cities and suburbs of the "New South"—Atlanta, Winston-Salem, Baton Rouge. In those settings, for whites anyway, race was simply *not very important*. Of course, all of them knew—and a few of them were—white supremacists, but (the undergraduate reflected) race was clearly not the obsession that it should have been if it was as central to their lives as everyone assumed it was. And yet they were Southerners—as they were often reminded, and soon began to insist.

There were, in addition, a couple of newfound black friends—like him, young men from the South, displaced in New England. He did not discuss his musings with them—in fact, he tended politely to avoid the subject of the South; and they did, too, probably for the same reason. But he came to realize, and to hope that they realized, that he and they had a good deal in common, at least compared to the Northerners around them. They spoke with similar accents and in a similar allusive, anecdotal way; they knew the same Baptist and Methodist hymns and had the same trick of quoting or paraphrasing Scripture in outrageous contexts; they liked the same foods (although these blacks, like most of those he came to know later, preferred Scotch whiskey to bourbon, for some reason); and they seemed to share a good many assumptions that he couldn't quite put his finger on. Whatever Southernness was, he came to believe, it obviously included them—unless they chose to reject it.

So, he concluded, his Northern friends were just wrong. The South no more depended on segregation than it did on subsistence agriculture. Both had been fateful influences on the South, both had left their marks, but neither was the *sine qua non* of Southernness. Sometimes he was tempted, when under attack, to adopt a line from the Southern comedian Brother Dave Gardner: "I love everything about the South. I even love *hate*." But it wasn't really necessary to defend segregation in order to defend the South. To be sure, he thought, white supremacy could be defended by thoughtful and humane people (he knew some); but that observation merely proved to his satisfaction that thoughtful and humane people could be wrong, and unintentionally wicked. Perhaps because he was very young, this conclusion struck him as both profound and depressing.

But he was no closer to learning what *did* define the South. Off and on, as his circumstances allowed, he had begun to read and, in a most un-Southern way, to theorize about it. He rejected out of hand one possibility suggested by his reading. The South no longer depended (if it ever had) on the myths and imagery of the Lost Cause. The Stars and Bars, "Dixie," the whole Confederate heritage—all were dandy to use for annoying Yankees, and all served as a kind of Masonic code for white Southern boys, especially outside the South. But these symbols did not seem genuinely to move most Southerners of his generation. The last Confederate veteran had died, in his own home town, while he was in high school; what he remembered of the event was the amused local speculation that the old boy's war record was fictitious, invented to chisel a veteran's pension from the Commonwealth of Virginia. The United Daughters of the Confederacy soldiered on, but they were as remote from the real life of his town and as faintly ridiculous as the D.A.R.—to whom, he realized dimly, they were somewhat inferior, as these things are reckoned. People still stood up for "Dixie" at football games, but they would give that up without protest a few years later. Some of his high school friends once ran the Stars and Bars up the school flagpole on the anniversary of Appomattox, but they'd have flown the swastika or the hammer-and-sickle, if they'd had one, with the same fine, thoughtless, apolitical desire to raise hell.

No, time and Yankee textbooks had eaten away the core of Confederate sentiment. The little they had left was being undermined, in the early 1960s, by the Southern defenders of segregation, who had pretty well appropriated the Confederacy's flag and anthem. Their considerable success in identifying their own lost cause with the earlier one was, he felt, a shame.

He recognized that—like agriculture, like white supremacy—the War had helped to form the South he knew. But, he believed, it had long since ceased to play an important part in sustaining it. Once again, it seemed his conclusions were only negative.

Time passed, several years' worth. The undergraduate became a graduate and married a Southern girl. His penchant for brooding about questions of little practical consequence led him to drift more or less inevitably into graduate school, in New York City, where something he had noticed in Cambridge finally sank in.

In New York, even more than in Cambridge, it was borne in on him that, in the urban Northeast, almost everyone had what he thought of as a backup identity. Not just "some of his best friends" but *most* of his best friends were Jewish. Those who weren't were Italian, or Irish, or Puerto Rican, or Polish. Everybody was *some-thing*, even if only "WASP"—a label applied to those who couldn't do any better. What was he? Didn't being Southern mean much the same thing to him, serve many of the same functions, social and psychological, as his friends' ethnic identities? Wasn't there at least an analogy there?

This wasn't a particularly original idea; other people had been saying much the same thing for years (although he was pleased with himself for figuring it out independently). Still, it seemed to offer a key to understanding many of the things that had puzzled him since his first months in Massachusetts.

For one thing, relations among Southerners in the Northeast were very much like those he observed among his Jewish friends. It wasn't so much that they *liked* each other better than they liked non-Southerners (although, other things being equal, they probably did). Rather, they knew more quickly whether they liked one another or not. Because a background of understanding and shared experience could be assumed, interaction could proceed without the preliminary, tentative sort of negotiation that characterized their initial relations with non-Southerners. Even at a later stage, there were fewer surprises, fewer misunderstandings. They understood each other's humor to be humor, for instance, and usually found it funny—which was not always the case in relations with non-Southerners. There was just a lot less explaining to do.

There was, in addition, the relation between a group's identity and its past. Clearly, his Jewish friends had no more to do with the *shtetl* than he had to do with sharecropping. The Troubles were no more an ever-present burden to his Irish friends than Reconstruction was to him. His "Forget, Hell!" cigarette lighter had about as much historical significance as a "Kiss Me—I'm Italian" button. It became evident, to him at least, that ethnicity as he came to know it in New York was an American creation, and a recent one. Group identity had been forged and reinforced in interaction with other groups, and its relation to the group's actual history (as opposed to the *myth* of that history it created for itself) was very tenuous indeed.

But these other groups, he observed in New York, resisted the melting pot, just as the Agrarians would have had Southerners do. Various social scientists were starting to document the cultural differences that American ethnic groups maintained, in the aggregate—differences that presumably explained the greater "easiness" of relations within particular groups. Clearly, though, while a group's culture might reflect its origins in some refracted way, that culture was being sustained and employed in quite different circumstances.

Like other ethnic identities, he concluded, Southernness had two aspects: on the one hand, an undeniable core of shared meanings, understandings, and ways of doing things (particularly evident in the presence of those who do not share them); on the other, outsiders' insistence that his group membership was significant, and their expectations based on that datum. This conclusion was somehow comforting: locating Southernness as a special case of a more general phenomenon not only seemed to explain a lot, but it made the whole business more normal, less troublesome, and—in an odd way—more "American."

So he had found at least a partial and tentative answer to one of his early questions. What was Southernness to him? It was an important answer to the question "Who are you?"—a question common in a fluid and pluralistic society. And it was a label for a cultural community where he could be relatively sure of being understood—not necessarily accepted, but *understood*.

But the content, the organizing principles and the shared assumptions, of that cultural community still remained tantalizingly out of reach. He thought of Southernness, inelegantly, as something like an onion. He had, to his own satisfaction at least, peeled away the dry brown outer layers that first met the eye but that had lost their former vitality, and he was left with a solid, pungent nucleus. But while he felt he *knew* what made up that core, he was not much closer to being able to *describe* it. The observables—food, speech-ways, music, and the like—were signs, markers, symbols of that quiddity, but not the thing itself. Later, he was to read and listen with a sense of recognition as blacks strove to articulate the mystique of *negritude* and of "soul," and he came to realize that for Southerners, as for other ethnic communities, the essential qualities of the group may be, finally, ineffable—although to allow that possibility was far from allowing that they might be illusory, or that there was no point in trying to identify them.

It may seem that this third-person account has led us rather far from *I'll Take My Stand*, and indeed it has. The point is that Southernness is a more complicated business than it appeared to be in 1930. It's no longer a matter of taking one's stand in the lower right-hand quadrant of the United States and hurling defiance at an alien industrial civilization. For better or for worse, the South finally has "rejoined the Union" (as journalists are fond of saying). The region is increasingly and, it appears, irreversibly bound up with the rest of the country. It has become more and more difficult for Southerners to live out their lives entirely in the South, entirely with other Southerners. Unreflective, reflexive Southerners can still be found, and perhaps we can be thankful for that, but they are like the snail darter—threatened by the advance of that modern regime the Agrarians warned us about. We might wish it otherwise, it may yet be a Southern characteristic to wish it otherwise, but to believe it otherwise is to display the sort of romanticism and wishful thinking that lost us a war.

But perhaps this case history, this narrative of a young Tennessean, can serve as an example, if not an argument *a fortiori*, suggesting that the implications of "the facts" are not straightforwardly antipathetic to the continued existence of Southern culture and identity. Like other "primordial affiliations" (in Edward Shils's phrase), other ties based on blood and soil, Southernness provides a substrate beneath the overlay of functional and utilitarian relationships imposed by a modern industrial economy. Its evidences can't be kept down; it continues to crop up here, there, and everywhere, like grass through concrete.

One particular aspect of our region's culture seems to be not only surviving under these new conditions, but actually thriving. This trait has always been present in the South's cultural ecology, but (like goldenrod along new highways) it benefits from the elimination of its natural competitors by urbanization and industrial development. I am referring to our regional variant of what used to be seen as the *American* trait of individualism. This characteristic has always coexisted uneasily with some other "Southern" traits—in particular, those that the South has shared with other "folk cultures," traits that characterize all rural, village, and peasant societies—which is what the South has been, in the American context, until very recently. Such characteristics as parochialism, fatalism, authoritarianism, ethnocentrism, and categorical resistance to innovation have been "Southern" characteristics, in the sense that Southerners have been more likely than other Americans to display them. But the same catalogue could be (has been) applied to other "premodern" societies, to Iran, Turkey, Sicily, Mexico, and Ireland, among others. This bundle of traits, which one sociologist has called *the* traditional value orientation, is menaced everywhere by urbanization and industrialization. The Agrarians knew this: that list of deceptively Latinate, "scientific" and ostensibly non-evaluative terms includes some of the things they cherished most about the South. These characteristics are indeed linked, as effect to cause, to rural and small-town life and to agricultural pursuits. In the South, as in other modernizing societies, they survive most strikingly among the rural, the poor, the uneducated, those who are isolated from urban life, the industrial regime, and the media of mass communication.

The same traits survive, in attenuated form, among many other Southerners: the majority of us, after all, are no more than a generation removed from the countryside. But the prognosis for these aspects of Southern distinctiveness is not favorable. In many of these respects, the South's urban and suburban middle classes are already well-nigh indistinguishable from their non-Southern counterparts; in others, a difference remains, but who can say for how long? It may be that the South will hang on to a residuum of these cultural characteristics, a souvenir of its agrarian past. But such a vestige will only provide a traditional, folkish flavor to the standard industrial entrée; it will not be the foundation for a competing civilization, not the sort of thing manifestoes are made of.

Alongside the folkish, organic strain in our region's culture, however, there has always been a stubborn, individualist, "I'm as good as you" outlook, a collection of cultural themes that competed with and undermined the demands of prescription, hierarchy, and organic community. The openness of early Southern society, the possibilities for individual mobility, meant that the would-be hierarchs of the South had to resort to slavery to keep their retainers in place. The varieties of Christianity that were equipped by their histories to legitimize a prescriptive order never fared well among those folk who needed encouragement to do their duty in the station in life to which it had pleased God to call them, at least not after they had the opportunity to choose something else. Throughout the South's history, those whites who seemed intended to fill the lower ranks of Southern society showed a disturbing tendency to take off for the hills or the frontier. If they stayed around, they lingered not as humble servitors, but to display the prickly independence of men whose God has told them they are as good as anybody else, and better than the unsaved. Many Southern blacks adopted the same stance, as soon as they were able. It is significant, for instance, that after 1865 the new freedmen widely refused to work in gangs under supervision and forced Southern landowners to turn to a sharecropping system based (in theory, at least) on a contract between two autonomous parties.

These two competing visions—the individualist and the organic—can be illustrated by a series of oversimplified contrasts—Jefferson and Fitzhugh, Baptists and Anglicans, yeomen and planters, Huey Long and Harry Byrd, perhaps uplands and low-country. One of the unresolved contradictions of *I'll Take My Stand*, some critics have observed, is that of which South it is defending. In fact, the combination, however unstable or philosophically unsatisfying, may have something to be said for it, if each of these tendencies served to check the excesses of the other. But that question is neither here nor there, if I am right: the erosion of the folkish South by twentieth-century economic and demographic changes has left the South's version of laissez-faire free to develop relatively unchecked by prescriptive obligations and restraints based on family position, rank, class, or even race. (Sex remains, perhaps, a different matter.)

The characteristics that I am clumping under the label "individualism" differ from the traits that Southerners have shared with those from other folk societies in at least two ways. In the first place, they seem to exist *sui generis*, so to speak, reflecting the unique circumstances of the South's settlement, development, and historical experience; they are by no means universal among or unique to "traditional" societies. In the second place, indicators of these traits "behave" differently when examined statistically: they differentiate educated, urban and suburban, *modernized* Southerners fully as much as poor, rural, and uneducated ones. Regional differences in these respects show little sign of disappearing—indeed, they often seem to be increasing.

These cultural presuppositions are easier to illustrate than to list. They are displayed with greatest clarity, perhaps, in the dominant religion of the South, a brand of evangelical Protestantism that cuts across denominational lines and, for that matter, probably characterizes the beliefs of most of the unchurched. Students of the subject agree that the South is unique, religiously, because it is dominated by low-church Protestant groups—notably the Southern Baptists, but also Methodists, Presbyterians, and other denominations that tend to imitate the more successful Baptists. These groups emphasize the individual's salvation and his role in accepting it. "The Hour of Decision," as the Reverend Mr. Graham tells us, is *now*, and it is up to the individual to choose, to accept the freely offered gift of salvation. Nobody else can walk the Lonesome Valley, as the old song has it. You've got to walk it by yourself. Others can and do help, but ultimately you're on your own. The Catholic doctrine of the church as the Body of Christ is, in this view, an elegant metaphor at best, a mystery (in the simplest sense of that word) at worst. The church is seen as an inorganic aggregate of individual congregations, themselves convenient gatherings of voluntarily associated individuals, each of whom maintains his own unmediated personal relation to transcendent Deity. The South's economic life increasingly relies on a complex hierarchical and specialized division of labor, but its religious economy is what the textbooks call a Robinson Crusoe situation.

Whatever else can be said about it, there is no question that this individualistic emphasis in Southern religion is comfortably consistent with other aspects of Southern culture. Just as Southerners are expected to work out their own salvation without calling on the formal institutional apparatus of church, priest, and sacrament, so we have often been inclined to work out our own justice without running off to the legislature or the courts. In the South, the state has no more monopoly on the means of justice than the church has on the means of grace. To concede all legitimate coercion to the state would be repugnant to many Southerners, if not to most. Ultimately, individuals must have the ability—indeed, may have the obligation—to settle such matters for themselves. A closer look at the South's homicide rates, perennially twice as high as the rest of the country's, bears this out. The sort of murders the South specializes in are not assaults on innocent and inoffensive citizens going about their business; they are, rather, responses to attacks—on someone's person, honor, or self-esteem. They are in fact private attempts, however excessive or misguided, to redress grievances. Collective violence has followed much the same pattern.

Some historians are now emphasizing the strong "Celtic" strain in Southerners' ancestry, and it is pleasant to recall that another Celtic nation has as its motto *Nemo me impune lacessit* (in Southern, "Nobody messes with me and gets away with it"). Although this handsome boast expresses for Southerners—as for the Scots— an ideal rather than a fact, what it threatens is clearly not a lawsuit.

A respect for individualism and self-reliance is also increasingly evident in Southerners' economic views. Let me tell another story. I asked an older man recently what had happened to a brilliant black athlete from his town who had played outstandingly for four years at a Southern university, only to have his professional career cut short by injuries. He had returned, I was told, to the middle-sized Southern city where he'd gone to college, as an executive in a predominantly white business. "He married a white girl, you know, but he's doing very well." Fifty years ago, that would have been one dead black man. No amount of athletic or commercial success would have offset his breach of racial etiquette; success, in fact, would have compounded the offense. But my friend mentioned the man's marriage as he might have alluded to some bad habit, and his tone in general was one of approval, even of pride in a local boy made good.

I don't pretend that this reaction would be universal, or even typical, but it is increasingly widespread. Particularly among the Southern middle class, we find a belief system which Fitzhugh and probably some of the Agrarians would have despised: an individual is entitled—indeed, obliged—to work out his own well-being; he is free to compete, without prescriptive restraints; and he is free to enjoy the fruits of success—even a white wife—if he succeeds. Public opinion polls have shown a substantial increase of late in the proportion of Southerners who support "conservative" (that is, laissez-faire) economic policies, along with an increase in those who support "liberal" social policies. The apparent contradiction is only in the cockeyed terms of American politics: in both respects, Southerners increasingly display a version of libertarianism, the natural political expression of an individualistic ethos long evident in other institutional spheres.

Cynics may argue that this represents merely another strategic retreat, a new and more sophisticated stance in defense of race and class privilege. If top-dog Southerners can no longer get away with holding back other groups, as groups, their new ideology assures at least that those others will not be helped, categorically, to threaten the top dogs' "hegemony." There may be something to this argument. It must deal with a great deal of false consciousness on the part of Southerners who are hardly top dogs; but it may be, for example, that the truly incredible rates of individual upward mobility that have accompanied the South's recent economic development are encouraging people to have aspirations that will eventually prove unrealistic.

In any case, the increasingly dominant Southern doctrine is an internally consistent one, perhaps for the first time, and it is a form of libertarianism. When middle-class Southerners tell us, as most now do, that blacks should not be held back economically by Jim Crow laws or employment discrimination, that they'd be pleased to have as a neighbor anyone who can afford to live in the neighborhood, that their neighbors' children should go to the same schools as their own—when they say all this, their sincerity is not impugned by their practical indifference to those, black and white, who fail the sink-or-swim test of a laissez-faire economy. They believe that well-being is ultimately a man's own lookout, and he ought to be able to work it out without the help of institutions like government, unions, and the like (although other individuals—kinfolk, neighbors, and Christians generally—ought to help him if he needs it and they are able). Like those who achieve salvation, those who achieve economic success are entitled to the benefits, regardless of what they were before. Those who don't succeed—well, they may get helped, but, like the unsaved, they will get exhortation and Christmas baskets, and hardly as a matter of *right*.

If, as I believe, the South is refining and beginning to exemplify a worldview that puts individual responsibility at the heart of things and insists that individuals should—and, by and large, do—get what they deserve, it presents some interesting, homegrown features. One of the most common theoretical objections to pure libertarianism—that it destroys community—simply does not seem to apply to the Southern variety, as it is actually put into practice in most Southern towns and institutions. Community seems at least as healthy in the South as elsewhere, and I don't think it is merely as a residue from the region's preindustrial past. Here again, we can look at Southern churches as a useful microcosm of Southern society. If we can understand their cohesiveness, perhaps we can see the same processes at work in other Southern settings.

Southerners, I have said, incline to the view that churches are simply voluntary associations for the benefit, in the last analysis, of the individuals who make them up—a view so taken for granted that many Southerners cannot conceive that there is any other way to think of the church. The proposition "Love it or leave it" seems perfectly reasonable to many Southern churchmen. From time to time groups *do* leave, to set up their own congregations or to found entirely new denominations. This mode of response results in both homogeneity and considerable group loyalty—in the new groups, obviously; but also in the old.

The same phenomenon can be observed at the community level: congregationalism in the churches of the South (whatever their formal polity) is echoed by *localism*, especially in smaller communities. Southerners' relations to their communities are not merely utilitarian: loyalty is expected and is usually forthcoming, but it is also freely chosen. The prototypical Southern sentiment may be the bumper-sticker admonition, "Get your heart in Dixie or get your ass out." That sentiment applies, *mutatis mutandis*, to churches, communities, and even business and industrial enterprises, as well as to the region as a whole. But, paradoxically, this species of apparent intolerance is not wholly antithetical to individualism. In a way, individualism is its prerequisite, for the individual is free to choose: salvation or damnation, right or wrong opinions, loyalty or treason, to stay or to go. "Love it or leave it" is said only to free men. "Leaving," of course, need not be physical (although it often is). As Southerners have shown repeatedly, it is no longer necessary to go to Rhode Island or to Utah to set up a new religious denomination, and someone willing to be lonesome can usually withdraw from the life of a Southern town without heading for points west or north. But in order to be part of a community one must adhere to community standards, or else start a new community with like-minded individuals. In theory, nonconformity can be dealt with by suppression, by abandoning group standards altogether, or by excluding the deviant from the group. It seems to me that Southerners usually prefer the last of these solutions, although the first gets more publicity.

The old joke about both of our churches worshipping God—you in your way, we in His—summarizes an anomaly that has puzzled many observers of Southern life. Theoretical hostility toward other groups, other communities, and other regions is often combined with a sort of workaday pluralism that lets folks get along pretty well most of the time, although it wouldn't satisfy the sponsors of National Brotherhood Week. Southerners quite often tolerate the theoretically intolerable from "outsiders," reasoning that what those people do is of no concern to us. An element of circularity defines outsiders, in part, as those who think or do the intolerable. Whatever else may be said about this solution, it seems to me that it's usually preferable to trying to make outsiders conform to insider standards, and always superior to concluding that there is nothing that could be called intolerable.

In return, Southerners would like a similar toleration for themselves. Nashville's Charlie Daniels sings about it in "Long-haired Country Boy," suggesting that his critics just leave him alone. The coiffure has changed, but the sentiment is as old as the hills to which Daniels's ancestors migrated, in order to be left alone. And, it should be noted, today's long-haired country boy is likely to be a loyal member of a group of long-haired country boys who are tolerated by the rest of the community, as long as they keep their intolerable tastes and habits to themselves and only knife each other.

What has always particularly annoyed Southerners is not what others do among themselves but others' attempts to make us do differently. My reading of the defenders of slavery and later of segregation is that they were genuinely puzzled by the attitudes of their opponents. After all, Southerners didn't approve of the way other Americans ran their affairs, but they didn't try to make those others change. Southerners, it seems to me, are usually willing to let the rest of the country (the world, for that matter) go to hell any way it pleases, and won't interfere unless invited—an attitude learned at home. But it's only reasonable, in this view, to expect that others will keep their missionaries, inspectors, revenue agents, soldiers, and outside agitators at home. If they don't like the way we're living, what's it to them? *Nemo me impune lacessit.*

So what we have, I am suggesting, is a nested set of communities—a region composed of states, composed in turn of cities and towns, themselves made up of groups and associations and neighborhoods, down, in good Burkean fashion, to the level of the family and perhaps beyond. At each level, the criteria for membership and the definitions of the intolerable differ, but everywhere the "love it or leave it" principle applies—even, if we examine the divorce statistics, at the level of the family. The result is communities and groups which enlist the loyalty of their members, so long as they remain members, precisely *because* they are free to leave. Cash's "savage ideal" of conformity may well characterize relations *within* many Southern communities, while *between* communities a certain rough-and-ready tolerance (indifference, really) prevails.

Of course, this mode of association is, by its nature, centrifugal. The history of the Confederacy, like its existence in the first place, attests to this. The internal tensions, the struggles among the composite states, would have torn the young nation apart, had it not been held together by the common adversary. Just so, the churches of the South have exaggerated the natural tendency of Protestantism to go to seed, dividing over and over again. Groups break away from larger groups, rather than compromising or accommodating. Individuals take their leave as well. But things somehow don't fall apart all that often, or all that disastrously. What holds them together? What countervailing forces check this inherent tendency toward disintegration?

In the first place, there is some measure of self-selection. Although nonconformists don't usually *have* to leave, many choose to do so. The South has always exported a large proportion of its population to other regions, and it still does. Those who remain, it has been shown, are culturally more "Southern" than those who leave. Although Southern fiction is filled with cranks, grotesques, and weirdos, the South itself doesn't seem to have a great many more than its share. No doubt many have joined the outward migration, and they are now California's problem, or New York's. Similarly, there has always been a great deal of migration *within* the region, originally to the Southwest, more recently from the countryside to the South's cities. It is my impression that misfits and dissenters from the South's smaller communities now tend to migrate to Southern cities, along with the many who go for other reasons, thus helping to preserve the homogeneity and cohesion of the groups they have left behind.

What this means for Southern cities is a different matter. It may mean that big Southern cities will become downright *strange*— nothing new for New Orleans, but surprising to observe in Atlanta and Houston, Nashville and Memphis. The fact that oddballs from the small-town South can often link up with communities of likeminded deviants, and the fact that different communities within Southern cities pretty well succeed in ignoring one another may mean that most residents of these cities can overlook this development. (In any case, it is an urban phenomenon, and not specifically a Southern one.)

The fact remains that the Southern city is not simply one large community; I am suggesting, furthermore, that the Southern small town was not simply one community either. The two racial groupings are only the most obvious of the many subcommunities within most Southern towns, subcommunities with the ability to mind their own business and to cooperate when circumstances require. The monolithic small-town community may be a New England or a Midwestern phenomenon, but the Southern reality has usually been more complicated than that.

Also operating to offset the tendency toward fragmentation is the frequent presence, sometimes contrived, of external "threat." The South is never more united than when it feels the North is picking on it or pushing it around. I will leave the anthropologists to analyze the solidarity-producing functions of competitive sports, but will note simply for example that the heterogeneous state of North Carolina is seldom unified except when one of its universities' basketball teams faces outside opposition. At a lower level, the disparate and often hostile subcommunities in small towns unite to support their high school teams against those of other towns. At a higher level, we see the Atlantic Coast Conference *contra mundum*. The structure of Southern athletics, like that of Southern religion, both mirrors and reinforces more general patterns of social organization.

The importance of outsiders in holding things together is reflected in the narrative of the young Tennessean. His background was far from "typically Southern," even in a statistical sense. He came from a part of the South whose Civil War loyalties had been, at best, equivocal; an area with fewer blacks, proportionately, than Boston. His hometown was a busy, dirty industrial city with few reminders of any history before the 1920s, populated mostly by first- and second-generation migrants from other parts of the South. He was raised as a Republican and an Episcopalian (the former minority more acceptable than the latter, in his neck of the woods—an inversion of the usual Southern pattern). Yet all these atypical attributes, however important and telling for Southerners, were of no consequence to most Northerners, for whom the overriding datum was simply "Southerner." It could be said that his sense of himself as a member of the regional group was very largely the result of his experiences *outside* that group. Indeed, his friends who stayed in the South for their educations were generally a good deal less self-conscious about their region than he; many—particularly those who went to the "better" Southern schools—were inclined, in an unreflective way, to be vaguely ashamed of their origins and apologetic about them, anxious to avoid the stigma of "provincialism." Paradoxically, it seemed that, for this young man and others he knew, travel and residence outside the South led not to "assimilation," but to a heightened sense of distinctiveness and solidarity with other Southerners. (The best antidote for a sense of regional inferiority seemed to be exposure to Yankees.)

Finally, the South and its constituent groups and communities show more cohesion than we might expect because they aren't really organized all that consistently with the social ideology I have been describing. The old prescriptive ties, obligations, and hierarchies are disappearing, where they have not already vanished, and with them is fading the ideology that justified them and served to offset the implications of the principles of individualism and voluntarism. But the old patterns have been replaced by hierarchies and restraints of a different order, no less real for going unrecognized and unlegitimated by custom and traditional principle. Southern churches, like all formal organizations, exhibit hierarchy and differentiation of function. Southern communities, like all communities, reflect social stratification. And the South's economy is, perhaps more than ever, a complicated, interdependent system in which some command, others obey, and most do both. Whether acknowledged explicitly or not, power remains power, and, within the broad limits established by the "love it or leave it" principle, it can still be used to keep others in line.

It is interesting to see how Southerners deal with the facts of stratification, facts that some would say contradict an image of society as made up of autonomous individuals freely acting and in some senses equal. Of course, someone's position in the various hierarchies of Southern society can be attributed partly to his own efforts and decisions. Success, like salvation, has its rewards. On the other hand, Southerners are at least as aware as other Americans that many things are outside their control, that much of what happens to people results from external forces, or chance. Since fatalism is one aspect of the now-evaporating "traditional value orientation," it may be that Southerners will become more consistent in this respect. Still, it seems to me that we shrink from inflicting on those at the bottom all the scorn, or according to those at the top all the deference, that should follow from our conviction that they deserve to be there. We do not follow through; the harsher implications of our individualism are mitigated by a set of manners that leave a great deal implicit, that even tend to deny the existence of a top and a bottom.

Authority in the South is often veiled by a style that pays lip service to the useful fiction that all men are created equal, whatever the private opinions of those who exercise the authority. W. J. Cash wrote of the oldtime Southern industrialist whose back-slapping manner as he mingled with his employees, speaking of hunting and fishing and college football, denied that there was any sharp distinction, much less a qualitative difference, between capitalist and worker. Southern workers have often returned the compliment by refusing to listen to outsiders who insist that there *is* a difference. Similarly, a friend who left the Southern Baptists for the Episcopal Church allowed that he preferred a denomination where the bishops were visible (a most un-Southern taste). The Baptists can camouflage their elite; while Anglican bishops may shun the trappings of prelacy, they can hardly escape the designation.

This style is also evident in politics. When President Carter walked in his inaugural parade, when he was sworn in wearing a business suit and came on television in a cardigan sweater, he was solidly in the Southern tradition. (Jefferson's inauguration was also informal, and he was condemned for lacking dignity.) Southerners know who's the president, but we appreciate his not rubbing it in.

Consider as well the folkways of tipping. Expatriate Southerners who have had a New York mailman return all their mail marked "Addressee Unknown" when they didn't know to render a Christmas tribute will recognize that there are regional differences in this matter. Any Northern headwaiter or parking lot attendant will attest that unassimilated Southerners are notoriously poor tippers, and some Southerners more concerned with service than with honor have been known to have friends with less obtrusive accents call for restaurant reservations, or to tip various flunkies in advance.

The point is not that Yankees are greedy or Southerners tight. The difference in customs reflects, rather, a Southern conviction that expecting and receiving tips is demeaning, and somehow unmanly; that giving them can be insulting. Another story: When I got my first Southern haircut in some years, I asked cautiously whether North Carolinians tipped barbers yet. "Some do," I was told. "Had a doctor, used to come in here a lot. Always gave me fifty cents." The barber clipped thoughtfully for a while. "Went for a physical one time. Gave *him* fifty cents. 'This is for you, Doc.'" He chuckled. "Seems to me if I want more money I can raise my price." Like the doctor, this man had his skills, his independence, and his pride. He didn't need or intend to depend on the charity of his customers.

Times and mores are changing, perhaps, but the underlying attitude persists. Presents are all right: a present is from one friend, one equal, to another. But tips are for servants, and who would want to be a servant? If you want more money, raise your price. If you don't like it, leave.

Finally, it may even be that the same tendency to deny hierarchy—hierarchy, to repeat, that may very well exist—is evident in Southerners' conversation-starting style. It seems to me that the ice-breaking "What do you do?" is heard less often below the Mason-Dixon Line. Southerners, I think, prefer "Where are you from?" ("What's your sign?"—the West Coast standard—hasn't caught on, even among the singles-bar set.) If Southerners do avoid "What do you do?" this avoidance may simply reflect the survival of an older belief that what you *do* is a paltry way to indicate who you *are*. But it's also a matter of manners. To ask that question is to ask someone to brag if he's successful, or to confess failure if he's not. One can like "Where are you from?" for the same reason Melbourne liked the Order of the Garter: because there's no damned merit about it.

In any case, everyone knows there are hierarchies everywhere, in church, state, and economy. But that fact is unpleasant enough for those at the bottom without being reminded of it all the time. Those at the top may (in fact, certainly do) feel superior to those at the bottom—why else would they be at the top? But they're obliged not to assault the self-respect of their inferiors by ostentatiously putting them down. Similarly, members of a group may agree among themselves about their group's social or moral superiority to other groups, but they tend to follow forms that keep those opinions tacit, forms that, like the entente among Southern churches, disguise indifference as cordial respect. If, as I believe, race relations are now better in many respects in the South than anywhere else in the country, it may be simply because whites are now prepared to follow these forms in their relations with blacks, as they have always followed them in relations with other whites. And blacks are willing to return the favor.

A final story. A black North Carolinian, now living in New York, once tried to explain why he saw more anti-white sentiment among New York blacks than among black Southerners. "Lots of people came here because they wanted to be treated like white folks," he told me. "What they still don't realize is that New Yorkers treat everyone like niggers." Most Southerners are raised to want others to feel at ease, at home, part of the community. Even if we believe their part is an inferior one, even if they are newcomers still on probation, even if they are transients never to be seen again, well-mannered Southerners will try to *include* them, unless we have reason to believe that they are unassimilable. (Then, of course, we can be as savagely rude as anyone else.) Californians might say we are not "sincere"; New Yorkers and others who are friendly only to their friends sometimes accuse us of hypocrisy. But it seems to me that we are just trying to deal with the peculiarly modern problem of how to reconcile liberty, equality, and fraternity—a fine but obviously unstable combination. If Southern principles increasingly exalt the first of these, our manners emphasize the second, and the result is a workable version of the third.

What I have been describing is not an abstract blueprint but a way of life, a set of unexamined axioms about the nature of association that I believe are widespread in the South and are likely to remain so. People are free to choose in many important matters, and should bear the consequences. Association is based on shared values and beliefs. People are free to leave associations they find onerous, and should do so. It is impolite to emphasize unavoidable differences in rank. Groups, like individuals, should be free to choose in many matters. Consequently, pluralism and decentralization are desirable policies (a Southern refraction of the Catholic principle of subsidiarity). . . . It is impossible to make a systematic list of these convictions, since they are not so much articulated as lived. Like any way of life, this one embodies contradictions, evasions, and blind spots that rigorous ideologues of any persuasion will likely find intolerable. Never mind: it seems to work, and many of us like it.

More than that, it seems to me that these are among the more important "shared understandings" that set the young Tennessean and his fellow Southerners apart from their Northern friends. Not that I claim that this mode of association has always been distinctively Southern. I don't know in what respects it has been that: many features of it strike me as things the South resisted longer than the rest of the country, that the South adopted only after they had been pretty well abandoned elsewhere. But that doesn't matter. The point is that these are now "Southern" understandings, in the American context; they are, for the time being, at least, principles that many Southerners find almost instinctively congenial. No doubt many other Americans find those same understandings quaint—or more likely repugnant, since (I have noticed) people who can be perfectly dispassionate when discussing infanticide among the Toda cannot bring a similar detachment to their view of Southern folkways.

I don't insist that these understandings are somehow at the heart of Southern identity, or that all else depends on them. I doubt that that is true. Details and emphases have changed and will continue to change. Southerners who don't share this view of things, though, may well be uncomfortable in the South (increasingly so, if I am right) and might be happier elsewhere. Recall the bumper sticker's advice to those whose hearts aren't in Dixie.

Clearly, one thing this set of understandings does is to provide a solid rationale—perhaps "underpinning" is the better word—for Southerners' continued insistence on our right as a regional and quasi-ethnic group to keep on doing some things *our* way, to hold out as a large and gristly lump in the national stew. One thing that sets Southerners off from many other Americans may be the conviction that groups like ours are *entitled* to be set off from the rest.

But however much Southerners may find Southern identity and Southern culture congenial and downright *useful*, the question remains whether the South has anything to offer the rest of the country. It is an article of the liberal pluralist faith that every group, no matter how apparently degraded, has something to offer the rest of us, that we can all learn from each other. Doesn't this axiom apply to Southerners? To be sure, many who assert this principle most vigorously can, in the next breath, deplore the "Southernization" of America, by which they mean the proliferation of everything from Kentucky Fried Chicken stands and country music to fundamentalist religion and high homicide rates. But they may be right in their assertion, even if inconsistent in its application. The South may indeed have something to offer the rest of the country—something other than a bad example, that is.

Alas, as I have explained, it is presumptuous to tell other people how to order their own affairs. Some have abandoned or never subscribed to the principle of individual responsibility, have no respect for self-respect, and regard the worldview I have described as hopelessly retrograde. They may have taken a wrong turn, but that is their prerogative. If they have, the consequences will be on them and on their children. So long as we are not obligated to save them from those consequences, they're entitled to the same toleration we have always asked for ourselves. For our part, we should refrain from preaching at them and should seek to construct a society pleasing to man and to God. If we succeed, others can draw the lessons for themselves.

The Distinctive South

Fading or Reviving?

William C. Havard

EVEN IF THE LONG QUEST for understanding the meaning of the South as a distinctive entity has not produced a characterization of Southern society or culture that commands consensus among historians, social scientists, journalists, and various other literati, we have succeeded in making a major academic enterprise out of the project. As one of the minor entrepreneurs, I often find myself wondering whether I continue to pursue my interest in the South because my vocational investment in it has been so heavy that I am not sure I could cut my losses if I got out, or whether the higher motivation of intellectual curiosity for its own sake still impels me to try to get a firmer objective grasp on the elusive concept of Southern identity—an identity that is also deeply personal and subjective.

What follows, then, is an effort in all too brief a compass to come to grips with some of those social characteristics and casts of mind that, in Donald Davidson's terms, "render understanding among Southerners immediate, spontaneous, intuitive; that bind them, whatever their incidental differences . . . so that they are conscious of a mutual interest that needs no definition and is beyond argument; and that, finally, rest upon principles of life . . . rather than on the series of pragmatic adjustments, capable of easy rationalization and also capable of quick change, so characteristic of modern life." Those elusive elements that have grown out of a common experience cannot be expressed with total clarity through the use of any set of language or other symbols of which I am aware, and they cannot be readily confided to a list of codified propositions that we may apply in the conduct of our moral and political lives. They are too deeply embedded in our consciousness and observable in our behavior to be denied, yet they are fraught with all of the ambiguities and contradictions of life itself. If we are to make our experience of life as a whole coherent (as all of us are compelled to do—if not intellectually, then in some other way), we must continue to search for their meaning for both the individual and his society.

As a political scientist of a rather old-fashioned sort, I am convinced that interpretations of human experience through the philosophical, historical, and artistic modes offer greater possibilities for understanding the practical areas of morals and politics than do the analytical modes of the mathematicized sciences, although I do not reject the applicability of natural science methods to some problems with which the social sciences are concerned. Thus I make no apology for my self perception as one whose consciousness and behavior have been shaped in ways that I cannot always penetrate intellectually, but also cannot deny affectively, by the fact that I was born and brought up as a Southerner. The late A. J. Liebling said that his taste in the architecture of public buildings had been permanently fixed by his initial visit to Napoleon's tomb. The older I grow, the more I realize that my assessment of both aesthetic and moral matters is rooted too firmly in the Southern environment to permit much flexibility in adapting emotionally and cognitively (and thus phenomenologically) to abstractly conceived objectives of change that cannot somehow be related to the formation of my concrete experience of time, place, and historical perspective.

The Southern accent, without respect to the broad range of dialects in various parts and among different populations of the South, falls more softly on my ear than do most other American speech patterns. I prefer the food of the South to the general run of American cuisine, although this preference is certainly affected by the fact that I was raised in South Louisiana, where Creole cookery adds a certain fillip to the heartier fare produced in the typical Southern hunting and fishing grounds, barnyards, and pea patches. And I certainly favor Southern manners over the patterns of conduct I observe in the supposedly more sophisticated urban agglomerations of the Northeast, where attempts to pass the time of day often seem to be regarded with suspicion, if not downright hostility. I also prefer traditional New Orleans jazz (with its unique combination of individual improvisation and harmonic blend of the collective performance) to the so-called modern stuff, and the country music that came out of the tradition of the English ballad and folkdance to the gaudy commercialized product that is now one of Nashville's main exports. And for concreteness of image, deftness in characterization, and capacity to assess moral worth in a context that subtly evokes the universal in the clarity of the particular, without attaching condemnatory judgment, I think Eudora Welty is unsurpassed among living American writers.

While such preferences may seem to be mere trivialities that characterize me as the stereotypical provincial who confirms the validity of that patronizing sense of superiority displayed by cosmopolitan intellectuals, they are really subliminal reflections of more general social and cultural traits by which both Southerners and non-Southerners distinguish the South and the Southerner from other components of a pluralistic, perhaps even polyglot, nation. Paradoxically, both tolerance in the face of perceived differences and the capacity to accommodate to change without destructiveness seem to me to depend as much on awareness of the distinctiveness of one's own formative experience as on the effort to understand differences in others.

The fact that the vast literature on the South has produced so many different (often contradictory) interpretations of the central historical, social, and ideological features that are supposed to make the South a separate society or "culture" (in the anthropological sense) has not caused us to reject the quest for the meaning of what Southerners and non-Southerners understand viscerally to be distinctions that make a difference. As Frank Vandiver rather poignantly puts it, "Surely there lurks somewhere a South, a tangible, knowable, living South, with traditions and meanings and ideals to serve the present and future as well as the past. . . ." If we cannot accept, without what amounts to refutational qualifications, U. B. Phillips's "central theme" that the presence of blacks in the South shaped the region's history and culture into unique configurations, we certainly find it even more difficult to accept any other single concept that would account for the particularities (some would say "peculiarities") we associate with the South. If there is an anachronistic, romantic South, there is also, as T. Harry Williams has strikingly informed us, and as Faulkner, Warren, O'Connor, and other Southern writers have made palpable in fictional form, a South that is incontestably realistic. If there is a South that seems hopelessly strapped to the rule of a Bourbon oligarchy, as both internal and external critics have avowed, there are also the Whig South, the Democratic South, and the Populist South so ably portrayed in the works of such leading recent and contemporary historians as C. Vann Woodward, David Potter, George Tindall, Dewey Grantham, and Charles Roland, among others. If we have a monolithic South in which the rigid mind-set characterized by Wilbur J. Cash is so pervasive that it makes (or once made) for virtually total conformity among all segments of the white population, we also have the pluralistic South in which not only do the various states (and sections of states) differ from one another, but in which the tolerance of eccentricity and capacity for producing bizarre characters exceeds that of any other part of the United States—at least according to Henry Miller, who may have tested the case as thoroughly as anyone who has spoken publicly to the question.

To all of these and other contradictions we may add the ambivalence that still attends the question of the Southerner as American. And that question is currently being totally reshaped by the shock of recognition that the South can no longer be treated as the isolated, inward- and backward-looking section to which the Puritan conscience, working out of what Robert Penn Warren called the Northern "Treasury of Virtue," could consign American guilt in confident expectation that the region's collective ignorance, primitive social customs, lag in economic development, and other evidence of moral blight would continue to reflect the wages of sin that preclude the possibility of a real share in the bounties of the "City on the Hill." In the wake of the American confrontation with certain brute facts of history that called into question its innocence and its elect status among nations—loss of a war that was widely perceived as morally degrading, the exploitation of nature to the point of destroying much of our national heritage, institutional corruption, urban blight, and increasing social segmentation—the South not only seems less disaffected than the rest of the country, but in Faulknerian terms seems also to be infused with a strong will not merely to survive, but to prevail over these times of trouble. Perhaps as much to the surprise of Southerners as to the outside world, the South even managed to accommodate the *de facto* enforcement of civil rights for blacks somewhat better than the Northern cities that had earlier been the recipients of black flight from the South.

The main issue facing those who monitor the health of the South, with perhaps a sublimated desire to preserve it not only as part of the nation, but in its own right (and even to restore it to the place of leadership it held at the outset of our national experience), may be cast in the form of yet another paradox. Is the current state of optimism about the region a result of its final capitulation to the forces of industrialism and urbanism that produced the American industrial revolution in the post-Civil War era, that provided the moving spirit of the country since that time, and that have long had a partial hold on the region by way of the New South Creed? Or is the South emerging, after partial purge of its long affliction, as a bona fide carrier of some of the original virtues that made the American experiment in establishing a new nation more successful than most? Another, and perhaps vaguer, way of putting it is to ask whether the South, having been arrested in a preindustrial state for the greater part of America's century of "modern development," may have preserved some traits and accumulated some useful experience that can be brought to bear on the effort to cope with the region's steadily increasing industrial growth, as well as on the possibilities for a decent post-industrial society in America at large.

My personal inclination (or moral sentiment) leans toward the latter interpretation. It is reinforced by the gloomy projections set forth in John Egerton's warnings about the threat of homogenizing the nation by interchanging the worst social characteristics of North and South, and by more optimistic but still qualified suggestions from such sources as Charles Roland, Grady McWhiney, Louis Rubin et al. that we badly need to pay conscious attention to some of the social and character traits that are closely identified with the Southern heritage. As others have observed many times, every time the death knell for the distinctive South seems about to ring, the hand at the toll ropes is stayed by a resurgence of vital signs.

I regret that I have no central theme to offer that would reconcile all the contradictions and contingencies I have been talking about; indeed, I do not know of a characterization of any society that manages to do that. The mythical self-interpretation that undergirds any social order is probably not reducible to a single "worldview" out of which such a characterization could proceed. In lieu of singular explanation, I fall back on those general characteristics most often associated with Southern distinctiveness in the historical and other literature about the South: a sense of place; an awareness of the past and the way it influences the conduct of life in the present; a preference for the concrete over the abstract that places the consideration of personal, family, and community relations above legal, contractual, and formal bureaucratic arrangements; and a persisting attachment to organized religion. Contrary to the assessment of Michael O'Brien in his recent book, *The Idea of the American South*, I do not think that the distinctive South is solely a matter of perception and that the social structure of the region lacks any traits to differentiate it from America at large. The identifiable features I just mentioned seem to have grown out of a particular historical experience unique to the South, and the interpretation of that experience has shaped the social configurations of the South in the attempt of its people to cope practically, i.e., morally and politically, with it. Here I can do no more than suggest some of the effects worked on Southern identity by the abstract characteristics under consideration; to try to spell them out in detail would constitute an agenda for the next wave of historical revisionism.

Sense of place, historical awareness, and personalism are all related in complex ways to a pattern of individualism, attachment to the extended family, localism of the *Gemeinshaft* sort, and a tendency to accept, often with good humor and a sense of satisfaction, the world as it is rather than as it might be in some utopian progressivist transformation. One is reminded of John Egerton's story of his conversation with a middle-aged black man who was a fellow passenger on a Chicago-Miami run under the auspices of Amtrak. After the introductory amenities had been observed, his new acquaintance asked John where he was going. Upon being told that he was headed for Montgomery, Alabama, the man said he was getting off there, too, but that he would go on to Tuskegee if he could catch a bus. He added that he went there every year for at least two weeks. John then asked, "Is that your home?" The man replied that it was, and that he worked in Chicago and was on the way to visit some of his people. He avowed that in five more years, though, he would be going back for good. On being asked how long he had lived in Chicago, he made the following telling reply: "I been there twenty-five years. Chicago ain't where I live, though. It's where I stay. Chicago's *existin'*. Tuskegee is livin'." The argument over the relative influences of time and place—the sense of historical memory (especially recollections from youth) as compared with the persistence through change of the concrete geographic identification—as parts of the constitution of the Southern sensibility is sufficiently answered (for me, at least) in this brief vignette. The two are so inseparable as to nullify the question of predominance of one over the other. One might compare this attitude with that of a substantial portion of the British population, who have been urban for nearly two centuries but who somehow manage to identify themselves with pastoral England and specific locations of family origin.

The stress on kinship (including fictive kinship) and local origin is still strong among Southerners, even of the most recent generations. And Southerners, no matter how far from home or how widely separated their places of birth or home places may be, will, upon meeting, find some way to establish personal connections. I am not implying that Americans in general do not have something of this identity of place and personal relations, or that Southerners have not in recent years become almost as peripatetic as our fellow countrymen. But I am suggesting that the sense of a "place to come to" for Southerners—black and white alike—is especially strong. Perhaps this is because the South remained rural, sequestered and less affected by waves of immigration long after the rest of the country (except for a lingering nostalgia for the small town) had seemingly accustomed itself to urban anonymity and ceaseless physical mobility.

Partly because of this identity with place (and the memories associated with it) Southerners tend to be acutely conscious of scale, both geographic and populational, as something that greatly affects the possibilities of the good life, and especially a largely self-directed life. A classical sense of proportion prevails: one's social responsibilities start with the family and extend to the local community in a face-to-face way, if not much beyond that point. Of the ultimate case—Mississippi—Walker Percy has noted that "one peculiar social dimension" really differentiates Mississippians from other Americans. It "has to do with the distribution, as Mississippians see it, of what is public and what is private. More precisely it is the absence of a truly public zone, as the word is understood in most places." Percy made this judgment in the 1960s as part of his explanation of the complex psychic reponse to the eventually successful effort on the part of James Meredith to secure admission to the University of Mississippi. Ole Miss, according to Percy, was not (and may still not be) a public institution in the ordinary sense of that term. Therefore Meredith's fellow students not only cursed and reviled him, but they also "wept with genuine grief" because "it was as if he had been quartered in their living room." Percy saw in this event an application of the old experience of the "hypertrophy of pleasant familial space" (extending to the entire state) that "accounts for the extraordinary apposition in Mississippi of kindliness and unspeakable violence." If one wants to see direct democracy at work in its devolutionary Jeffersonian extreme, where private and public are virtually indistinguishable even in the political sense, he should observe a county supervisor's election in a rural Mississippi district where fewer than two hundred neighbors and voters are involved, and all but the nearly expired are turned out on election day.

The implicit assumption that a face-to-face relation is a better way of resolving both individual and social conflicts than resorting to more abstract (and legally institutionalized) means has ambivalent results. If this complex and deep-rooted attitude has played a

shabby part in race relations and has obstructed public programs
that might have relieved some of the poverty, economic dependence, and repressiveness attending social structures and mores in
the South, it has, contrapuntally, served as a constraint on the evolution of the "modern" or "new" South into that anomic condition of
urbanized mass society in which individuals seem reduced to interchangeable parts of a machine operated by faceless bureaucrats, corporate or governmental. The proclivity toward violence in the South
is also related in no small part to Southern personalism. Within that
realm in which the private takes precedence over the public, a code
of honor came into being that insists on personal redress of individual grievance or on overt protection of individuals or private groups
who have a claim (whether asserted or merely assumed) on one's paternal, maternal, fraternal, extended familial, or neighborly responsibility. Even in the pure form of Cash's "savage ideal," such direct
violence may be more easily understood and eventually less difficult
to control than the abstract, depersonalized violence that now seems
endemic to the American megalopolis, old North and new South
alike.

Other personal and social attributes flow from these and related
Southern characteristics. I am conscious, for example, of a continuing sense of deference among Southerners that relates to the acceptance of familial authority. There remains an awareness that it is
not personally degrading, but uplifting, to be able to acknowledge
that which is meritorious and deserves respect, or even calls intrin-
sically for special consideration, as in the case of age and its association with wisdom, lineage, or simply length of survival in an often
inhospitable world. Not only do such habits reduce the extent to
which the insidious envy factor intrudes on personal relations in the
South, but they have also helped ease the tensions among social
classes in the South right into the present.

Cash recognized the extent to which personal and familial relations elided class differences, although he saw the inferior position
of blacks as the catalyzing agent in establishing this "Proto-Dorian"
bond among whites. I would go further by suggesting that the reci-
procity inherent in a cultivated respect for who and what one is,
both in himself and in his relation to others within an admittedly
circumscribed orbit of daily life, even helped in its strange, pater-
nalistic way to ease the common pains in the old caste system and
assisted with the transition to somewhat more equable justice in
race relations. As a former student of mine in Massachusetts once
said about those of his fellow graduate students who were blacks

from the South: "I am always surprised at how much more Southern they are than simply black."

Little need be said about religion in this context. After ancestry and place, and well before occupation (which is an identification ordinarily sought early by Northerners in new acquaintances), Southerners are likely to want to know what church you attend—not just *belong* to, but *go* to. Despite the ubiquity of religion in the South, Allen Tate was skeptical about the possibility of a cohesive culture without the unifying influence of a *common* religion to displace the fragmented religious pluralism of the region. Richard Weaver, on the other hand, held that the universality of religion in the South (despite the variety of sectarianism) was sufficient to provide an awareness of the finiteness of the world and the constancy of man's quest for the meaning of transcendence. Although heavily Protestant, the South's "attitude toward religion was essentially the attitude of orthodoxy: it was a simple acceptance of a body of belief, an innocence of protest and heresy which left religion one of the unquestioned and unquestionable supports of the general settlement under which men live." In Weaver's view, the religious commitment of the South was characterized by doctrinal innocence; its unifying centrality "was the acknowledgement, the submissiveness of the will, and that general respect for order, natural and institutional, which is piety." Religion in this respect was a matter for profession, not a matter for discussion in casuistic terms. Once one had professed belief, he was a member of a religious brotherhood, "but this did not encourage him to examine the foundation of his creed, or to assail the professions of others." The unifying effect was such that "a religious solid South preceded the political solid South."

Certainly enough of a common Calvinist and Old Testament quality remains in the fundamentalist South to make for a strong sense of the imperfections of the world and a fairly pessimistic view of the nature of man. In interpreting the meaning of the grotesque elements in Flannery O'Connor's fiction, Thomas Daniel Young notes that under the "weird and startling surface, her work is unrelenting in its insistence on imperfect men living in a world that reflects their imperfection. Man's only means of salvation is through the redeeming grace of Jesus Christ. This kind of creed has persisted in the South, for Protestant and Catholic alike. . . . This is the region that produced Jimmy Carter, who would believe, with Flannery O'Connor, that man's lost innocence is available to him only through the redemption accessible to him by his participation in the conviction of a slain and risen Christ." This dogged attachment to faith has brought consolation and hope, as well as a sense of reality, to the lives of those who often seem to have little to hope for, at least in this world. It has also, in combination with personalism, provided something of a barrier of compassion and charity against the potential excesses in some of the other collective attitudes with which we have so often identified the South as a whole.

Of course, these and other ostensible Southern attributes may appear to be nothing more than a naive clinging to outmoded or even romantic notions of an older, simpler, and more innocent America. If so, they now seem to be exerting a strong appeal, not just to Southerners, but to all Americans. For professional South-watchers, and especially for those of us who look inward as well as outward for the Southern identification, the question still is: How much of the best of the tradition can we preserve, without dragging too much of the worst along with it, as we move beyond the expectation that all our moral, political, and economic problems are amenable to solution by technology alone?

A South Too Busy to Hate?

FRED HOBSON

THE SOUTH has risen again all right, just as we all said it would, but nobody quite imagined the manner of its rising. Certainly not the Southern Agrarians, and probably not even their adversaries of the 1930s, the sociologists and liberals of Chapel Hill. For what has risen is a South neither of them would know: suddenly washed, scrubbed, dressed up—in double-knit, not overalls—guiltless, optimistic, and on display; part Sun Belt (the Agrarians would wince at the term), part museum, a sort of subcultural curiosity shop for Yankees to visit just off the interstate highways on the way to Florida and New Orleans. The part that is Sun Belt is slick and polished, air-conditioned and comfortable, corporate and wealthy, extending all the way to the Pacific. Donald Davidson would not recognize it. The part that is cultural museum he would recognize, but only as a distortion of what indeed had been, not something preserved so much as something enshrined: Opryland, Kentucky Fried Chicken, "Hee Haw," red-faced sheriffs, good ole boys. We are coming to see a packaging and marketing of those Southern values—a regard for the land and the individual, a certain casualness and love of leisure, a protest against bigness, bureaucracy, and abstraction—which suit the mood of America at the present time. In the process of being marketed, these values are losing some of their original meaning, much of their integrity. They became rustic, quaint, cute—plasticized charm. Southern is chic. The irony is that the packaging, commercializing, advertising, and popularizing of those values long considered Southern is—or at least would be in the eyes of those who best defined those values, the Southern Agrarians—antithetical to the original Southern tradition. If there was anything the

Agrarians hated, it was commercializing, public relations, slickness. But no matter: the selling of the South continues, and public relations replaces racism as the compelling Southern vice. Peachtree Street succeeds Tobacco Road. What once was natural becomes self-conscious; what once was organic becomes stylized.

It happened largely in the 1970s, a decade in which the South, having survived the 1960s, having exited better than it entered, was caught up in a frenzy of self-congratulation. It had come through, had not only endured but prevailed. For the first time in a century and a half it could face the nation without the taint of racism (not more than the rest of the country, anyway). Its 1960s mood of self-scrutiny gave way to celebration. The plain white, the last holdout, finally received his due; his folk culture—music, religion, and stock-car racing—was exhibited for all the world to see. The good ole boy had first been defined in a 1965 *Esquire* article by Tom Wolfe, but not until the 1970s was he certified. Junior Johnson, then Richard Petty, became the Last American Hero, and Johnny, not W. J., became the notable Cash. It all culminated in the election to the presidency of one of the South's own, not one of the singing Carters but one of the preaching and witnessing ones. And he was of the folk culture. In his TV ads, Jimmy Carter of Plains stood on his land, held up a handful of peanuts, and proclaimed himself a product of soil and place, roots and family, all the timeless verities. His people had been in Georgia for two centuries. He belonged. In fact, he *did* belong—but something was lost when all the virtues were cataloged for TV. What was authentic became corrupted. The Grand Ole Opry, authentic, becomes Opryland, slick. Jimmy Carter, part farmer, becomes packaged agrarian. His election was the triumph of public relations, the quintessential selling of the South.

Certainly the South today looks better—more successful and prosperous, less defensive—than it has looked for more than a century. It is a comfortable place to live, this newest of New Souths. The shopping centers continue to go up: one might call it the "malling" of America, and now of the South. Movie theaters and discos replace lynching and nightriding, and the Klan moves out of the cornfield into the Ramada, meeting next to the Rotarians and the Lions. (Even its violence is conducted on city streets, not on country roads.) It is a confident South, a diversified South that advertises itself: Virginia is for lovers, Alabama is the Heart of Dixie, North Carolina—or that part of it around Chapel Hill–Durham—is the Mind of the South: in all seriousness, someone should undertake an anatomy of the South. But it is modern with the Southern accent. If there are many Souths, there is, as W. J. Cash wrote in 1941, still one. Cash named his book *The Mind of the South*, suggesting a definite unity of thought. Rare is the man, by contrast, who would presume to isolate the Mind of the Midwest or the Mind of the Pacific Northwest; and the "New England Mind" is discussed only in historical terms. It would be impossible to define a twentieth-century New England mind, because the English cultural tradition created that mind in the seventeenth century. In the twentieth, the WASPs in New England are far outnumbered.

The South in 1981 feels it has the best of both worlds: pleasant and comfortable, but possessing at least a mild sense of its tradition and heritage. But is it a South to which one can really be committed, which one can regard as distinctly different from the rest of America, which one can love or hate? Can one really feel that strongly about the South anymore? Can there exist a passionate desire to either defend *or* reform it? Does even writing about it become primarily an intellectual exercise? I refer to a particular Southern tradition, one stemming from certain other cultural legacies, which held that the Southerner *felt* very strongly about the South and in many cases expressed his feelings in words. For a century and a half, from the first response to abolitionist sentiment in the early 1830s to the civil rights battles of the 1960s, Southerners took the South seriously indeed. The South defined and explained itself in and through adversity; the Southerner who wrote about it wrote in love and in anger, in pride and in shame. He agonized and brooded over the South, its failure, its promise and sometimes its mission, and he felt compelled to pour out his feelings about the South and about himself as Southerner. Not only the writer but many other Southerners as well took very seriously their Southernness. Edmund Ruffin of Virginia, at the end of the Civil War, scrawled in his diary his "unmitigated hatred" of "the perfidious, malignant and vile Yankee race," then fired a bullet into his brain. Faulkner's Quentin Compson, the fictional prototype of the Southerner who took his South seriously, sat in his cold room at Harvard, telling about the South with pride and anguish, love and hate. Many other Southerners, unchronicled in biography or fiction, have lived and died knowing first of all that they were Southern.

The particular world this Southerner inhabited led to his depth of feeling. It was a world outside the national mainstream, always resistant to it. To outsiders the South was spectacle, enigma, paradox, the most innocent part of America to some, the guiltiest to others. But the greatest paradox was that the Southerner, though defeated in war and humiliated in peace, was proud—proud not in spite of being defeated and downtrodden, but because of it. He perceived a certain value in his defeat, in his poverty, even (if he were a writer) in his guilt and shame. There existed a perverse and defiant spirit in the Southerner, a sense of distinction, even superiority, stemming from what should have been his inferior status. The Southerner wore his heritage of failure and defeat as his badge of honor. He would not have it any other way. He also bore his legacy of failure with an attitude akin to arrogance, and was impatient with less sensitive beings who lacked the tragic sense, who failed to understand and feel the complexities of life. "You would have to be born there," said Faulkner's Quentin, impatiently and with a certain condescension, to his Canadian roommate at Harvard.

That was a South that Southerners *could* take seriously. Loyalists defended it, and native critics attacked it with particular intensity. It was a South whose very self-image *stemmed* in part from its presumed inferiority and its reaction to that presumption. Its legacy, as C. Vann Woodward has reminded us, was one of defeat, poverty, failure, and guilt; its most distinctive thought, and certainly its greatest literature, grew out of that tradition of tragedy. But what becomes of the Southerner who finds himself transported from this savage and benighted South of pre-1970 to a land suddenly become successful, optimistic, and progressive—a region which boasts of being cleaner, less crowded, more open and honest, more genuinely religious, and suddenly more racially tolerant than the rest of America? The South assumes a curious new role in America life. It becomes to America what America in the beginning was to Europe: the nation's second chance, a relatively unspoiled land whose cities, according to the myth, are new and sparkling, and whose people retain the mythical innocence and simplicity of an earlier America. Not a Savage or Benighted, but a Superior South.

I call to witness Atlanta, for despite its recently tarnished image it is still the Southern city to measure up to. Since 1880 and Henry Grady, Atlanta has been the spearhead of whatever New South happened to be current. If the religion of the New South was advertising, as Gerald Johnson wrote in 1924, Atlanta was its Mecca. Nothing has changed, or at least not until recently. Atlanta has been the Southern City on a Hill, the city to emulate. Birmingham and Charlotte and Donald Davidson's Nashville have wanted nothing more than to equal it in size, power, and sophistication. It is literally a city on a hill, and each skyscraper and Portman-designed hotel seems to have been constructed with the vision of the beholder in mind. Approaching Atlanta on I-20 from the west, from the wilds of Alabama and Mississippi, you see its shining towers from fifteen miles away, just about the time you hit Six Flags. You have seen Byzantium. You have left the hinterland and touched the East. You have come to civilization.

It was Atlanta, I recall, which in the 1960s proclaimed itself "The City Too Busy to Hate." An admirable sentiment in some ways. Atlanta did lead the Lower South in racial progress; the city fathers, progressive liberals, genuinely desired racial harmony, not hatred. But why? Let Atlanta answer. It was the city too *busy* to hate. Not too humane, honorable, ethical, or even courteous, but too busy. Busy as in business; as the Oxford English Dictionary shows, the two words are related. Hating would be reported on CBS and would discourage Northern industry and commerce. "The times demand good haters," arch-Southerner Robert Lewis Dabney insisted in the 1860s, but a century later Atlanta assuredly did not. Hatred in the 1960s was left to Birmingham, the fire-breathing rival Atlanta had finally outdistanced. The contrast was evident to anyone who looked: Birmingham's public relations consisted of police dogs and fire hoses, Atlanta's of full-page ads in the *New York Times*. Atlanta was right, of course, but for the wrong reasons. Birmingham was wrong, but, a Birminghamian might have said, for the right reasons. It did not sell its soul for business as Atlanta did. For all its cruelty and inhumanity, racism possessed a certain integrity, a commitment, however distorted and twisted. It would never sell out, never compromise simply to please. By contrast, public relations, to which Atlanta was committed, possessed no soul at all; it held only to the integrity of the dollar. Business required that Atlanta give up racism, so it did. But might not the City Too Busy to Hate also become, in other times and other circumstances, the city too busy to care, to help, to hold to anything in its tradition that did not benefit it in a purely economic or utilitarian way?

I am being too hard on Atlanta. Whatever its motives, tolerance was better than hatred. Besides, Atlanta now has problems enough: its public schools deteriorate even faster than those elsewhere, and the City Too Busy to Hate records nearly a homicide a day. Even its boosterism, the spirit of Peachtree Street, should not be singled out. George F. Babbitt of Zenith has also moved to Charlotte and Nashville and Birmingham, and he has emerged indigenously in Roanoke and High Point and Spartanburg. If image-making is Atlanta's besetting sin, the same is true of the entire South. In one sense, such a phenomenon is explicable, even defensible: the South looked so bad for so long to the progressive, educated American that it naturally wants to look as good as it can now that it has a measure of wealth, sophistication, and racial tolerance to show off. After years of the Benighted South and the Savage South, the Superior South has a nice ring to it. Following upon the Bible Belt, the Hookworm Belt, the Chastity Belt—all supplied by Mencken—the Sun Belt sounds fine after all.

If the metaphor for the inferior South, the dependent colonial South, was that 1886 decree by which all left-hand tracks of the Louisville & Nashville Railroad were moved three inches west in order to accommodate Northern rolling stock—Northern being considered standard—the point at which the South began to rise from colonialism and back toward equality was that moment in 1966 when major league sports crossed the Potomac heading South. First was baseball, which was altogether appropriate, since baseball was the national sport and the South had contributed more than its share of stars: Ty Cobb, Dizzy Dean, Willie Mays, Hank Aaron. But Dixie itself had no major league teams. It had only *farm* teams (the word was appropriate: bush league was its synonym), the Atlanta Crackers, the Birmingham Barons, the New Orleans Pelicans. The South served the same function in baseball that it served in the nation's economy: it was the colony, producing the raw materials— Cobb, Dean, Mays, Aaron—to be shipped north. Southern fans chose a favorite team from above the Potomac and the Ohio, sometimes (particularly at World Series time) the Yankees or Dodgers or Giants, but more often those teams geographically closest to the South—the St. Louis Cardinals or the Cincinnati Reds. It was not so much that the South lacked the population to attract major league baseball—Atlanta was bigger than Milwaukee. But it was a colony, and besides, it was segregated. The Dodgers with Robinson, Campanella, and Newcombe could hardly come to Atlanta first-class. Until 1966, that is, by which time an integration of sorts had come South, and the Braves moved down from Milwaukee. The football Falcons and the basketball Hawks soon followed in Atlanta, and other major league teams came to Miami, New Orleans, Dallas, and Houston. The South had left the farm, it was no longer bush league. The wrong done when the tracks were moved in 1886 had been partially righted: the South had joined the big league and (in one respect) the Union.

But something was lost in the process. In one sense, what has happened to major league baseball in the past two decades is what has happened to the South: it has been cleaned up, homogenized, gone from cotton and wool to double knit. Baseball is now a slick game, with ladies' nights, scoreboards flashing, and pitchers riding in from the bullpen. Most of the dirt is gone: the infields are now grass. Some of the real grass is even gone, replaced by synthetic. The regional identity is gone as well. The Atlanta Crackers were a team with a Southern accent; they were *of* Georgia. But what is Southern about the Braves, the Falcons, the Hawks? They could as easily be— might be any day—in Des Moines.

Most important of all, the dugouts are now air-conditioned. No one can estimate the role of air-conditioning in bringing the South into the Union, or the effect of the summer heat on what the South was or seemed to be before 1950. George W. Cable believed that Southerners never developed the habit of reading because the weather was too hot. One can speculate beyond this. Can one imagine the Scopes trial in an air-conditioned courthouse? The 100-degree heat, the florid faces and sweating bodies were what made Dayton, Tennessee, seem savage to Mencken and the outsiders, nearly as much as the fundamentalism. Can one imagine Faulkner writing *Absalom, Absalom!* under the spell of central air? One might, indeed, discover a direct relationship between the rise of air-conditioning and the decline of the creative fury of the Southern writer. And could the Yankees have come to an un-air-conditioned Atlanta or New Orleans or Houston—and stayed? The Sun Belt is an air-conditioned South.

Of course, the Sun Belt is not precisely the South. Rather, the Sun Belt civilization is one that in some respects has been lifted out of the Northeast and placed in that geographical area designated "the South." It is in large part a transplanted, imposed civilization, its goals having little in common with the goals of Jefferson, Edmund Ruffin, or Donald Davidson; it happened to land in the South primarily because the South had oil, water, forests, military bases, good tax rates, cheap labor, and air-conditioning. But the Sun Belt philosophy has had its effect on traditional Southern thinking. Its optimism and confidence have replaced, or at least modified, the Southern legacy of failure, pessimism, and looking backward. Indeed, one might be tempted to say (if it had not been said and disproved half a dozen times before) that what has been claimed since 1875 might now really be true: this most recent of New Souths really *is* different, because it is based on a different set of assumptions. For the first time since 1930, the South has dropped its defensive stance and speaks from a position of strength, even presumed superiority. The nation's confidence has declined—a decade of Vietnam, racial unrest, and Watergate assured that—while the South's has increased correspondingly.

But, to come back to my original question: Is this a South about which one can feel deeply anymore? Could true commitment come only in adversity? In all this homogenization of Southern and national traits, is there anything left that is distinctively Southern? If we are to judge by Southern literature, the Southerner still *seems* to feel deeply, still seems to write in that particular tradition which requires that he probe deeply and painfully his relationship to his homeland. Willie Morris's *North Toward Home* (1967) and Larry King's *Confessions of a White Racist* (1971) seem, for example, to be in the love-hate genre, their authors latter-day Quentin Compsons. But are they? They are eloquent and interesting, but do they really *mean* it, as Ruffin and Hinton Helper and Dabney and Davidson and Cash did? Or are they merely writing in a particular Southern mode, writing the obligatory love-hate-pride-shame memoir more out of custom and habit than from true rage, indignation, love, hate, or anything else? Can the Southerner, no longer severely afflicted by an inferiority complex, released from the savage ideal, besieged neither by critics from the North nor in his own backyard, write with that same intensity and conviction, even fear and trembling, that drove Ruffin and Dabney and Davidson? Will what was once natural become stylized? Will what was once deeply and painfully experienced become ritualized? Will the passion disappear and only the form remain?

Perhaps not. Perhaps the writers in the present volume are proof that it will not. But I wonder. The times may not be right for the making of impassioned Southerners. Whatever the South of 1981 is, it is not a likely partner for a love-hate relationship. That, for its general health, is good. It is good that the South is more tolerant than before, more open, prosperous, integrated, successful, and air-conditioned. It is good that symphonies have replaced night-riding, and no one could really have defended the "integrity" of racism. So I am not saying that the South of 1981 is not better; just that it is softer, less vital, less *interesting*. Jimmy Carter is a case in point. He is a decent man—the term becomes the cliché—not a wild man, an all-or-nothing man like Vardaman, Bilbo, or Huey Long. But he and his presidency may have done more to endanger the livelihoods of South-watchers than anything else could have done. One would not have thought it; one would have thought that the South-watching industry would prosper with a Georgian in the White House. But only at first. Soon Carter served to destroy the Southern mystique—

by being decent, moderate, industrious, colorless, always the technician. He might as well have been from Nebraska.

But could he be? And is he any less Southern for being temperate and colorless? Have we perhaps misled ourselves all along by dwelling on the extremes of Southern life, rather than on its norms? Are there certain qualities the Southerner retains that are subtler, more muted, less flamboyant than racism, hedonism, violence, and dramatic oratory? I think so, and it is in those qualities—qualities that cannot be marketed, at least not successfully—that we find the continuing value of the Southern tradition.

What the South has to offer goes beyond fried chicken and country music and stock-car racing. It is related to those features of Southern life and thought that the Agrarians and their successors identified—a sense of time and place, a religious temper, a suspicion of material progress, a tradition of manners, a fury against abstraction. One must be careful not to overstate the uniqueness of the Southern character, not to mistake as exclusively Southern what is in fact traditional American rural. I would bet, for example, that more than a few farmers and small townspeople in New Hampshire, Indiana, and Ohio are religious, have a sense of tradition, and love the land. One must also be careful not to exaggerate the presumed Southern rage against abstraction: Jefferson and Calhoun and George Fitzhugh were devoted to system-building, and William Faulkner is more abstract than Hemingway. One must be wary as well of glorifying those traits that might indeed exist in the Southern temper but which one finds (at least, I find) not really very admirable: an aversion to reasoned argument, or a distrust of analysis, reform, and social change. Finally, one must realize that certain Southern virtues resulted from historical accident or even from Southern shortcomings as much as from moral superiority. The South's anti-materialism arose in part from its poverty, its distrust of progress partly from its realization that progress would bring painful racial change, even its religious sentiment partly from its rural isolation and lack of exposure to other ways of viewing life. But whatever the origins of the virtues, they were virtues nonetheless, and they remain even in those parts of the South that have become urbanized.

It is in his way of viewing the world that the Southerner has something to offer. His is a view, has been a view, in which man is not always at the center. Whatever else it does or does not do, Southern religion engenders a habit of belief which allows one to transcend both self and the purely material world self has created; it also provides a barrier against cultural fragmentation. Likewise with the

Southern view of history, a history not learned so much as felt. The past lives in the present. The American, a progressive creature, lives in his subdivision, drives on his interstate highway, shops at his mall, a captive of the moment, the present. He gives little thought to what occupied any particular spot fifty years before, to what happened there. The Southerner may not, either—but, with his tradition, he should.

It is finally in his attitude toward leisure and work—and, related to it, his heritage of manners—that the Southerner has something to offer. The Southerner has always appreciated leisure: from the poor white of Lubberland to the gentleman of Virginia, the colonial Southerner was more likely to prize a leisured way of life than was the New England Puritan. But what Southerners saw as a virtue (a love of leisure) Northerners often saw as a vice (laziness). When Yankees traveled in the antebellum South, "sloth" and "idleness" offended them, even more than slavery fired their passion to reform. A Southern Benjamin Franklin was rare indeed—Walter Hines Page, a generation after Appomattox, perhaps came closest—but as a rule the Southerner found a measure for the good life other than utilitarian activity. It had to do with his ability to absorb himself in life, to take it as it came rather than trying to design it. He was not too *busy*, that is—to hate, to help, to enjoy or to produce those elements of a vital folk culture: art, crafts, music, food. If his purse was not rich, his life assuredly was, in those things that were the fruits of his leisure.

But whither the South now? Whither Southern virtues? Are they merely ripe for exploitation, for packaging and marketing? I am reminded of W. B. Yeats's division of three "cultures": high (classical art, music, literature; i.e., the learned and shared possession of people of diverse backgrounds), folk (the organic and often unconscious expression of the folk in music, art, and crafts), and, somewhere in the middle but lacking the distinction of either, popular, or mass culture—that shared domain of all who take their values from television, advertising, popular literature and music.

Until recently, the South—except in certain parts of the Tidewater—had relatively little high culture, but it can claim a vital and abundant folk culture, white and black. Its promise now for a rich and vital life is that it will welcome the high culture and at the same time retain as much as possible of the folk. Its danger is that, being prosperous and busy, it will fall into the amorphous middle.

II

IN JUSTICE TO SO
FINE A COUNTRY

The Enduring Soil

Hamilton C. Horton, Jr.

THE SOUTHLAND. A region analyzed, quantified, described and explained, caressed with honeyed words, condemned as a hopeless anachronism. Does it still exist, or has it passed into myth?

Perhaps it was always as much myth as fact. Certainly the region we think of as the South has changed profoundly since you and I first saw it, though we still tend to think of it as it was when we first opened our eyes to it. But myth is often as real as statistics. And if a majority of us hold to the same myth, why then, it's real enough to the extent we act on it and live by it.

So let us simply say that, to whatever degree and for whatever reason, a region exists that has been, and is, stubbornly different.

But just where is this Southland? Various lines have been drawn, of course. The Mason-Dixon line comes to mind. Some suggest that the South consists of those states which seceded in the War between the States. The late Jonathan Daniels argued for a ma'am line—below which "all nice children say 'no ma'am' and 'yes ma'am,' and on the other side of which they get laughed at for saying it at all."[1] That definition is pretty close, but I would contend for a harsher test, perhaps more restricted, but with the advantage of self-identification. I suggest that the true Southland is that territory within which, when asked by an outsider whether he is a Southerner, the reply almost invariably is "Hell, yes!" This "Hell, yes" line has the advantage of eliminating the ambivalent wishy-washy fringes, and leaving the unquestionable defiant, hard-core Southland for our study.[2]

1. Jonathan Daniels, *A Southerner Discovers the South* (New York: Macmillan, 1938).
2. Strangely, it seems the "Hell, yes" line defines that region in the Eastern United States where the growing season is 200 days or more.

Within this Southland, the soil retains an ineluctable hold.

Countless others have commented on the Southerner's attachment to his soil, but they have tended to picture this as an agricultural attachment, a love of land that a man and his forebears have watered with their own sweat. And, of course, this special connection exists among those on the farms. The evidence suggests, however, that there is more.

For in the past few decades, the number of those earning a living on farms has radically declined, so that now the farmer is a minority in most of the region. Indeed, in most of the South a man can't earn a living on a small farm.

Yet the Southerner, though his family may have lived for several generations in town, typically declines to consider himself a town dweller. His vision of the good life is not a penthouse, but a place in the country. He is exiled, perhaps, to town. But home remains the land.

Of course, other people in other sections of the nation feel the same way. I argue only that this affection for the land is a characteristic in the South. We see its aspects, good and bad, in many ways: We see it in the springtime when the population, like lemmings, march out of their homes and begin scrabbling in the soil of their fifty by one hundred foot lots, planting gardens. By summer's end, the land may or may not have yielded a few scrawny tomatoes, at great expense to the household and great profit to the local garden store. No matter: the urge to dirty fingernails, to feel the soil in the hand has been met. The annual tryst with the land has been kept.

During the growing season, the factory laborer and the bank president become kin to the farmer. Talk during lunch hour is dominated by rainfall, fertilizer, mulch, and a comparison of crop yields that would cause a fisherman to blush.

We also see this tie to the land in an obsession with hunting and fishing. In the South, a youngster of whatever education or social background expects to learn to hunt as a part of growing up. More than twice as many hunting licenses per capita are issued in the South as in the North. I suspect what keeps calling the hunter to the field and the fisherman to the river may not be so much the meat as the chance for communion with the land. When the crisp air moves across a stubble cornfield in the lowering yellow light of an autumn afternoon, and dove hunters are crouched against the fringing pine woods; when the deer hunters separate in the gray mists of dawn and walk, alone in the woods at last, to their stands; when the outboard motor is cut and the boat drifts, catching the water's own tempo, the Southland calls its own unto itself.

Up in the Appalachians, bear hunting calls clans like the Hugheses and the Boones and the Wilsons away for weeks. The mountain forests were never fenced, never really "owned" by those who held title to them: they have belonged for centuries to the mountaineers as a vested ancestral right, a sort of commons. So whole families go out gathering galax and herbs in the vast forests.[3]

In a very real sense, the land *is* theirs. And while the Appalachian Southerner has not fallen for the dry logic of environmentalism, he is a true conservationist: Genesis tells him that he is to have dominion over the beast and fowl and the harvest of the earth, but piety tells him that there is a great difference between dominion and destruction.

Roan Mountain is a "bald," on top of which are broad meadows and vast natural gardens of rhododendron. In the springtime the massed blooms and the panorama of circling mountains brings tears to jaded eyes. Long before tourists discovered the Roan, the people of the towns at its foot would climb to the top every year to sit and contemplate God's handiwork. They still do. And these same people have kept the mica and feldspar mines from polluting their rivers.

In Virginia and North Carolina, the families along the New River were offered more money per acre than they ever would have dreamed when a power company wanted to build a hydroelectric dam and flood the valley. Jobs, visions of tourist dollars, were dangled before them. But most of them figured that money could not buy their homesteads, their graveyards and churches. They fought the power company up to and through Congress—and won.

The point I hope I am not laboring is that within the South there remains a tendency to view the land as something more than just a commodity.

Indeed, many of those people in the New River Valley are not there because they make livings farming the land; only a large landowner can. They live there because that land is somehow special— and they commute as much as a hundred miles a day to factory jobs.

Which leads us to a development in the South not foreseen by those who despaired of her survival fifty years ago.

Industry is coming—has come—to the South. After centuries of

3. A recent tentative proposal to turn the Mount Mitchell area in North Carolina into a national park—an action which would curtail hunting and "galacking"—nearly brought on riots in Yancey County, where free ranging in the mountains is viewed as a prescriptive right.

economic dominion by the North, whether by rigged freight rates, tariffs, or bankers, after centuries of being fed (in Andrew Lytle's pungent phrase) "at the hind tit," the South is booming.[4]

Partly because of the new availability of industrial jobs, in the 1950s the South shifted from a net out-migration of her population to a modest in-migration. In the 1960s this became a moderate influx, and in the 1970s a substantial flood. Young and old, poor and non-poor, retirees and climate seekers, black and white are coming South—reversing a pattern extending back to the early 1800s.

But for once, history has been kind: the very delay in our industrialization has been a blessing.

In past societies, vast industrial cities—the Liverpools and Manchesters, the Pittsburghs and Buffaloes, the Stuttgarts and Bolognas—grew beside waterways and railway tracks. Factories run on energy, whether coal or waterwheel; and raw materials had to be brought in and finished goods shipped out at the cheapest price, thus usually by water. Typically, the workers left their homes in the villages and farmsteads of the world and moved to the factory towns. Uprooted, without the comfort of that rural sense of continuity and identity, dependent on strangers for their bread, compelled for lack of transportation to huddle close to the factory itself, the masses of industrial employees, as much as the cheap factory goods they produced, changed whole societies.

Only recently have the network of highways and the ease with which energy can be delivered, made it feasible for the first time to move the factories to the workers.

And this moving of the work place to the labor supply has become the pattern in the South.

The South is creating an industrial society unlike any the world has ever known.

There they are: squat, flat, almost sterile factory buildings next to the corn, the soybean, the cane fields throughout the South, with neat parking lots and broad manicured lawns. Not as romantic as pillared mansions, perhaps, but evidence of an industrialization with minimal social impact.

This happy result is not planned (what would have been more un-Southern!). It comes about as a sort of bargain in which all parties gain, and typically takes place somewhat in this way: the town fathers of Culpepper Crossroads, seeing their young people leaving town to find jobs, and seeing the effect of a decline in agriculture reflected in lower mercantile sales and an eroding tax base, decide to

---

4. So much of their industry is moving to the South that Northern states are forming regional caucuses in Congress to oppose Southern "piracy."

entice an industry to come in, provide jobs, create a payroll, and ultimately pay taxes. To do this, after consulting the state industry-hunting office (which salivates just as readily, but on a larger scale), Culpepper Crossroads offers an industrial site free (land has always been comparatively cheap for us), taxfree revenue bonds to build a plant, a moratorium on *ad valorem* taxes, an entire social and political structure anxious to cooperate with the new industry.

Meanwhile, up in Titus Falls, Connecticut, Ethan Ames, industrialist, looks out a frosty window at a ninety-year-old grimy brick factory. It is inefficient, drafty, expensive to operate. Moreover, the union shop steward has just left the office after making demands that border on the rapacious. Taxes are up, employees resentful and surly, labor department regulations more and more difficult to comply with. Ethan Ames's thoughts drift Southward.

So it arranged. And after the ribbons are cut and the high school band has packed up its instruments, Ethan Ames finds himself in a modern air-conditioned concrete block factory on the interstate highway outside Culpepper Crossroads, with the pick of the county youth at his machines. (It seemed the whole county lined up, he recalls, when he began hiring.) Whether it is the new machinery or the new laborers he's not sure, but production is higher. He knows his overhead is lower; and, for the first time in years, when Ethan Ames walks down the lines of machinery, he meets quick smiles and open faces. The second-shift line foreman is taking him fishing Saturday.

There are drawbacks, of course. As for Ames, he misses not being within a couple of hours of New York and Boston. As for Culpepper Crossroads, Ames's industry is the only one so far. With a labor surplus and no competition for it, there is little incentive to pay more than minimum wages.

But note the point: the new factory in Culpepper Crossroads has meant no significant increase in the community's population. It has become no industrial warren, no mill town. The new factory has simply stabilized Culpepper Crossroads's population, offering jobs to those already there who might otherwise leave. The Crossroads remains a small, rural community, where everyone seems to know everyone else.

And the industrial workers at the factory are unlike any others in history: they have not been proletarianized. The factory came to them, not they to it. They have not left their homes, their churches, their ancestral cemeteries. Their roots in the Southern soil are intact.

Indeed, the jobs to which they commute have *saved* the family farm. Thousands of Southern farm families today supplement the income from their farms with income from industrial jobs. They could not otherwise have earned the cash to invest in improved equipment. Nor could the farm alone have provided more than a marginal standard of living.[5]

So the South by and large will remain as most Southerners would want it: a region of small, rural communities in which the Atlantas and Houstons are unnatural growths, albeit benign. By and large, the new highways have not so much beckoned our people to factories as they have beckoned factories to our people.

For the Southerner has an ineradicable sense of place. He stays put if he can, but if he must leave, he is afflicted with a homesickness, a sense of being forever an alien. So the displaced Southerners in Detroit and Cleveland gather in their own taverns around jukeboxes playing those sad country-western ballads that speak of home. And the bright young college graduates in New York somehow find each other and crowd to places where they can shag and drink bourbon and tell each other those self-deprecating, hyperbolic tales that mark Southern humor.

And they, most of them, come back. Some more than once: among the poignant proofs of the pull the soil exerts is the number of families that, not able to make a living on the farm, rent the homestead and move away, saving every penny they can in order to move back and try to make it on the farm once more. And the cycle is repeated, again and again.

Now, at last, there is hope for employment near home.

The significance of this can hardly be underestimated: Through historical reasons not of our making, the South may well be the first major region of this world to be industrialized and yet preserve the human dimension. Megalopolis can be rejected.

The Agrarian writers of fifty years ago were rightly concerned that industrialization of the South could mean the end of those values that made us more than economic ciphers. I suspect it was not the regular paycheck they abhorred; it was what one had to give up in human terms to get that paycheck. And it was not the factory they opposed, but the factory of inhuman scale.

So far, we've kept the human scale. And at a time when individual citizens feel they have lost control of their own lives, that their personal destinies may be decided by pork futures posted in Chicago,

5. Industrialization throughout the region is proceeding so rapidly that by the later 1980s the historic per capita income gap between the South and the industrialized, urbanized North will have disappeared.

by international wheat prices or oil-producing cartels, that scale maintained in Southern growth holds special charm.

The smaller Southern community, whether urban or rural, can preserve that sense of continuity that stabilizes societies. When you are known not by your income or your job but as a person, when your friend's fathers were friends of your father, when you have a name and a known heritage, cousins and the familial responsibilities and all those imply, you know that your status and that of your family is based on more important things than mere income.

In the Culpepper Crossroads of the New South, the factory owner, farmer, teacher, laborer, go to the same churches and their children go to the same schools. Acknowledged class distinctions exist. They have throughout history, but here they need not be divisive or antagonistic—especially when the bosses and machine operators, the lawyers and farmers hunt and fish together.[6]

So an agrarian industrialization has become the Southern pattern, made possible by developments in energy transmission and transportation over which the South has had minimal influence. It was worked out by dumb luck. (Even a blind sow stumbles over an occasional acorn.)

That may be just as well, for in the past, when we have attempted to plan prosperity, we have often been inept.

Agriculture is an example.

Nature was prodigal to the South. Originally the region was magnificently forested: it was said that a squirrel could travel from the Atlantic Coast to the Mississippi River without touching the ground. The soil was deep and rich. Except along the Appalachian Mountain salient, growing seasons were a generous two hundred days or more. A multitude of rivers drained the interior, and rainfall was plentiful: more than in any other region; more than double that of the West.

But over the decades we Southerners have stumbled from one agricultural disaster to another. We have been poor custodians of the land and worse forecasters of the markets.

Monoculture seemed natural to the broad acres of the Southland, but it forced the planter to wager everything on one cast of the dice.

---

6. Much has been said about the intransigence of the South in accepting labor unionism. It has been put down to oppressive laws, backward social customs, and racism. The truth is simpler: *Klassenkampf* is difficult when you've cussed and gotten drunk together, when you've cheered one another's children on the local football team, when you've followed each other's family caskets to the old cemetery plots. Moreover, when the worker can raise enough meat and vegetables on his own land to face economic depression without panic, there is a sense of security and independence unknown in the megalopolis.

In good crop years, there was too much to sell, and prices were down. In bad crop years, prices were good, but there was little to sell. Each season was a hope that somehow the law of supply and demand would be suspended and that there would be both a big crop and a high price.

Indigo, rice, naval stores, cane, cotton have each taken their turn, sending more topsoil into the rivers and away.

They say Cotton was King: but more, it was a tyrant. Leaving the land of the east coast exhausted, it moved gradually inland, depleting the land in its path. Even before the War between the States, it ruined as many planters as it made rich. And after the War fluctuating markets and uncertain prices pushed the South deeper and deeper into an agricultural depression. Then in 1913 the boll weevil arrived. Only World War I saved the cotton farmer. Even when wartime scarcity led to record high prices in 1919, the resulting overplanting glutted the market and threw the cotton-growing South into a depression from which it has never recovered. The boll weevil continued its migration northward; synthetic fibers later came into use. Today what was the "land of cotton" has largely gone back to forest and broomsedge. The main production has moved to the far Southwest and California.

The other major Southern cash crop was tobacco. It remains one of the few that returns enough per acre to make a small farm profitable. But even this is possible only because of a federal quota system that allots how much each farmer can produce. If this prop were taken away, the large farms would promptly drive the small ones out of production. The gnawing if unspoken question in the grower's mind is how long will the federal quota system for tobacco be retained when that same government proclaims that smoking is harmful to the health?

And what of the moderate-sized family farms of the upper and Piedmont South, those self-sustaining yeoman farms that in past years provided meat and vegetables for nearby communities? They are gone, most of them, victims of a loss of their markets. The supermarket chains purchase by 40,000-pound truckloads, not by bushels. So once-productive fields are reverting to weeds and woods: the South has more forest cover today than it had a century ago.

And a region that could provide vegetables in boundless quantity, that could provide year-round pasture, instead imports meat and vegetables from a thousand miles away. California produces more than five times as many peaches as the "peach state" of Georgia. New York produces twice as many string beans as the entire South.

Eighty percent of the asparagus and cauliflower, nearly all of the broccoli, grapes, pears, and plums, more than half the cantaloupe, carrots, celery, lima beans, spinach, and lettuce come from the West Coast. Even in corn production no Southern state approaches California. We do not even feed ourselves.

And this in a region with the climate, the soil, and the water resources to feed a nation. We should rightly be outraged: Are our people not as able farmers, as intelligent, as willing to work, as others?

The truth is that Southern land and Southern farmers *can* grow small fruits and vegetables. But where will they sell them?

The smaller farm simply does not produce the truckload quantities that are the units in which fruit and vegetbles move from farm to market. For all the evils of cotton and tobacco monoculture, the farmer at least knows that he can sell what he grows.

A diversified agriculture for the average farm must await adequate competitive markets.

Of course, there do exist, in those few places where vegetables and fruit are grown in the South, "markets" where farmers can bring in a pickup truck and sell their small load to brokers, who in turn amass the necessary amounts to sell by the standard truckload. But the farmer is at the mercy of the market, and when the reckoning is made, with the commissions, handling charges, and freight charged back to him, the return often is disappointing.

Yet on the West Coast small farmers grow and sell fruit and vegetables successfully, often on less acreage than their Southern counterparts have available. The important difference is that they have learned to process, pack, and market their crops—most often cooperatively. Indeed, in every farming area except the South, farmer-owned cooperatives dominate the marketing process, often under their own labels: labels such as Welch's, Sunkist, Donald Duck, Land 'O Lakes. These coops were started by farmers themselves in response to years of being victimized by the marketing system, the kind of victimization Southerners know only too well. It's been part of their history since before the Revolution.

The difference is that the rest of the nation's farmers have fought this exploitation with reasonable success. The Southerner has railed and cussed but done practically nothing.[7]

The shame is that our Southern schools of agriculture, our state

7. Today the eleven Confederate states together market a mere $7 billion through cooperatives. Excluding Florida and Texas, the remaining nine states market only $4.5 billion through coops. California alone markets $4 billion cooperatively, Iowa $3 billion.

departments of agriculture, have given diversification little more than lip service. They have catered to the big crops and the big farmers, while offering the small farmer sympathetic cluckings that his day has passed, and that the family-run farm is doomed. Effort after effort by small farmers to grow fruits and vegetables has failed because the problem of marketing has been ignored. It is no wonder that Southern farmers are leery of committing an entire year to a new crop.

But even lazy extension agents, unimaginative agriculture schools, and moribund departments of agriculture cannot delay forever the diversification of Southern agriculture. It will come.

The question is: *Who* will reap the coming prosperity from our farms? Will it be native Southern farmers, or the Californians and Arizonans and New Mexicans who will have moved to the Southeast? That, too, will happen: because the farms of the far Southwest are destined to become progressively less productive and profitable. The essential reason is that the Western United States is water deficient; by the year 2000 its water use will exceed its water runoff. Already the irrigation water on California cropland contains three times more dissolved solids than Southeastern water. Salinity levels are rising due to repeated use of the same water in agricultural irrigation. As available water is diminishing, their demand for it continues to grow.

Meanwhile, the Southeast has a comfortable water surplus, a rainfall more than twice that of the West, a long growing season, abundant land, and proximity to the major markets of the North and East. So, evitably, Southern soil will feed the nation during the next century. Whether numerous family farms processing and marketing their products cooperatively will survive alongside the super farms producing enough volume to market efficiently by themselves remains to be seen.

Even Southern forests are destined to a new prosperity: climate and rainfall have conspired to make our timberland the most productive in the nation. Here, too, the problem is that, since three out of four timber tracts in the South are of less than seventy-five acres, efficient harvesting and marketing methods must be found if the landowner is to receive his due.

In fact, each element of the Southland's current and coming prosperity has its problems. The rural and dispersed industrialization pattern often means absentee ownership. The continuation of the family farm is as often threatened by estate taxes imposed on inflated land values as by crop prices. Even the Southerner's romance with the soil carries its own penalty: the demand for land has driven the price so high that a young man can no longer afford to buy a farm that will provide him a good living.

But even so, after long waiting, we are in the catbird seat. The South, with its forests and broad acres and storied rivers, will endure. The political stranglehold of the Northeast and Central states is gradually being broken as each census gives more congressional seats to the South, at their expense. And our newcomers are becoming Southerners, too, snared in that multitude of tendrils by which our land makes men its own. Their "Hell, yes" has the authentic ring of conviction.

At Daniel's Mountain

DON ANDERSON

And so at Daniel's mountain the year dies,
A cold sets in, the warmth of body goes;
The quiet, soundless season then comes on.

The dead leaves and leafless trees
Lead us to talk about "what was"—
Like examining old fossils
We talk about last summer.
The fire is out on the campsite.
I hear the voices on the tennis court.

Spring comes as if we were forgiven.
The sprouting leaves evince a Resurrection,
The beaver rushes out to mend his dams
And we repair the road.
I hear the voices of the woods,
The crows in the cemetery
The lone piper on the campsite.
We get to know the river.
The shadows in the distant mountains
Make us all one.
And at night, above the candles and the wine
Laughing and talking
Making our recordings upon time.

I do not dream about next summer
For the peacock's full maturity
Nor can I believe with assurance
I shall see again the Autumn leaves
But be content to know the corners of
Each minute, each hour, each day.

At Daniel's Mountain 'til I go home.

ONE CAN SEE, as one drives through the South, the pale outline of its history. One strays from the modern interstate highways to old plantation houses or to households whose decor dates them back a century or so. There is a constant longing for former times, and the heart is stirred that here a village withstood a Federal advance, there a hero was born. The pendulum swings from the past to the present, and back into the past.

For much of my life I was a stranger to this sentiment. Although I spent most of my youth in the South, I went to college and law school in the North, then to the army and then to school in London. After a law clerkship in Pittsburgh for a couple of years, I began to work with the Congress. I was working in this cloistered atmosphere when, in 1965, I got a call from my father. He had, he said, a piece of property in a remote area of Virginia; he wanted me to survey the place. Such a task was burdensome for me, since I had recently been given a large responsibility on a House subcommittee; besides, I had little interest in his proposal. I contacted a Washington surveying firm and, through them, found a surveyor within a convenient distance of my father's land. When the survey was sent to me, I forwarded it to my father, having, I thought, fully satisfied the paternal command.

Within a few weeks my father called again. I should, he said, at least look at the survey lines and permanent markers. I could not do so immediately, but on a cold November day when Congress was out of session I motored to Fincastle, Virginia, to meet with the surveyor and have him guide me to the property.

We went into the place from the back. It was untouched wilderness with heavy undergrowth, and with great difficulty we made our way on a path that was ceasing to be a path. As we walked along, I learned that my grandfather had left the place as a youth nearly seventy years earlier and that it had not been lived on since. We pushed through one secluded section of the land, and we saw gravestones. We were looking down on what I learned later was a half-acre of graves, the graves of several score of the former slaves of the plantation. One read, "Harris Anderson, Born October 7, 1821, died August 4, 1891." It began to dawn on me that I was looking at the graves of my forebears.

At that moment we heard a rather urgent bellow. A friend who had accompanied us, and had walked ahead of us, cried out in a voice which signified injury. We rushed to the spot where his voice came from and found him almost transfixed, looking down on a magnificent view of mountains.

From that moment there crept over my spirit a feeling akin to patriotism for this piece of land—for its history and for its beauty. From that moment I have been drawn to it as to a magnet. From that month and that year I have not strayed from it for long. I built on the place three years later, just in front of the graveyard; today it is my home.

During my first visit I met a relative and a resident of what I now realized was the plantation upon which my forebears were slaves. Mrs. Arbullah Mack is my grandfather's first cousin, and represents that part of our family that never left the old plantation. A woman of strong character, witty and intelligent, she lives alone (her husband had died seven years earlier) on her $125 monthly Social Security check, on her hill with what an insurance salesman had told her was a $100,000 view of mountains. So gracious, so interesting, so entertaining is she that I regularly take my guests across the valley just to listen to her. She constantly monitored what I did with my part of the plantation. Soon after I had completed my house, she called me up.

"Donald," she said, "did you build that house in the graveyard?"

"No," I replied, "just on the verge of it."

"I was just about to say, Old Gabriel blow the horn and those folks would have a great deal of trouble getting up through that concrete."

From Mrs. Mack I learned the history of the land insofar as it touched my close relatives. They were slaves of a small plantation of roughly five hundred acres. The plantation house is still used; it stands in the next valley, though not on our property. The father of my grandfather's mother, a circuit minister, established three nearby churches in the 1870s. (His picture still hangs on the wall of one of those churches.) He had been born in slave quarters near the plantation house, a son of the plantation owner and a slave. He is buried in the backyard of my house. He had never been a slave, but even before the Civil War had traveled throughout the valley on his ministry.

My forebears had been devoted to the property. At the end of the Civil War my great-grandfather and his brother, newly emancipated, went eighteen miles north of the plantation to work on canals and five years later were able to purchase ninety-two acres of the place. My grandfather had said he thought his father owned the world because he owned that property.

I now call the property Daniel's Mountain, after one of the ancestors who purchased it in 1869. The name was suggested to me by Mrs. Deirdre Barber. She and her husband, Stephen, loved Daniel's Mountain and visited it often. I was deeply touched that, when Stephen Barber died, one of his last wishes was to be buried at Daniel's Mountain, as he was on April 3, 1980. Stephen had been a great journalist; for the last eighteen years of his career he was a bureau chief for the *London Daily Telegraph*. In a tribute in the *Washington Star*, Barber was said to have been "one of the best." He had covered the messier part of World War II, always the "man on the spot," the first man to tell the world that Mussolini was dead. He had been around the world and had seen the beauty, the majesty of much of it; yet when, in his last days, he was compelled to think of a final resting place, he chose Daniel's Mountain—because of its beauty, and because, as a London newspaper stated, I had been the first in America to befriend him and his family. And because of the opportunity which America had afforded me.

Throughout his life, according to Mrs. Mack, my grandfather had made regular pilgrimages to the place. She said he would walk around it all day. I had been on the land for ten years before I discovered the remains of his house; the thick growth of vines had shielded it from view, and, in any case, not much was left of it. The deer bed down where the house stood, and there is a hand-dug well that has fallen in. But in the front yard several rows of daffodils return every year, though my family has been absent.

The former owners of Daniel's Mountain—the white owners, those who had given us their name and some of their blood—had been Scotch Presbyterians from County Donegal, Ireland. They had settled the place in the 1790s. They had done some things of importance for the state of Virginia. One grandson of the original immigrant had served on the Court of Appeals of Virginia; one of his cousins had been rector of Washington and Lee University and in that position had been a pallbearer at Robert E. Lee's funeral. We know not how much runs in the blood, nor what this Scottish ancestry did to me; yet when I was traveling in Scotland in 1969, I heard bagpipes for the first time. I was hypnotized by them, and I rushed out and bought a set the next day. I have been playing them for a decade, and recently won a medal in the competition at Grandfather Mountain, North Carolina—the largest gathering of Scottish clans on the east coast. I have been told that people in the valley near Daniel's Mountain sit on their porches in anticipation of my playing on summer evenings—a strange transplant in what must be the right atmosphere.

As time went on, I learned that I had hundreds of relatives in the valley. Like Mrs. Mack, they were low-income people, but all were supremely conscious that they belonged to a single clan fathered by named patriarchs. All were conscious of the influence of my great-great-grandfather on the religious institutions of the valley. Thus I learned of the importance of the church in the lives of rural blacks. It is, of course, the dominant institution of their culture, and (aside from music) the only institution that is not imitative. It is so much a reflection of their past. The analogy of the Jews coming out of Egypt is a perfect parallel of these people's own emancipation and their eventual achievement of equality. Their complete knowledge of the Bible has lent richness to their language, a complete moral code, fastidiously adhered to, and a philosophy judiciously applied to their own closed world. They knew the difference between good and evil, and although they knew that there was evil among them, they saw no good at all in the white man.

"You notice," one of them once said, "in that hurricane down in Mississippi, it only killed white men. The Lord knows what He's doing."

Their religion made them a community. (No other meetings were so regularly attended.) Their religion was also a source for traditions, the mold for which had to begin with the exigencies of slavery. In times of slavery, when the fields lay fallow and were in little need of attention, ministers took advantage of the slack period by holding church services every night; thus the tradition of revivals began. Starting in July and ending in early September, it is strongest in August, when church revivals are held every single night of the week. This period has become a sort of homecoming for people now living in the North, and August will find people trailing back from Pennsylvania, New York, New Jersey, and elsewhere to the Southern rural areas of their origin, in order to see their families and attend the revivals.

I visited the church, just down the road a bit, which my grandfather not only had attended, but in which he had also been educated. I saw in the service the same traditions which he had observed as a deacon in a Baptist church in Pittsburgh. It was a bit like living beside history, and I reflected upon the difference between his life at Daniel's Mountain seventy years ago and my life there now.

Sylvestor Anderson, my grandfather, left Daniel's Mountain in 1898 and established residence in Pittsburgh. He was, by trade, a tile-setter, but the whites had formed a union and excluded him. He became a chauffeur to a vice-president of Westinghouse Electric, and ended his life as a night clerk at the Pittsburgh YMCA. Sylvestor had seven sons and one daughter; one of his sons (my father) earned three degrees, including a Ph.D. in genetics, from the University of Pittsburgh, which was then tuition free. It was not easy for my father to finish college, because he had to work full-time in the city's steel mills while doing so. He told me he had to stand or walk about when studying in order not to fall asleep.

My father got his Ph.D. in 1932, the year my twin sister and I were born. Although he had studied under and published a joint work with a Nobel Prize winner, he was unable to find work in the North. He went to Johnson C. Smith University, a Negro college in Charlotte, North Carolina, where he taught for thirteen years. At the age of thirty-five, realizing that he would be unable to educate his four children on his salary of $3,000, he went to medical school, and thereafter established his practice in Florida.

The color bar and prejudice dominated our lives from beginning to end, but my earliest memory of the race question goes back to when my father was asked to attend an international genetics conference in Edinburgh, Scotland, in 1939. The war broke out while he was there, and the British were placing the American conferees on the first ships out. One such ship was the *Athenia*, but my father was prohibited from taking it because his intended cabinmate refused to room with a black man. In a sense it was a voyage of some importance, for, as Winston Churchill mentions in his war memoirs, the Germans accused Churchill of personally having placed a bomb on board the ship. The *Athenia* went down, drowning over a hundred people, twenty-eight of them American, including my father's intended cabinmate. For three weeks we believed that my father had also perished. Afterwards I remember, as a child of seven, believing prejudice to be a virtue, for it had saved my father's life.

During my youth, the all-black world forced upon us by the color bar caused us to believe that that was the whole problem for black people in the South. All of our thoughts were directed toward ridding ourselves of bars to our legal rights. Yet, when these bars disappeared, I began to see the more trying problem confronted by a large part of the black race, a problem which before that time had appeared to me only in abstract form. This was the problem of poverty, and it remains the primary racial problem today. I have found that the poverty confronted by Mrs. Mack and my relatives in their isolated church communities is a story which is retold many times in the South. Across the state of Virginia, stretching down into North Carolina, thence to South Carolina through six more states to Louisiana is an area called the Black Belt. The residents of that area are predominantly black—the black population of the counties ranging from 30 to 82 percent. They are desperately poor. The median family income for the three hundred counties of that region ranges from $2,200 to $5,000, with most between $2,700 and $3,200.

The lives of the people in that area reflect their very low incomes. Homes often have cardboard walls and tin roofs. Some people live in converted stables or former chicken coops. Many have no toilets, indoors or out. Often they must transport water for long distances. A large proportion of their babies are born without assistance or any medical advice. The sleep of residents is sometimes disturbed by children crying from hunger, and I have witnessed that hunger pacified by the sugar and water on which an entire household has existed for days.

It cannot be said that these people have been forgotten, for most Americans would not believe that they exist. Their place in society is not of their own making, but is inherited directly from slavery. In so many senses these counties resemble the isolated church communities near Daniel's Mountain. Most of these people live on or near the land on which their forebears were slaves.

Those residents of the Black Belt who do move off the land have, for the most part, found their ways to the dark slums of Northern cities. Statistics indicate that they are now returning to the South. Individual initiative has allowed some who moved away to enter the mainstream of American life, but for black people in the United States, both North and South, opportunities have been rationed. A few have made it to the top, but the great part of the population has not moved from the bottom.

The problems of people in the Black Belt are reflected in patterns which endlessly repeat themselves. The problems confronted by the black residents of Washington, North Carolina, are the same as those confronted by the black residents of Washington, Louisiana. Common problems require community effort—this is true for a county; it is true for a city, and it is also true for residents of the Black Belt. For that huge community, confronting as it does that colossal problem, a plan is needed to enable people to take their last step up from slavery.

I had worked for the House of Representatives when the federal government took on the task of attempting to deal with the problem of poverty for the nation. A 1964 bill, the Economic Opportunity Act, recognized that community effort was a most efficacious method for dealing with the problem. But its proposed model for community effort was not sufficiently broadbased to elicit communal activity in the truest sense. The problem the bill confronted was enormous. It may be a simple matter to obtain communal activity on the part of ten or twenty, or even a hundred people, but when the numbers get into hundreds or thousands how is it possible to get that many people to engage in a common undertaking?

As it happens, this is precisely the principle involved when we are considering whether democracy is a possibility: how can the residents of a whole county, city, or state engage in decision-making on matters common to them?

Many modern political thinkers believe democracy to be unworkable in the huge nations that have developed, or think it is at best a doubtful experiment. Democracy, they say, was intended for a simpler, smaller social system; the greater population will ultimately be controlled by a small minority which possesses organization and unity of purpose. Gaetano Mosca, the well-known political scientist, says, "A hundred men acting in concert, with common understanding, will triumph over a thousand men who are not in accord and can be dealt with one by one."

This is not to say that great numbers of people never engage in a common undertaking. To achieve such an objective among large numbers who are not in direct communication with each other requires bringing them into some sort of relationship with each other. Events can perform such a function, and such common action is frequent in a nation's history, as when a hero is mourned, or when a nation is invaded, or at other times of war. The simultaneous activity is due to the common experience, the common reaction to events.

Many community groups, realizing that events *do* bring about common action, use events to construct permanent organizations. This approach is referred to as organizing around issues. Such simultaneity tends to be transient, for it is based upon emotions which seldom endure in their intensity. When the issue fades, so does the organization, once the symbolic moment has passed.

Most societies take care of their arrangements in a manner arising not merely from momentary impulses or passing desires. All long-term planning is done in terms of institutions, and all societies are consciously (even self-consciously) engaged in institution-building. For most of us, an institution is a habit, a practice, a way of doing things which can be transferred to succeeding generations, enabling them to take advantage of the experiences of others. In the dispensation of justice, in the delivery of mail, in the education of our children, one has a choice not simply of one set of options, but of a whole range of options, heavily reduced by experience. The purpose of an institution is to hold these possibilities within limits, to profit from the mistakes of others, to eliminate the need for planning on each occasion, and to avoid the undesirable consequences of acts whose implications, without experience or a close examination of history, we cannot foresee.

The question which confronted me over a decade ago when I wanted to implement a plan which could deal effectively with the problem of poverty in the Black Belt was: Was it possible to create an institution which would enable large numbers of people to engage in a common undertaking and thus, by self-help, vitiate the poverty which was the central fact of their lives? It seemed appropriate to me, in attempting to solve the main problem confronting the Negro people in the South, that I should put to work the ideas of Virginia's greatest political philosopher, Thomas Jefferson. He believed that the salvation of the idea of democracy lay in his ward republics. "Just as Cato ended every speech with 'Carthage must be destroyed,'" he said, "so do I every opinion with the injunction: divide the counties into wards." And again: "Among other improvements, I hope they will adopt the subdivision of our counties into Wards. Each Ward would thus be a small Republic within itself, and every man in the state would thus become an acting member of the common government, transacting in person a great portion of its rights and duties, subordinate indeed, but important, and entirely within his competence. The wit of man cannot devise a more solid base for a free, durable, and well administered Republic."

And so, three years after I discovered Daniel's Mountain and Mrs. Mack and the rest of my relatives of the valley and the poverty of the Black Belt, I left the marbled halls of the Rayburn Building for the remotest rural areas of Virginia and North Carolina to put, with some precision, the ideas of Jefferson to work. Under the scheme which I developed, a county was divided into manageable groups called conferences (instead of wards). A conference is a group of fifty people. Each conference is represented in a central decision-making body for each county, which I call an assembly. By this means the poor of a large part of Virginia (roughly half of the Black Belt of that state) and North Carolina (roughly one-third of that state) would have a vehicle for solving their problems, and for taking the last step up from slavery.

It is a point that has intrigued most observers of these assemblies that, by mere arrangement, by a logical structure of organization, the habits and even the whole way of life of a community can be changed. This type of institution *can* be planted in the most difficult soil, that is, among the unsophisticated rural poor. It is as if

I had found some missing link which, when put into place, brings masses of people in such relationship with each other that they produce, in nearly every case, collective and communal activity.

I fully realize that black people are not the first in history to suffer. I realize also that, although much pain is involved in this type of suffering, all is not bad which comes from pain. The saints extracted from their pain and suffering a special grace which has illuminated our civilization. It would be a special blessing to the Negro people if, in their efforts to achieve social and economic equality, they might impart fresh vigor to our democracy, providing an example for the South, the nation, and the world.

III

THAT THIS NATION
MAY ENDURE

A Southern
Political Tradition

George C. Rogers, Jr.

JOHN LOCKE and Lord Ashley envisaged a society for South Carolina in which the Agrarian Rule would be the linchpin. Power would reflect property, but property itself would be divided among three groups: the proprietors, the local nobility, and the commons. The instruments of government would reflect this three-fold power. There was to be a balance among the political institutions, and that balance would be everlastingly maintained. Thus liberty would be preserved.

When the Glorious Revolution occurred in England in 1688–89, there were similar hopes for the settlement. King, lords, and commons would balance each other, providing a harmony which would secure for the landholders of Great Britain a continuing stability as estates descended from fathers to sons over countless generations. If J. H. Plumb is correct, it took twenty to thirty years to achieve political stability, but once secured it was hoped that it would be enduring.

When, in the 1720s and 1730s, Sir Robert Walpole harnessed new forces, the financial power of the Bank of England and the patronage of the Crown, to disrupt the balance and to rule in the interests of the great Whig magnates, an opposition was born. Out of the pages of Trenchard and Gordon's *Independent Whig* and Bolingbroke's *Craftsman* an ideology emerged that would long do battle with the centralizing influence of national institutions and their tendency to the corruption of power. The country ideology, as it has been called, represented the thoughts of the landed gentlemen of England, the group who considered themselves the chief architects, beneficiaries, and preservers of the Revolution of 1688.

When, in the 1760s, the Americans needed arguments to parry the greed of aristocratic factions, those who manipulated funds, pensions, places—the corruption of London—they knew where to go to find their arguments. John Mackenzie wrote in the *South-Carolina Gazette* in 1769: "In every free state, when government cannot, or will not, protect the people, they have a right to fall upon such measures as they may think conducive to their own preservation. This is a truth, founded on revolution principles, which a man need not be ashamed or afraid to avow." Gerald Stourzh has pointed out that Mackenzie, by invoking the formula of "revolution principles," "shows how basic the Glorious Revolution was to the colonists' constitutional thinking." But it was William Henry Drayton who fitted the American Revolution most clearly into the pattern of the Glorious Revolution. In his charge to a grand jury on April 23, 1776, Drayton justified the revolutionary government of South Carolina in words patterned after the Resolution of the Lords and Commons in Convention of February 7, 1689, which declared James II's abdication.

Convention, 1689

King James the Second, having endeavoured to subvert the Constitution of the Kingdom, by breaking the original Contract between King and People, and, by the advice of Jesuits, and other wicked Persons, having violated the fundamental Laws, and having withdrawn himself out of this Kingdom, has *abdicated* the Government, and that the Throne is thereby become vacant [italics mine].

Drayton, April 1776

The king's judges in this country refused to administer justice; and the late governor, lord William Campbell, acting as the king's representative for him, and on his behalf, having endeavoured to subvert the constitution of this country, by breaking the original contract between king and people, attacking the people by force of arms; having violated the fundamental laws; having carried off the great seal, and having withdrawn himself out of this colony, he *abdicated* the government [italics mine].

And so Drayton concluded: "Wherefore if James the second broke the original contract, it is undeniable that George the third has also broken the original contract between king and people."

The American Revolution, at least in the South, was designed to correct the imbalance that had grown up amid English institutions. The corroding agent was favoritism: the handing out of offices on the basis of connections, not on the basis of merit. "Placeman" was the chief term of opprobrium. Great wealth generated corruption among the rich; moderate estates would be the basis for a new distribution of power. There was still a fundamental belief in the connection between property and power, but it would henceforth be a connection in a land dominated by myriad middle-class property-holders. But if power was to be reflected from a mass of fifty-acre freeholders, what would happen to the balance in government so dearly beloved by the patriots? Not having a highly structured or hierarchical society such as the one they were leaving behind, they found their safety in the doctrine of the separation of powers. John Adams taught John Rutledge the mechanics of constructing governments; Rutledge, learning his lesson, brought his knowledge to fruition in the Constitution of 1776 for South Carolina. But the South Carolinians, understanding human nature and thus fearful of their own leaders (a triumvirate of three Rutledge brothers was a possibility), wrote a self-denying ordinance against nepotism into their second constitution two years later.

Safety at first seemed to rest on the existence of thirteen distinct republics, all (except Franklin's Pennsylvania) recognizing the separation of powers and all abhorring the growth of too strong a central government. Yet weakness in the 1780s forced the confederation into a federation. A period of sharing was needed. As David Donald has recently suggested, the history of the South is not written in a straight line; rather, it is a cyclical story, punctuated by periods of entry to and withdrawal from the national stage. The year 1787 was the ideal moment for a sharing. As J. G. A. Pocock has perceptively stated, it was the "Machiavellian Moment."

Thomas Rhett Smith's Fourth of July oration of 1802, delivered in St. Michael's Church, Charleston, had as its theme the preservation of the republic: "How far we have conformed to the principle with which we set out, and how long we are likely to retain the prize for which we struggled so hard. . . ." The American Revolution, according to Smith, was unlike any other revolution in history, for it had not consumed its leaders. It had occurred at just the right time. If it had taken place sooner, America would not have been sufficiently inhabited to sustain the fight; if later, it would have been sucked into the maelstrom of the French Revolution and would not have stopped "at the precise point of temperate liberty." "Our severest trials" had come after the fighting was over. We needed the period of humiliation in the 1780s; we needed to *feel* before we *acted*. Thus the Constitution was also made at the only possible time. If the

Constitutional Convention had been postponed three years, the document would never have been put together. The date of the birth of the republic is less important than the date on which it was saved: 1787 was therefore more important than 1776.

But what was agreed upon in 1787 was not only a doctrine of separation of powers for the federal structure, but also a balance of power between the states and the new central government. This twin accomplishment had always to be honored or the nation would fall apart. It was a double safety-lock for these republican-minded gentlemen—and they were gentlemen. They thought they could trust each other implicitly, not only in the present generation, but that sons of such fathers would not go back upon sacred pledges. Charles Cotesworth Pinckney said as much when he acknowledged that the New England men had behaved handsomely in agreeing to the compromises over slavery. "He had himself, he said, prejudices against the Eastern States before he came here, but would acknowledge that he had found them as liberal and candid as any men whatever."

In 1776, the men who signed the Declaration of Independence pledged their lives, their fortunes, and their sacred honor. Those who met at Philadelphia in 1787 were equally willing to make similar pledges. Their signatures to the document were sufficient evidence. Having based their own revolution on the charges that the king had broken his contract, they were certain that their colleagues would honor the contract thus agreed upon. Men of honor, their word was their bond, and they expected their sons to be worthy of them. A great civil war occurred only when enough people failed to remember and to honor the Constitution.

But, long before then, a new engine had arisen which seemed to sweep all the balances under the carpet. Just as Sir Robert Walpole had used Funds and places to triumph over the balance of the revolutionary settlement of 1688, so Alexander Hamilton by his funding schemes and his Bank and his control over the numerous new federal customs and postal positions seemed to jeopardize the victories just won. As early as 1794, John Taylor of Caroline made arguments reminiscent of those of Bolingbroke; if not by name, then certainly in spirit he passed the country ideology into the minds and hearts of Southerners. The new creed was spelled out in his *Arator* and his *Construction Construed*. Of course, what was needed to make the new government truly work was a group of virtuous men. Southerners have always known that only character can make constitutions work.

The most serious threat to the philosophy of John Taylor of Caroline was the series of decisions rendered by John Marshall between 1819 and 1821. They clearly emphasized the full panoply of federal power, power which Marshall reiterated reflected the will of "one people," the nation. Although the concept excluded Indians, free blacks, and women, it did imply one national entity, rather than twenty-four separate sovereignties. The Virginians led by Spencer Roane, Thomas Ritchie, and John Taylor of Caroline saw in these great substantive powers reflecting the will of a new national majority a threat to the concept of the republic as they understood it. Marshall, however, in his greatest decision *Cohens* v. *Virginia*, apparently had the last word. Yet it was Calhoun who perceived how the concept, only a legal fiction in the hands of Marshall, became a reality in the hands of Andrew Jackson.

Jackson led a really national party. It was the new instrument of the political party, an institution not favored or expected by the men who met in Philadelphia in 1787. As Calhoun so clearly pointed out, by the exchanging of quid pro quos a party could unite a congeries of diverse interests until there was a coalition that could capture control of all three branches of the federal government. What Marshall cherished as "one people" Calhoun feared as "King Numbers." In a two-party system, one party could secure power with only 51 percent of the votes and then institute a program which would be destructive of the interests of one section of the country. In order to parry this new danger, Calhoun fashioned his doctrine of nullification. It was designed as another check, a gadget to make the constitutional engine run more smoothly.

Another fundamental concern of Calhoun's was that a party, once in power, could use federal funds and patronage to maintain itself in power for long periods of time. In the spoils system Calhoun perceived the old English practice of places and pensions. This hatred of a new form of corruption led the Carolina planter to focus more fiercely on the ideal of the independent man in office. A man should not campaign, should not spend money in order to secure office, should be known for his past achievements, should be visible without the aid of anyone to tout his accomplishments. Elevation to office depended upon honorable standing in society. This promotion of virtue depended upon limitation of power, and upon a social situation where men's relationships were close enough to allow the recognition of virtue. The opposite implied the manipulation of office to achieve dominance in society. Thus the concept of the unconnected figure was thrown up against the new Jacksonian system of patronage and rewards.

William Freehling has called our attention to this side of Calhoun's politics: "The theory of spoilsmen, like the theory of interests, is based on the primordial selfishness of human nature. However, the focus shifts from the economic interests to their politicians, and the servants become masters. Spoilsmen, breaking free from the control of the interests which selected them, emerge as the primary historical force. This time, the pot of gold which turns men into plunderers is the spoils of office rather than the riches of minorities." Freehling shows that Calhoun's thought represents a natural evolution from Bolingbroke, the Revolutionary generation, and John Taylor: "As a political philosopher well versed in the ideology of the Founding Fathers, Calhoun inherited that strain of late eighteenth-century thought which considered democratic politics the pursuit of gentlemen and disdained legislative cabals and mass parties." Thus the sharp differences between a Calhoun and a Van Buren.

A man was visible by virtue of his property and by his personal characteristics, which would be known among the other leaders of his own region; this was why the electoral college had been established. The best men in each state would be selected, and they in turn would select the best man in the nation to be president. There would be no campaigning, no electioneering—the process would work through the ties of recognized achievements. This was why South Carolina refused to send a delegation to any of the Democratic nominating conventions until 1856. This stance also explains why, in the antebellum South, the duel was a key institution: one must be sure that no unkind references to character would be left unanswered. (James Hamilton, nullification governor of South Carolina, fought fourteen duels in his lifetime.) This political ethos was summed up by Francis Lieber when he wrote that the art of politics was the code of the gentleman.

Nullification was a failure as a constitutional theory; that we know. Yet in another form—that of the concurrent majority—Calhoun's ideas did endure for at least one hundred years. David Potter, perhaps the wisest of the historians produced by the South in the last two generations, told this story in *The South and the Concurrent Majority*. When the Democratic party adopted the two-thirds rule for nomination at its convention in 1836 and retained that rule until Franklin Roosevelt broke it in 1936, there was brought into being a way that Southern interests could not be ignored. Thus the march of "King Numbers" over the balance of power was retarded and delayed. In a republic, power must continually be broken up. The march in the world today is against republics and in favor of totalitarian regimes. Perhaps this is the destiny of all mankind. Thus what is important is to delay that march for as long as possible. As differences in property are erased, the rage of envy becomes ever more compelling, and thus the minds of men who exhibit talent and genius are smothered. The duty of the republican is to emphasize structure so that the final unanimous cry shall never be heard.

Potter also demonstrates that Southerners worked to amplify their voices in another way, by adapting the new committee system of Congress to their own needs. Once standing committees were organized and the rule of seniority followed, then persons who served for long periods could obtain more than ordinary effectiveness. This system emerged in the third and fourth decades of the nineteenth century, not to be broken up until the 1970s. Within this almost 150-year period, and especially after the Civil War and Reconstruction, Southern leadership was to make itself a potent force in the republic, one exerted for the preservation of a limited federal government.

Another institution used by Southerners was the convention. The genealogy of this institution is perhaps more ancient than that of any other political institution. In February, 1776, James Wilson and John Dickinson attempted to prove the constitutionality of the Continental Congress on the grounds of analogy to the "assembly of the barons at Runningmede, when Magna Charta was signed, the Convention Parliament that recalled Charles II, and the Convention of Lords and Commons that placed King William on the throne." Thus the line of conventions ran back to Runnymede and forward to Philadelphia, to the state ratifying conventions, and to the nullification and secession conventions. On these occasions the ablest men came forth with a mandate, fresh from the sovereign people, to settle the most important questions. Ordinarily such men might not be willing to take seats in legislative bodies merely to suffer the tedium of endless debate and few accomplishments, necessary as such day-to-day work was. But when the republic was in danger, they would answer the call and appear to give the joint wisdom of the community some force. Certainly the ablest men were more willing to come forward at such times, and perhaps the people were also more willing to vote for recognizable talent. Can it be that we do not make use of this institution any longer because we have lost the ability to recognize talent—or is it that we do not produce men of talent anymore? Nothing has been more conducive to the emphasizing of the irrelevant and the downplaying of the perennial than television; one shudders to realize that it may now make possible a pure democracy, something which the Madisons and the Hamiltons both abhorred. (Teheran, of course, is the future, a frightening illustration of the mob shouting down reason.)

Thus the Southern political tradition was fully established before the Civil War. It consisted of a belief in republics guided by the best talent of the community. Within this tradition the hardest political thinking must be devoted to creating new political institutions designed to break up any growing aggregations of power. Men must be trained to perceive dangers and to sound alarms. Certainly in 1860 and the winter of 1860–61, Southerners thought they were following the examples of their forefathers who had fought the British. Robert Barnwell Rhett, the father of secession, consciously modeled his career after those of Christopher Gadsden and Patrick Henry.

There was nothing wrong with this political creed *per se*. However, the greatest tragedy in American history is that it was used to defend slavery. One purpose of this essay is to disentangle the creed itself from the uses made of it. The first is absolutely necessary for the continuation of our form of government; the second cannot be defended. Where Southern leadership failed was in not knowing when (and perhaps how) to give way. As indicated above, because the march of history is against this form of government, one should never do anything to hasten the march. The South has been guilty, twice, of doing just that: once when it did not yield before the need to abolish slavery; and the second time when it did not give way in time to end segregation. Being obstinate in the first instance made the Civil War inevitable and in its train brought the Fourteenth Amendment. Being obstinate in the second instance made it possible for the Warren Court to launch its activist phase of social engineering, to move from declaring an end to discrimination to insisting upon a forced overhaul of society. Together, the Fourteenth Amendment and the Warren Court have made it almost impossible for any voice other than the federal one to be heard. Insofar as the platforms from which men speak are whittled away and reduced, the cause of liberty suffers.

The Warren Court by its school decision and its one-man-one-vote decision has done more than any other force to erode local power. It is true that segregation should have come to an end long before 1954, and that blacks should have had the full opportunity to vote long before 1962—yet these decisions have made the neighborhood school impossible and the continued practice of some limitations upon mass democracy not viable. The mixture of the social with the constitutional has damned the constitutional. We desperately need clearer thinking about the structure of government and the need to preserve that structure.

Did the Southern political tradition fail, or did Southerners simply fail to rise to the message of that tradition? James F. Byrnes was one of those Southerners who had a golden opportunity to solve this problem. Upon his return to South Carolina from the national stage, he became aware that there was a need to tackle the segregation question. But his response was to obtain, by passage of a state sales tax, increased revenues which might be used in making the black schools actually equal to the white. That was too little, too late. What he should have done (and he had the opportunity, with his national standing) was to urge the abandonment of segregation by the local authorities before it was pushed upon the South by the federal government. Then there would have been no need for the Warren school decision, the hinge upon which so many social changes have swung. The art of the leader is to preserve the essence of institutions amidst change. Byrnes could have drawn valuable lessons from the post–Civil War period, but perhaps he could not perceive the lessons, or was not articulate enough to present them. The common mistake is to observe these matters in terms of contemporary necessities, and not in terms of the founding fathers' concerns. The men of 1787 thought not for themselves, but for posterity.

The most vivid example of how pernicious results can flow from what many would consider a positive step is the threat posed by affirmative action programs. We have affirmative action because the South was too slow in ending segregation and race discrimination (and the South should be ready to accept these criticisms). The point is that affirmative action will be around after discrimination has gone, a woeful legacy for a republic built upon a foundation of virtuous people. Just like the spoilsmen of Jackson's time, the Warren Court has reversed the relationship between power and virtue. To insist upon a national search every time there is an opening in a state university is damaging to the concept of character as being important in the management of affairs. Character cannot be judged in dossiers or in two-day visits; it is something to be scrutinized in the long run and evaluated in a local context. This whole procedure is against the Southern tradition because it prevents the analysis of character at close hand over long periods of time, which is the only way to be sure that we are getting honorable leaders.

Today one cannot select a person for a job because one knows that person; rather, one must select a person whom one does not know. The fact of acquaintanceship is in itself damning. The specious rationalization for this procedure is that one thereby gets the best possible person in the nation for the job. This is patently ridiculous. It is true that the best person in certain fields is recognizable, but in the most important positions he is not easily discernible; furthermore, many of the best people already have jobs and do not want to leave them. What we get is someone from a pool of the discontented—persons willing to go to any port in search of advancement, with no loyalty to the new port except insofar as it serves as a launching place for something more grandiose. These are the present-day placemen. Thus we rake in the flotsam and jetsam from the national pool.

Fortunately, the states still have some mechanisms inherited from their republican past that have not yet been wiped out by federal edict. Governors must meet a residency requirement and generally are limited to one term, or at most two. Thus we have had a succession of good Southern governors. There must be a loyalty to the people of a state and a desire to enhance their unique cultures. The attempt to wipe out all local flavor and variety in our institutions so that every institution is the same throughout the nation must be opposed. The national voice seems to say that we are all interchangeable and that everything is a matter of politics, of government decision—not of quality, or of social tradition.

The Southern political tradition must be brought back, first by protecting the state governments from edicts from the federal bureaucracy—the attempt to mould each state government into one form certified at the center. The Constitution guarantees each state a republican form of government, but the courts have wisely never tried to spell out what this means. This ideal recognizes implicitly the value of diversity. Second, the South must recover the idea of a neighborhood school where the same students proceed with fellow students and friends over the years. If students are shuffled every year, no one becomes a friend of anybody, and no one cares what others think of him or of her. There is a loss of self-respect and a sinking into anonymity. The republic and character-building are still important. They are related, they rise or fall together, and in the South there is still an awareness of that relationship. This is the heart of the Southern political tradition—as important now as it was in 1776 or 1787.

Foreign Policy and the South

Samuel T. Francis

NEARLY ALL OBSERVERS agree that American foreign policy is undergoing a crisis. Indecision and lack of direction seem apparent in the formulation and execution of our relations with the world. From both the right and the left we are given advice on how to deal with other nations. It is America's business, say conservatives, to resist Soviet expansion and "adventurism"—in Africa, the Middle East, Central and Southeast Asia, and Latin America—and we are warned that our withdrawal from the world will only create a power vacuum into which Moscow and its surrogates will quickly move. From the left comes the admonition that America has been involved too much, and in the wrong way, with the world; spokesmen for this view assert that our investments, military bases, foreign aid programs, and diplomatic functions have been covert forms of conquest and exploitation as well as causes in themselves of economic, political, and cultural destruction. Only a drastic redesign of our international policy (and of our internal arrangements)—we are told—can realize a more just and peaceful world order.

Yet the drift continues, regardless of this advice, and the rest of the world observes, with a mixture of anxiety and satisfaction, the lack of coherence and leadership from the wealthiest and most powerful state in history, the chastiser of tyrants, the champion of the oppressed. Perhaps as remarkable as the incoherence of American foreign policy is the lack of concern on the part of our own citizens. Public discussion of the central problems of foreign affairs—SALT II, the instability of U.S. allies, the meaning and observance of human rights, the Mideast conflict, African and Latin American policy, the North-South dialogue—produces little reaction in a populace understandably obsessed with exorbitant taxation, uncontrollable inflation, and the uncertain availability of routine resources. America's proper role in the world has been a topic of intense debate for at least twelve years, but the discussion has taken place in learned journals, on editorial pages, at academic or professional conferences, and in other largely unread or unattended locations. Probably never before in its history has America stood at so important a crossroads in foreign policy; and rarely, if ever, has there been such apathy about what we should do.

It is possible that the demonstrable indifference of most Americans to the issues of foreign policy is a chief cause of the current crisis in our foreign relations. Any society governed by deliberative institutions must conduct its foreign affairs with the support and interest of its members, and if the citizens are indifferent to the world, there is little reason for the agencies responsible for foreign policy to follow a coherent course. American society—at the present time, as well as historically—has been reluctant to come to grips with the world as it is, or at least with the world as most human beings outside America have perceived it. Our apathy and drift today are the result of that most peculiar institution, American democratic orthodoxy. Alexis de Tocqueville noted our unsuitability for high designs in the world:

Foreign politics demand scarcely any of those qualities which are peculiar to a democracy. . . . a democracy can only with great difficulty regulate the details of an important undertaking, persevere in a fixed design, and work out its existence in spite of serious obstacles. It cannot combine its measures with secrecy or await their consequences with patience. These are qualities which more especially belong to an individual or an aristocracy; and they are precisely the qualities by which a nation, like an individual, attains a dominant position.

Most would agree that the immediate cause of our present discontents was the experience of Vietnam, and it is to Vietnam that de Tocqueville's insights are most applicable. In Vietnam the United States did indeed have great difficulty "persevering in a fixed design," and our inability to use secrecy effectively became notorious. A large portion of our journalism on foreign affairs, even at its best, has dealt with cover-ups and conspiracies, rather than with the substance of our policies. Nor were we able to await the consequences of those policies with patience. Perhaps the ultimate and most universal source of aversion to the Vietnam War was the apparent interminability of the conflict—an objection strange to Europeans, who have named their wars for the numbers of years they lasted, and stranger still to Asians, who have given up measuring war's duration. The discovery by millions of young soldiers that armed conflict is not as brief, clean, easy, or fun as a John Wayne film elicited more shock than one would have expected in high school and college-educated men eighteen to twenty-six years of age.

There is, in other words, a naiveté or childlike innocence endemic to the American character, a habitual expectation of quick solutions and happy endings. The belief in the natural innocence of America is a necessary prop for, the logical foundation of, modern democracy, which is unimaginable in a society that takes seriously the idea of original sin. The philosophical basis of contemporary American democracy is the Pelagian heresy of the natural goodness of man, and man is more obviously good where democracy has been the most developed. In the United States, according to this formula, man started anew and brought forth a new order of the ages to which the hag-ridden evils of the Old World were alien. When Americans have thought about the Old World, east or west, it has been with a mixed feeling of contempt for the unredeemed and solicitude for their continued burdens. In foreign policy, the Pelagian orthodoxy of American democracy received its most nearly complete formulation in the policies of Woodrow Wilson and his vision of the Old World redesigned in accordance with American legends, prepossessions, and illusions. (The South, with characteristic disdain for abstractions, supported Wilson's policies, not from philosophical affinity, but because of his accidentally Southern antecedents and its Democratic loyalty.) Yet the "fixed design" of the Wilsonian adventure dissolved when Americans discovered that the Old World did not share the axioms of the design; that its implications had certain unforeseen and undesirable consequences; and that the whole proceeding required more blood, sweat, and tears than it was worth—when, that is, the unpalatable realities of the world as it is stung the callow taste buds of American innocence.

The indecisiveness of American foreign policy, the apathy of citizens toward the world, and the decay of American power and of foreign respect for America itself have many causes: the rise of rival economies in Europe and Asia since World War II, the collapse of European empires in the 1960s, the development of nationalist and racial ideologies in the Third World, and the growth of the countervailing power of the Soviet Union. But the international decadence of the United States would not have occurred in such a precipitous and often humiliating way without the psychic experience of the Vietnam war and the implosion of the premises of American foreign policy to which that experience led. The psychic consequences of Vietnam were far more devastating to the United States than the material ones. As cynics have pointed out, the number of American lives lost in Indochina throughout the whole of the war was no more than the number of highway fatalities each year, and the total financial cost was comparable to the annual budget of a federal department of government. It is through the intellectual and moral realm that Vietnam will enter our folklore; unlike any other war in our history, it had many martyrs and few heroes.

What Americans experienced in Vietnam was not military defeat, but something more serious: the inability to accomplish a set purpose. Prior to the 1970s, the premise on which American foreign policy had been conducted since at least the time of Wilson was the belief that America was capable of teaching the world how to become like America. We assumed that the rest of the world did indeed aspire to be like America, and that the ultimate justification of American power was the practical fulfillment of this capacity—through American wealth, American example, and, finally, American arms. It was in terms of this belief in the historic destiny of American power that President Wilson expressed his ambition to make the world safe for democracy. To a large extent, this belief also animated our "Second Crusade" in World War II, and the benevolent internationalism of the 1950s. The Peace Corps, the Alliance for Progress, the Marshall Plan, and other U.S.-sponsored programs for the modernization (i.e., Americanization) of undeveloped nations revealed the same underlying assumption. Were not these lands inhabited by "teeming masses yearning to be free"? And did not freedom consist in either the actual passage to America or, if this was not possible, in the passage of America to the teeming masses in the form of American money, American products, American ideas, and American troops?

Historically, this belief in the unique capabilities and peculiar destiny of America had its origins in the Puritan Yankee establishment of the Northeast, and it is no accident that this same establishment has preserved its most entrenched position in the Department of State. In no other branch of government has it been as dominant, and in no other aspect of policy formation has it been as influential. Intellectually, the august credo of American destiny had its origins in the millenarianism of the early Puritans. The secularization of Puritanism led to the setting of what seemed to be more practicable

goals than that of a liberal rule of the saints. The perfection of man
would come about through his conforming to the model established
by the perfected elite in American society.

The millenarianism of American diplomacy has not been impractical in its implementation, however. Like the Northeastern mer-
chants who sponsored these ideals, more recent exponents have
possessed both a hard head for business and a shrewd eye for the realities of power. In the twentieth century, authors of our foreign policy have four times persuaded a reluctant and indifferent populace
that it should go to war—not for its own interests, but for the interests of democracy in Europe, Korea, and Vietnam. The lofty rhetoric of internationalism, world peace, and human rights has been
matched in almost every instance by ruthless bargaining for economic, political, and military power. But the pragmatic success of
millenarian idealism need not surprise us, for it was the very arche-
type of Puritan millenarianism, Oliver Cromwell, who successfully
combined sanctimonious idealism and brutal *Realpolitik*. If millenarianism in politics were to adopt a motto, it could not do better
than "Trust in God and keep your powder dry." Bible-quoting slave
traders are not so far removed from modern diplomats who cast a
tearful eye on the violations of human rights by our corrupt allies,
while at the same time carefully measuring our investments in the
Soviet Union and mainland China.

Ultimately, millenarianism collapses. To construct the City on
the Hill, it is necessary to bulldoze the less stately mansions of the
earthly realm. In time, for most men, the paradoxical dialectic of
millenarianism weighs too heavy. The conscience cannot bear, and
the mind cannot reconcile, the brutal (or at least mundane) means
by which the final vision is to be realized. So it was with the sensitive consciences and acute, finely educated minds of the American
intelligentsia of the 1960s and '70s. The seeming embarrassment of
the Tet offensive; the haunting brutality of My Lai; the toppling of
the millenarian heroes of the Kennedy Administration by the release of the Pentagon Papers; and the continuous, heckling, un-
answerable questions about Vietnam from even more radically
millenarian dissenters all led to the discrediting of the premises on
which U.S. globalism had proceeded. Had the Vietnam war been
presented to the American populace on its proper grounds—as a
geopolitically essential countering of the aggressive forces of North
Vietnam and its allies—millenarian ideals would not have been involved. Yet to have invoked strategic arguments would immediately
have led to the questioning of our own strategy of a limited war. If

the war were really a struggle against aggression, then why not put a permanent end to the aggressor's ability to make war? Avoiding this unthinkable implication, the authors of our Vietnam policy insisted on defending their course on the grounds that the war was a conflict for democracy and progress in the Third World, i.e., for the millenarian vision. They could not, of course, sustain this argument, given the realities of our allies and the necessities of counterinsurgency warfare. The only possible defense was that the millenarian omelette required the breaking of several terrestrial eggs, and this response immediately exposed the unreality of the final goal.

The result of the Vietnam war in the psychological history of America was the complete discrediting of the millenarian premises of U.S. foreign policy. With their discrediting there also collapsed any justification for American globalism. Dr. Henry Kissinger, who is possessed of few millenarian illusions, sought to construct an alternative foundation in the balance-of-power *Realpolitik* of his nineteenth-century European heroes. But this model was not adequate, as Kissinger himself came to see; it did not reflect the realities of power of the late twentieth century, and (perhaps even more importantly) it demanded too much of Americans, who disliked its cynicism and the slowness with which it achieved concrete results. In the end, even Kissinger had to admit that Americans were not suited to the pragmatic manipulation of power, and he privately advised that we reconcile ourselves to a more modest role in world affairs.

The Carter Administration also sought to avoid the millenarian illusion of omnipotence, but in its place developed an ideology of incapacitation. Power, so far from being a bulwark of security, was actually a hindrance; it had to be restrained if America was to play an effective role in the world. American power, the academics of the Carter Administration told us, had promoted only the jealousy and fears of the Soviets, who had tried to catch up and compete with us. Power had made us an object of fear and envy to the Third World as well. The United States should therefore modify its zeal to remain militarily superior to the Soviets, should seek a more equitable distribution of wealth throughout the world, and should work for an international order composed of cooperating peers rather than one dominated by conflicting giants with their retinues of satellites. This approach to foreign policy was also unsatisfactory, if only because no one could take it seriously. The rejection of power immediately led to results that had been unsuspected by and were unthinkable to most Americans. The devolution of American control over the Panama Canal was quickly followed by the escalation of Cuban power throughout the Caribbean. American criticism of the shah's regime and its subsequent overthrow in the absence of U.S. support led to a fanatically hostile and far more brutal regime. American mediation in Africa brought threats of oil embargo from Nigeria and the loss of initiative throughout the continent. In short, the Carter scheme for the peaceful abdication of American global potency did nothing to impress the world and did much to attract hostile reactions. At bottom, the policy ignored a simple law of political physics: power abhors a vacuum, and where one force withdraws, another will enter.

The collapse of the millenarian ideal of U.S. foreign policy has resulted in the rejection of the legitimacy and usefulness of national power itself, and with the rejection of power comes the disappearance of respect. What has come to be called the new isolationism—the defeatism, appeasement, and vacillation that seem to hold sway in our diplomatic counsels—derives not from any inherent material weakness of the United States, but from the absence of any viable principle that justified retaining power and exercising leadership.

Yet there is one part of the United States that has been only minimally infected by the millenarian orthodoxy that has dominated the rest of the country. According to its critics as well as its apologists, that region locates its roots and identity in the Old World, and has defied throughout its history the efforts of the millenarian vision to envelop it. This is, of course, the South, and no small part of the Southern message to America may lie in its instruction on international affairs. Its teaching consists not in instruction in the techniques of the high arts of diplomacy—although the Foreign Service might profit from observing the horse-traders of the Old South or even the used car salesmen of the New—nor in the content and purposes of policy. What the South offers America in international affairs is a reformulation of American expectations of the world.

It may be that the United States will decide that it does not want a "dominant position" in international affairs. Perhaps its own interests can be best served in a multipolar world with many different, sometimes competing, sometimes cooperating, centers of power. Whether this decision to surrender power would be wise is another question, but if such a decision is taken, Americans must be aware of its consequences and be prepared to bear them. The erosion of American power in the last few years has not been the result of deliberate decision. Although a modification of American might has been a goal of the Carter Administration, most citizens have not clearly understood it as a goal and have not even begun to explore its consequences. The erosion of power has derived from the frustrations, failures, inattentions, and indecisiveness of the U.S. government and citizenry, and from the discrediting of the political formulas that motivated and justified our national power.

What the South has to offer America in foreign policy is neither a recovery of nor a further diminution of power. It is, rather, a different framework of values and institutions through which we can approach the world with purpose and coherence.

Southern intellectual history and social institutions have yielded up little millenarianism and few expectations of a New Jerusalem. C. Vann Woodward, in a well-known essay, "The Search for Southern Identity," contrasted the dominant mythology of America with the realities of the American South. America has believed itself (and was in fact) affluent, in contrast to the historic poverty of the South. America was successful (might we say invincible?), and the South was unique in having experienced military defeat, foreign occupation, and the suppression of its institutions. Whereas America was innocent, a noble savage pioneering the untrodden solitude of the New Eden, the South had direct experience and consciousness of sin, in the abuses of slavery and racial hegemony. A culture whose identity is enveloped in poverty, failure, and consciousness of sin cannot easily formulate millenarian ideologies, though a culture mythicized in wealth, success, and innocence can formulate hardly anything else.

The South is thus far closer to the cultural values of the Old World than to those of the New, and it approximates the truths of the human condition more accurately. The legacy of the Southern identity in foreign affairs is therefore likely to be a far more realistic appreciation of what the rest of the world is like, and of what it expects, than was implied in the now-shattered millenarianism of the past.

A realism drawn from the Southern tradition should not, however, be confused with the *Realpolitik* of modern European diplomacy. The realism of the South is based on a pessimism about man and his works that is affiliated with religious affirmation. This kind of realism tends to distrust the ability of statesmen to reorder the world, because it ultimately distrusts man himself. By contrast, *Realpolitik* of the nineteenth-century European tradition tends to enlarge the ability of human reason to manipulate states and peoples, to divorce human affairs from restraining moral institutions, and to place unproven faith in power. There can be no doubt that America has placed far too much faith in power, and that it should regard it more skeptically. At the same time, the problem of American foreign policy has not been the amount of power at its disposal, but the uses to which that power has been put. A realism based on the Southern, tragic view of man would not hesitate to make full use of power to pursue legitimate national interests—the protection of security, the defense of our allies and of the lawful activities of Americans abroad—but it is almost inconceivable that it could lead to the kind of crusades on which millenarianism has several times embarked us, or to the expeditions for booty in which *Realpolitik* tends to indulge.

Southerners are able to draw their realism from another source as well. Poverty, failure, and sin may be alien to most of America, but they are the framework in which most of the world lives and has lived since neolithic times. Perhaps more than other Americans, Southerners are in a position to understand the racially oppressed and their oppressors, the exploitation of undeveloped economies, the persistent tribal and ethnic categories by which most non-Western peoples identify themselves, the stratification by status and kinship rather than by class and education, traditional patterns of deference, and the motivations for rebellion. The global complaint against the United States today is that capitalism and industrial technology, democracy, mass culture, and Western liberalism, have undermined traditional cultures. This complaint—far more than the economics of slavery or the legalisms of the Constitution—also underlay much of the Confederate revolt.

Another contribution that the South can make to American foreign policy consists in what may be called its tradition of command. Much has been written about the military tradition of the South: the use of "colonel" as a title, the number of military academies, and the statistics on Southern volunteers in the armed forces. These traditions have led some writers to describe the South as militaristic; yet "militarism" is a term that describes Prussian generals and Third World despots far better than it does the ragged followers of Lee or the volunteer flyers of the "Royal Texas Air Force" of World War II. Clearly, some distinctions must be made.

The military life is most obviously distinguished from a civilian career by its adherence to the principles of loyalty and command. The continued vitality of this principle in the South—more than any love of violence, or ornate uniforms, or marching music—probably accounts for the attractions of the military for the Southerner. It is difficult to reconcile the images of Southern social life (its informalities and laziness) with the ferocious energy of modern military machines, or to reconcile characteristic Southern forms of violence (most typically, the feud and the vendetta) with the calculated and undiscriminating massacres of modern warfare. The principle of loyalty and command, however, reflects the deferential and hierarchical patterns of the historic South. Social stratification in the South can be manifest in dialect, bearing, dress, and manners to a greater degree than in more bourgeois regions. Not merely the military heritage and usages of the South but also the entire hierarchical structure of its society have reinforced the tradition of command.

The egalitarian and pacifist residues of millenarianism are not present in this tradition, which combines moral justification of leadership with restraint of power. In the aftermath of the millenarian collapse, America lacks any justification for its power and any accurate perception of the limitations on what power can accomplish. The lack of leadership in the United States—the unwillingness to make hard decisions, the art of making decisions that please everyone, the fear of displeasing, and the dread of hurting and being hurt—all point to the absence of any sense of command or responsibility in American public life and render meaningless all efforts to formulate a coherent foreign policy. The very means by which public men acquire office—by pleasing enough people to gain their quadrennial vote—undermines those leaders' ability to face unpleasant realities and communicate them to the electorate. The method of acquiring leadership in contemporary America prohibits the exercise of leadership; the result is a foreign policy of vacillation and a domestic condition that resembles anarchy.

Leadership in Southern society, however, has not come about by amassing votes through cleverly designed and projected images, nor has it rested upon the mere accumulation of property and official power. Leadership in the South, of course, has been associated with property and office, as it has been everywhere; but they are not the sole sources of command. Given the South's vestigial and largely informal political order, it was unlikely that leadership could be acquired through the state. The apparatus of power for Southern leaders has traditionally been located in and virtually identical with the community itself. Church, family, and neighborhood are at the same time intermediary institutions of social life and the power bases for Southern leaders. The means by which influence within and over institutions is acquired tends to correspond with the necessities of exercising leadership, so that there is no disparity between the art of gaining command and the art of using it. And an instinct for loyalty, a vestige of chivalry, possibly survives more extensively in the South than elsewhere.

The zealous scandal-mongering of politicians and journalists in the recent past strongly suggests that Americans, having lost any justification for their preeminence in the world, have also lost the ability to distinguish between legitimate and illegitimate uses of power. The tradition of command and responsibility in the South, however, offers instruction not only in the use of power but also in its restraint. A central part of the tradition of command is the idea of the commander's responsibility. Whether this idea is manifested in General Lee's solicitude for his troops or in the plantation mistress's care for sick servants, it implies a limitation in the uses of authority and privileges. It implies a responsibility for those who are led, and their duty to obey is communicated to them to the same degree that the commander's responsibility is performed. The origins of power, leadership, and authority in the community thus provide legitimation for the exercise of power while at the same time placing restraints on its abuses.

The immediate application of the Southern tradition of command to foreign policy may not be clear, since the problems of leadership in a localized community are quite different from those on a national or international scale. Yet there are at least two functions that an individual trained to command can and will provide by the very nature of his character. First, he can recognize and translate to the community those sacrifices and risks that are always involved in the "important undertakings" of which de Tocqueville spoke, and which are indeed part of the human condition. The ability to induce one's followers to assume the consequences of their actions, to sacrifice willingly, and to inflict and endure suffering is virtually a definition of leadership and is not a trait for which mass democracies are noted. The supplying of this trait to America has been no small part of the Southern contribution to American achievements, not only in some of the most attractive Founding Fathers and in the Confederate leaders, but also in more recent figures such as General Patton. The Southern capacity to continue to provide this kind of leadership will be a test to which the aristocratic pretensions of the South may be usefully put. Second, the tradition of command can instill some responsibility, discipline, and coherence upon foreign policy itself, not merely within the country at large, but also within a particular administration and within the bureaucracy that oversees the formulation and execution of foreign policy. (It is not clear how much of our recent foreign policy has been the result of decision and how much has been due to the indirect and disguised actions of State Department bureaucrats.) A coherent policy cannot exist until the duly constituted leaders have effective control of the policy-implementing bodies. Moreover, whether America decides to continue dismantling its power or to retrieve it, it must make a deliberate choice and pursue that choice logically and consistently. It will not do so unless the alternatives and their consequences are made clear, and only highly skilled and trustworthy leaders can clarify these choices.

Finally, America may find useful to the future of its foreign policy the Southern ideal of community and the Southern concept of a public order. The United States today appears to be in serious danger of social and regional fragmentation. What is often called "divisiveness"—the conflict of generations, races, subcultures, or of Sun Belt and Frost Belt—is the manifestation of this fracturing. It has developed from two principal causes. First, since around 1960, a number of social categories have developed among themselves an awareness, a cohesion, and an ideology that disciplines them as distinct units of social and political action. This is true most obviously of blacks, but other sectors—women, youth, students, Indians, other racial and ethnic groups, and even homosexuals—have followed and emulated blacks. Usually styling themselves "liberation movements," these groups have challenged the conventional institutions of American society and government, have articulated "alternative lifestyles" that subvert the conventional American way of life, and have formulated doctrines and rhetoric centered around themselves, their own material and political interests, that do not hesitate to ignore any catholic sense of the public interest. Almost all political leaders, regardless of ideology, now must at least circumnavigate these liberated collectivities, and many politicians actively pander to them, knowing that their votes are numerous and their causes fashionable.

A second source of fragmentation derives from the increasing scramble for economic gain and political largesse. Virtually every identifiable sector of American society—old people and young, farmers and city-dwellers, professors and laborers, welfare recipients and corporate executives—makes some claim for special consideration of its particular interest. The regions, too, have their special interests and political champions pressing for federal assistance (i.e., for one region to pay for another) in different forms: land policy, energy allocations, subsidies for construction, education, renovation, or merely "bailout."

The result of this fragmentation and internal conflict is the collapse of any general perception of the interests of the public order, and even the ultimate denial that there *is* a public order with any legitimate claims. While every society is composed of groups that compete for special consideration, no determination of who should get what is possible unless all competing groups adhere to a consensus that affirms a hierarchy of claims and establishes regular procedures for realizing those claims. America lacks a consensus of this nature at the present time, and the collapse of the dominant millenarian ideology has only contributed to the confusion. It is doubtful that a new consensus will be established until a particular social force, or a new coalition of social forces, imposes one through its own domination.

The relevance of the fragmentation of America to foreign policy became obvious during the debate on the Panama Canal treaties in 1977 and 1978. A small but powerful coterie of banks and established business interests promoted the treaties for some time before the public became aware of them at all, oversaw their conclusion, and encouraged their ratification. Whether the treaties were good or bad, the immense influence of a narrow and unseen force on a question of national policy revealed the danger of special interests dominating foreign policy with little attention to public desires and interests. The same kind of influence could be demonstrated in the case of a number of economic, ethnic, and regional blocs that have asserted their own influence in foreign affairs for their own perceived interests.

The South, like other regions, has not abstained from this process. Perhaps Southern involvement in this scramble for protection and power should be added to the index of other sins with which it is taxed. Nevertheless, the South is in a unique position to instruct America in the meaning and importance of a public order, and not simply by trying to dominate in its own interests. The South has had the unique experience of trying to define its existence as a national and as a subcultural community, legal but in opposition, with special claims. While it would be futile to argue that the content of the Southern tradition is of direct use to America, ethical and philosophical problems that the South has sought to define and clarify are those that revolve around the nature of a public order, the legitimacy of its claims, and the legitimacy of the claims of the part as opposed to those of the whole.

The Southern mind has addressed these problems by asserting that a public order is the product not of rational design, but of nonrational and undesigned human activity. Hence the claims of the part—individual or collective—are subordinate to the claims of the whole, although the claims of the whole may recognize the priority of some particular claims. A social unit, community or nation, does not exist through its physical borders or the sum of its individual residents. Because its existence is necessarily historical, reaching into the past as well as the future, any calculation of its particular interests must not omit those of a historical (and therefore not entirely material) nature. In foreign affairs, therefore, it is not enough merely to establish the present material interests of particular sectors; rather, the primary concern in foreign (as in domestic) policy must be the protection of the historic character and identity of the community.

Yet even if the character of a society is known, there is no possibility of formulating and enforcing a policy predicated on it without the support of the community. The splintering of society has been an important cause of those problems to which de Tocqueville pointed, and they are indeed characteristic of a democracy, in which each component is encouraged to pursue its own interests and no central authority is able to enforce unity and common purpose. The formulation of foreign policy, then, is by no means a matter solely of "reason of state"—the calculation of the material interests of abstract national blocs. Rather, it is closely related to the whole range of intellectual, moral, and social institutions that provide a common identity for and definition of a people. The ability to transcend particular concerns and make sacrifices for the whole is the final test of any foreign policy. Indeed, without awareness of and loyalty to the whole, there can be no coherent foreign policy at all.

The definition of the identity of a community is not easy, especially if it has been forgotten. It requires a considerable immersion in the history, letters, and manners of a society. Moreover, the very notion of a public order is alien to most contemporary Americans and is even abhorrent to some. Yet America, for once in its brief and not always glorious history, must try to learn that its own experience is peculiar, that it has been unusually fortunate in coming to maturity in an epoch of untypical peace and prosperity, and that it cannot continue to judge the world by the norm of its own mythology. This lesson is perhaps what the South, and only the South, can teach America—has in a sense always tried to teach it, and has never succeeded in teaching it. The failure of the South in this respect is at least as significant as that other, bloodier, and more dramatic failure that has haunted and informed our region for the past century and more.

Southern Schooling

and the Ancient Wisdom

THOMAS FLEMING

THE TEACHER of the first Queen Elizabeth called learning "the fairest exercise of God's greatest gift." Such language betrays the gulf which separates the education of our own time from that of former days, when learning was viewed as a challenge, almost sacred, to young men of ability. That we should speak of "gifts" or "exercise" or even "God" in the context of schooling is now unthinkable for a generation reared to believe that competition is unhealthy, that religion and morality must not intrude upon the province of instruction. It has even been asserted that so vast are the differences between the two educations, ancient (roughly before World War I) and modern, that there is no basis for a fruitful comparison.

While we may freely admit that methods of education have changed a great deal, we need not, at the same time, deny that the goal of every educational system must be the same: to raise up a generation capable of taking up where the last one left off. We may also concede that no previous system of formal education has ever attempted mass education on the scale now practiced in the United States. But, in making such a concession, we are saying nothing about the need to turn out at least no fewer well-educated men than earlier generations.

I leave it to others to debate the social usefulness of educated men. For several thousand years we have been told—admittedly by teachers most of the time—that an education is a fine thing to have. Of course, it *can* be argued that every society needs leaders in the shape of statesmen and generals, clergymen, writers, and scientists—that the quality of a civilization (its tone, so to speak) is set by the intellectual and moral qualities of those leaders, and that such a leadership is produced only by a vigorous education. It is as difficult for a man of good will to quarrel with such arguments, when they are made, as it is for professional educationists to understand them. Official public thinking on all social questions has become so infected with the utilitarian ideal of "the greatest good to the greatest number" that the whole notion of excellence has been effaced.

For whatever reason, enormous sums of money are spent on public and private education. Most children spend from thirteen to seventeen years (between one-sixth and one-fourth of their lives) in school. Since it does not take thirteen years to learn to drive a truck or twenty to learn the tricks of the law, all this time and money must be for something beyond job training. If we, despite this tremendous expenditure of effort and resources, fail to turn out the kind of statesmen, generals, and clergymen we used to produce with very little public money, we should feel justified in asking for a look at the books.

It is enough to assume that we would prefer a learned priest to an ignorant one, humane generals and statesmen to mercenaries and stockjobbers. If so, it is hard to escape the conviction that our preference is not being taken seriously by those who are in charge of schooling American youth.

A great deal of journalistic attention has been directed at the problems of drugs, violence, and poor discipline in the middle and high schools, while the annual decline in English SAT scores is reported with almost the same dismal regularity as the rise in oil prices. However, it is a mistake to concentrate on the period of the past twenty or so years, as if the 1940s and '50s were a time of excellence—a mistake made by many in the "Back to Basics" movement. Jacques Barzun's polite but firm categorization of our "educational products" as "complaints and cripples" (1959) antedates the drug culture, as does Thomas Molnar's indictment in *The Future of Education* (1961):

Today we realize that there are no more (or fewer) educated men in the mid-twentieth century than there were in the mid-seventeenth [despite the enormous increase in population]. . . . Make no mistake about it: with a few honorable exceptions, the American grade and high school represent twelve wasted years in the life of youth. . . . To be frank, there are no more than ten or twelve universities in the United States worthy of the name. The rest are a disgrace to the concept of higher education since most of them are doing the work of more or less acceptable high schools.

As early as 1930, Albert Jay Nock, in an essay on "American Education," cited the opinion of the president of Columbia University that "during the past half-century the changes in school and college instruction . . . have been so complete that it is probably safe to say that today no student in Columbia College, and perhaps no professor on its faculty, could pass satisfactorily the examination-tests that were set for admission to Columbia College fifty years ago." Another fifty years has passed, and it is probably still safe to say that few university students or professors could pass the entrance tests of 1930.

The substance of much of the current criticism is that, measured by the standards set up by our schools of education, we are not doing a very good job. That is the meaning of the furor over SAT scores: one arm of our educational apparatus is saying that the other is not, for one or another reason, producing the most desirable results. If we are dissatisfied with the job being done by our schools, we have a right to suspect the qualifications and the motives of educationists who confine their criticism to statistics gathered by other educationists at the College Board and Educational Testing Service.

Recently, browsing through a PSAT test administered to high school juniors, I was astonished to discover that the test-makers did not, apparently, perceive the distinction between *impudent* and *impertinent*. If this were an isolated barbarism, not much could be made out of it; however, a lifetime spent in taking and administering the PSAT, SAT, Graduate Record, Stanford Achievement, etc., has confirmed me in the conviction that the people in charge of educational standards are themselves the victims of poor schooling. It is not simply that the tests are stupid and unreliable, or even that their main effect is to reinforce clichés (a point well made by Barzun in *The House of Intellect*). These tests are the highest expression of literacy among our educators, people who share a firm conviction that learning, intelligence, and wisdom can be freeze-dried down to dots, grids, and numbers on pages—to be reconstituted, presumably, in "real-life learning situations." We have hired one pack of wolves to guard our sheep against another.

The question that faces Southern schools today is not: What can be done to undo the results of twenty-five years of unsuccessful experimentation? By limiting the problem to our generation, we imply that the experimentation of the first fifty years of this century was justified. Even the best of the recent critics of higher education, Russell Kirk, in *Decadence and Renewal in the Higher Learning*, confines his attention to the past thirty years and projects an impression that the liberal arts curriculum of fifty years ago was a kind of Golden Age. There is no doubt that colleges of the 1940s did a better job of instructing their students than those of the 1970s.

Their emphasis on a central curriculum of humanities, math, and science was certainly preferable to our own supermarkets, where job training competes with the humanities and both are threatened by courses in ceramics, basketry, and recreational sexuality. But the liberal arts program existed for so short a period that one is tempted to regard its existence as a trick of perception. The liberal arts college existed in a period of transition from the classical curriculum—what Barzun even in 1959 could call the "ancient nursery" of intellect—to our own period of unrestrained libertinism.

For Southerners, there is only one sound standard with which to compare modern education: the fully developed model of, say, 1860. There is no mystery about the instruction received by Southern boys a hundred years ago; in its essentials it differed very little from the course of studies to be found in New England and Europe. It was the nineteenth-century version of the classical curriculum. At the log cabin academies and Georgian colleges of the South, the sons of the gentry (most often a frontier, homespun gentry) were exposed to arithmetic and algebra, theology, rhetoric (that is, composition), Hebrew (seldom), Greek (often), and always Latin, a great deal of Latin. Students at the University of Georgia, for example, were expected not merely to have spent one year on grammar and another trudging through Caesar's *Gallic Wars*, but to be able "to read, translate, and parse Cicero, Virgil, and the Greek Testament, and to write true Latin in prose" *before* they were admitted. Similar requirements were maintained at the venerable College of William and Mary, Transylvania University of Kentucky, the tiny College of Charleston (founded 1767), and Mr. Jefferson's University of Virginia. The latter expected graduates "to be able to read the highest classics in the language with ease, thorough understanding, and just quantity"—stiff requirements today, even for most American professors of classics.

It may seem paradoxical, but a classical background made educated Southerners of the last century more cosmopolitan than those of the present. Thomas Jefferson and Jefferson Davis shared a common education, not only with each other and with their Northern rivals John Adams and Daniel Webster, but with all educated men in England and Europe. Such training allowed Edgar Poe to be at once an ardent Southern patriot and a student of European literature. The learned languages afforded the studious a glimpse into the minds and lives of civilized men of other times, from Homer (eighth century B.C.) to Augustine (fifth century A.D.). For the curious, the world of the Middle Ages and the Renaissance was also opened by the knowledge of Latin, although most young men were content with a few standard authors.

The experience of this schooling was itself a link with the past. Jefferson Davis and Robert E. Lee were nourished on many of the same books Quintilian had recommended in the first century, and in somewhat the same manner. The aim of education, as Quintilian saw it, was to produce an orator—a good man skilled in speaking, a man whose literacy was at the service of his country. Few will deny that the South, which clung more tenaciously than other regions to the ancient learning, has produced more than its share of the country's leading orators. The Southerner's love of oratory has been variously traced to his agrarian society, to the love of storytelling, and to a keen interest in political affairs. These tendencies could not have produced a Jefferson, a Calhoun, or a Davis without an education strongly rooted in the rhetorical tradition of the classics.

Generalizations are unconvincing without examples. No better representative of the South could be chosen than the Confederacy's only president. Like his opposite number in the North, President Davis was born in a log cabin in Kentucky. His father was a small farmer whose migrations ended in Mississippi, where the family began to rise in the world. As a boy, Jefferson Davis experienced the rough and ready ways of a frontier where the old Persian virtues— shoot straight and speak the truth—were accomplishments more highly prized than a good Latin style or ballroom etiquette. He attended a variety of schools in Mississippi and Kentucky, some good (like the Catholic St. Thomas Aquinas), others not. He showed so little early inclination toward study that, rather than complete an "unfair assignment," he refused to return to school. His prudent father sent him to work in the fields, picking cotton, where—as Davis tells us—"the heat of the sun and the physical labor, in conjunction with the implied equality with the other cotton pickers, convinced me that school was the lesser evil."

Davis had little regard for the country schools he attended, where "the oil of birch was the proper lubricator for any want of intelligence." He attended the County Academy of Wilkinson "until I was sufficiently advanced to be sent to the college known as the Transylvania University of Kentucky." It was at Transylvania that Davis completed his "studies in Greek and Latin and learned a little of algebra, geometry, trigonometry, surveying, profane and sacred history, and natural philosophy (that is, science)." Not bad accomplishments for a college graduate who, at the age of fifteen, left Transylvania to attend West Point, where high spirits and inattention put him only twenty-third in a graduating class of thirty-four. (Davis did not undertake serious study until after his first wife's death, when he buried himself in his brother Joseph's library, seeking consolation in political philosophy and the English classics.)

By his own account, Davis's background was spotty until he settled in at Transylvania; yet his country schools prepared him well enough to complete his classical education by the age of fifteen. It is hard to take the measure of a man so long dead, but I think it is safe to say that for some time there has been *no one* in public life who may claim to be his equal in learning and eloquence, much less in the strength of character and principle which made him admired even by his adversaries—W. H. Seward, for example. This prodigy (for so we would now regard him) was merely *primus inter pares* for his generation of Southern leaders. It is particularly strange that our own statesmen, with their university degrees, wealth, and experience, make such a poor showing in the world and cannot suffer comparison with a country boy from Mississippi, a state that is now held up as the worst pocket of ignorance in the whole United States—a considerable claim, if true.

But what of the ladies, who were, after all, half of society? They were, we are told, sunk in such sloughs of ignorance as would befit the malarial land in which they lived. Schooling for girls was almost entirely informal. Mrs. Varina Howell Davis received very casual training under the tutelage of Judge George Winchester, a family friend originally from Salem, Massachusetts. She made the best possible use of her learning as a wife and companion, as a mother, and as the writer of her husband's biography. That Mrs. Davis was no isolated prodigy is shown by the spate of splendid Southern diaries and memoirs which poured out in the years following the war. Few, if any, modern American novelists can match the humor and lucidity of Mary Boykin Chesnut's *A Diary from Dixie*, and every section of the South can boast at least one "Patience Pennington" or "Southern Girl."

What are we, the beneficiaries of fifty years of educational decline, to say of that generation of Southerners—of the Davises, the Lees, of James Hammond and William Gilmore Simms of South Carolina, of Edgar Poe and Richard Taylor and Beverley Tucker? Should we claim that, judged by the highest standards of scholarship of their day, they were woefully unprepared to translate Lycophron or to compile a collection of Latin inscriptions? Or that, judged by the standards of our own time, they were giants of learning and eloquence? What education they had was for use, not for display. No one who had read the speeches, essays, memoirs, and diaries of that period can fail to observe that, as a class, the educated Southerners of 1860 were head and shoulders above our own college graduates, scholars, novelists, newspaper editors, and politicians.

Whatever virtues the Old South possessed were due in large measure to the effects of a curriculum which stressed, along with correct grammar and effective speech, straightforward political participation and moral principles. Young men of ability had their minds schooled by the best minds of the ages, rather than by those semiliterate denizens of teachers' colleges, the writers of textbooks. The less able received sobering instruction on their limitations.

The classical curriculum was not without its critics; indeed, it had been under constant assault throughout the eighteenth century, particularly in the most celebrated treatises on education from Locke to Rousseau. The classics were dismissed as elitist, impractical, not suited to young minds, and a waste of valuable time. Northerners like Benjamin Rush and Noah Webster added a new entry to the debits of Latin and Greek: a new, democratic society like America ought not to be burdened by the fripperies of worn-out aristocratic Europe.

Few American theorists defended the old tradition, although the exceptions were notable. The Marylander Samuel Knox, in his essay on "Liberal Education" (1799), insisted that attacks on the classics resulted from "vitiated taste" and "the negligence or indulgence of parents." (The rigors of Latin and Greek do not win supporters among the ranks of today's sensitive, child-centered educators.) Sir Walter Scott wondered "whether those who are accustomed only to acquire instruction through the medium of amusement, may not be brought to reject that which approaches under the aspect of study." (It is not that modern humane methods of schooling inspire our children with a love of learning—quite the opposite. Television and illustrated textbooks have succeeded in turning a contact sport into a spectator sport.) "The knowledge that is got without pains is kept without pleasure." The maxim is from Halifax, who continues: "The struggling for knowledge hath a pleasure in it like that of wrestling with a fine woman."

Samuel Knox's essay threw down a challenge still not taken up by the reformers: "That which has been well tried and approved by experience ought not to be rashly abandoned. It is surely entitled to a decided preference to mere speculative theory." But America, especially New England, has always been the natural home of speculative fanaticism and intemperate innovation: of the transcendentalists, the Shakers, the Oneida colonists, of the consumers of Graham crackers and natural foods, of Joseph Smith and his science-fiction scriptures, of abolitionists and prohibitionists, of Seventh Day Adventists, Jim Jones, Charles Manson, and Dr. Spock—all eager to rewrite the constitution, not of America, but of the human race.

Education, like all aspects of child-rearing, must be an essentially conservative enterprise, and a prudent man approaches schemes of educational reform as delicately as King Agag when he came unto Samuel. Since all childrearing aims at handing down to children *nothing less* than what their fathers received, experimentation is a risky business. A bacteriologist whose experiment has failed need only throw away the culture and start over. With a generation of children, it is not so easy; it is rather as if a dangerous microbe were created in the lab, a virus that could be neither killed nor contained. Hence Plato's warning that risks in education are run not on slaves, but on our sons and on the children of our friends.

Educational revolutions—I speak not of mere reformations like those which took place during the Renaissance or at Thomas Arnold's Rugby—are important events; they do not simply mirror social and intellectual changes. It is true that most educational revolutionaries are at best second-raters, but it is their very mediocrity which allows them to become the vehicles of social change, the middle term (so to speak) by which revolutions in thought are converted in the everyday attitudes and prejudices of the literate classes. Few intellectual revolutions succeed without gaining control of the schools. The Sophists of the fifth century B.C. posed a serious danger to the Greek polis not because they generated irresistible ideas fated to transform society; with few exceptions, these men were *alazones*—that is, imposters or mere *professors*. At best, they were intellectuals in the Latin American sense—men of indifferent talents with a commitment to being noticed. The Sophists took what was most attractive and provocative from the philosophical ideas in the air (distrust of tradition, reliance on speculative reason and the self) and spoonfed them to young men all too happy to be liberated from the bonds of obedience to parents, tradition, law, and common decency. The Sophists of the fifth century, the philosophes of the eighteenth, and the disciples of John Dewey in our own were all intermediaries between real (albeit dangerous) thinkers and society. They all preached a gospel of liberation, based on the hatred of tradition and restraint. The educational innovations of our own day—our child-centered schools—seem designed to illustrate Burke's dictum that "rage and phrenzy will pull down more in half an hour, than prudence, deliberation, and foresight can build up in a hundred years." Actually, it has taken almost three generations.

The attack on our old education began to have its effects up North by the middle of the last century. The South, for several reasons, was much slower to do away with Latin requirements in her colleges and high schools. In the North, Jefferson's elective system, designed originally for a university which required its students to have a thorough knowledge of the classics, gradually replaced the basic curriculum in the humanities. In later life, Jefferson himself always insisted on the central importance of the learned languages; he even went so far as to warn Americans against following the example of Europeans, who, he had heard, were giving up Latin and Greek.

If the South had won its war of independence, she might have preserved a unique and flourishing educational tradition to the present; or perhaps circumstances would have induced her to pursue the same broad path of industrial progress and enlightenment down which the North had walked. But the South lost, and in defeat her people suffered so terribly that they were neither able nor willing to worship the alien gods who had brought them to ruin. Places of higher learning like the University of Virginia, the ambitiously named University of the South, and Davidson College clung to the old ways with a sentimental tenacity that was only one part of the upsurge of piety to the traditions of the Old South. Thus President Davis on his deathbed might have comforted himself with the reflection that the South, although it had lost the war, had nevertheless survived.

The South held on well into the twentieth century, despite ever heavier salvos from the professional educators. School after school relaxed its requirements, it is true; but even up to the end of the 1950s professional classicists often reassured themselves that the high schools of the Southern states were still turning out students who could read Caesar, tell active from passive voice, distinguish between indirect objects and infinitives, and realize that years B.C. run backward—modest accomplishments, but increasingly rare among college graduates and their teachers.

All this has changed. There is no longer anything distinctive about Southern schools except their notorious inferiority. The hodgepodge of relevant courses, career education, sex education, and pseudo-sociology is producing the same sort of uniform subliteracy which characterizes the rest of the United States. Our educators have forgotten that we once had a workable method for training at least a part of our population to be good for something better than making money. We gave it up without serious examination of the consequences. Of course, exclusive concentration on Cicero and Sophocles will not prepare anyone for "modern life." (It never did.)

From time to time the classical curriculum has been bolstered by the addition of courses in ethics, theology, mathematics, and natural science. More science and history could have been added without seriously weakening or even altering the character of the curriculum. Even though much of the early propaganda against the classics came from the champions of science, no practical person could argue for a curriculum based on the teaching of science.

It is not an intrinsic failing of science and mathematics teachers that they cannot do that which they should not even attempt: civilize the savage children of our race. Indeed, they are the sterling exception to the general decline in educational rigor. Our science teachers, at all levels, do their jobs well, turning out, year after year, men and women capable of doing research which most of us take for granted as a kind of tribute to our own indolent superiority. Of course, the pursuit of science has its own set of temptations, as Faust and Frankenstein learned to their sorrow; in the end, "the study of nature makes a man at last as remorseless as nature." To train only a man's brain, to teach him to be relentless in pursuit of truth and ruthless in his questioning of received wisdom, will produce cases of arrested development—great thinking machines, perhaps even endowed with splendid bodies, but divorced from all those kind and familiar things that raise us equally above the ant and the computer.

The great apostle of science, Thomas Henry Huxley, in his debate with Matthew Arnold, claimed that "every Englishman has in his native tongue, an almost perfect instrument of literary expression, and in his own literature, models for every kind of literary excellence." I have heard it suggested even by an excellent classicist that a sort of English classical curriculum could easily be devised to meet the needs of the Greekless and Latinless reader. But the English classics are not "basic" to the whole European tradition in the same way as their Greek and Latin models. A familiarity with Shakespeare will not necessarily make a man keen on Racine and Molière. English literature is hard to penetrate without the assistance of a classical background. One may be able to elucidate Homer out of Homer, but Milton is a different story. In fact, the descent of Milton's reputation is due in large measure to the contemporary ignorance of Virgil. We suffer the same problem with the English language as with its literature. English has a kind of dual parentage, a German mother but a Roman father. We do not understand the better than half of our vocabulary which is of Latin origin, or much of our syntax, without a solid grounding in Latin. Without Latin, the English speaker "will certainly have less intelligence and probably less practical mastery of his native idiom than the Frenchman or the German. He will be more exposed to the mental confusion of dimly discerned meanings and imperfectly apprehended relations," as Paul Shorey preached (to deaf ears) in 1917.

What *has* replaced the classics then, if not the sciences or even English? The real opposition to any sound curriculum (that is, any mixture of Latin, math and science, modern languages, and history) comes from the pseudo-sciences of psychology, sociology, and education, all of which might fairly be described as an ideology rather than as disciplines. Their goal, which they have actually already reached, has always been the transformation of our image of man. Formerly, most of us would have agreed that humanity, however animal in its physical being and appetites, nonetheless possessed attributes of reason, conscience, and compassion which raised us above the brute. The new sciences have changed all that. We are now to regard our behavior as a predictable complex of innate compulsions and external stimuli, reducible, for practical purposes, to a computer model. Not only is man denied his divine attributes, but he is now seen to have serious competitors in the trained dolphins and monkeys that communicate their needs with buttons or sign language. If this "philosophy" had not taken over the minds of teachers, schoolmasters, and educationists, it could have been defeated by a clever schoolboy armed only with a copy of Aristotle's *Organon*. But where could we find such a boy today?

It must not be supposed that our distress could be alleviated by turning the schools over to members of the American Philological Association. Professional classicists, as Jacques Barzun pointed out some time ago, "adopted a 'scorched earth' policy." They "allowed themselves to be invaded by the scientific spirit and in trying to compete with it reduced their field to a wasteland of verbal criticism, grammar, and philology." I shall never forget the young Roman historian who told me that, while he and other classicists were dishing out a "quality" product to the undergraduates, he could hardly pretend that reading Virgil and Cicero was a pleasure to be compared with perusing mystery novels or television comedies.

Even if we had a host of qualified teachers learned in the classics and eager to teach the Southern youth, what state or local board of education would allow the classical curriculum to be given a fair test? Our schools are subject to such rigid control by teachers' colleges, state departments of education, unions, and a clutter of federal agencies that no elitist heresy could possibly creep in under the noses of guidance counselors and driver's education teachers.

What is to be done? One county school superintendent in South

Carolina recently (upon leaving office) estimated that it would take
thirty years to bring his district up to the national average: that is, to
reach the state of hopeless illiteracy. He was widely suspected of optimism. Teachers, we must remember, are the products of schools of
education, proverbially the refuge of the ineducable, whose professors have been, for three generations, cranking out their theories
about the nature of man and his "learning potential" without one
convincing scrap of evidence or proof. Just give us more buildings,
more electronic hardware, more time, and more money; just give us
the children at an earlier age (Headstart did not begin early enough),
and we shall transform this country, and "every valley shall be
exalted, and every mountain and hill shall be made low; and the
crooked shall be made straight, and the rough places plain." Archi-
medes' proposal that, given a lever long enough and a place to stand,
he would move the earth, seems modest in comparison.

To devote billions of dollars of the people's money, not to mention
their children's lives, to schemes derived from the philosophical
theories of Skinner, Freud, and Dewey is no less absurd than to dedi-
cate such sums to, say, an education based on Bishop Berkeley's denial of the material world. One might imagine a Berkeley university
(preferably in California) where the students, wearing no clothes,
would be instructed to walk through walls, chanting: "It's all in the
mind." Or a Nietzschean institute of higher learning, where gladia-
torial games would be staged to weed out the unfit, as a substitute
for the more gentlemanly doctoral orals. There is no need, alas, to
imagine Dewey U.

There is no easy way to free ourselves from this curse, which is
already reaching the biblical third generation. The ideologues' control over public education is almost complete. Although their desire
to produce a nation of two hundred million unaggressive Navahoes
has not been entirely fulfilled, success, they tell us, depends only on
one more round of appropriations and a new wave of experimentation. The new federal Department of Education provides the necessary regrouping of forces before mounting the final offensive.

Our only hope lies in the restoration of some measure of human
control and in abandoning all grand schemes and giant projects in
favor of more modest local ambitions. If federal bureaucracy is
evil—a "metaphysical evil," as Gabriel Marcel would say—then
state or county bureaucracy is only a little better. In this respect the
Southern gospel of states' rights holds out little hope. Progress can
only begin in our own homes and our own circle of friends. We
must, as Marcel has expressed it, "Fight as actively as possible

against the kind of devouring anonymity that proliferates around us like cancerous tissue." A war against radical ideologies and depersonalizing bureaucracy will force us to abandon the whole notion of public school systems.

By suggesting that we abandon our public schools, I do not mean to imply that public education did not do the South a great deal of good, especially during the first fifty years of its existence. The South's innate conservatism prevented her public schools from going the way of those in the North and Midwest, but the 1960s saw the forces of radical ideology at last triumphant throughout the school systems of the South. Many Southern public schools still are considerably better than their Northern counterparts, but their days are numbered.

Fortunately, there is something uncongenial to the Southern spirit in the idea of bureaucracy. The people of the South have always preferred informal arrangements between family and friends to the abstractions of governmental machinery. The South's long-standing prejudice against public education was based on a frank appraisal of the perils of government interference in the very private matter of rearing children. It is true that men like Jefferson and Francis Marion believed that public school systems were the only hope of our infant republic, and that, throughout the nineteenth century, writers on education in North and South rarely failed to advocate tax-supported schools. However, for practical purposes, the creation of public school systems in the South was achieved under Reconstruction and on imported models.

It is not that there was no opposition. In 1876 the Reverend Robert Lewis Dabney—once Stonewall Jackson's chief of staff—debated the issue with William Ruffner, the leading proponent of public education in Virginia. Among Dabney's points were: while "there can be no true education without moral culture and no true moral culture without Christianity," in America, "the State's money cannot be used to teach one religion in preference to others"; state schools would level the classes which "providence, social laws, and parental virtues and effort do inevitably legislate in favor of . . . and if the State undertakes to countervail the legislation of nature, the attempt is wicked, mischievous, and futile." Finally, "the use of letters is not education," but leads to the degraded condition of European and Yankee society, where

Every manufactory is converted into a debating club. . . . The objection is that when the State interferes in the work of common school education, it inevitably does not enough, or too much. To give that large learning and thorough discipline necessary for setting the mind to deal independently with the corrupt labyrinth of modern current opinion is beyond the State's power. What she does give usually prepares the victim for literary seducers and political demagogues.

That many Southerners now recognize the truth of Dabney's prophecy is demonstrated by the independent and Christian schools that are flourishing in nearly every city and town. Some of these schools are as small and (comparatively speaking) as ill equipped as the log-cabin academies of the Old South; like those earlier schools, they are often staffed by overworked and underqualified teachers. Often the curriculum is no better than a dreary rehash of public education circa 1955. But for all their faults, imagined and real, these new schools and the associations which protect them are the future of the South.

Although many of these schools were created in the past twenty years, it would be a mistake to attach too much importance to problems engendered by integration and forced busing. Questions of race were simply a wedge to be inserted by the reformers into the cracks of social and intellectual divisions, a handy tool for demolishing the structure of society. It was necessary to divert attention from the dangerous notion of excellence, by replacing it with the obviously superior goal of racial harmony. The point of busing and affirmative action is not that they benefit minorities (they patently do not), but that they destroy traditional and personal responsibility, along with the basis for any healthy competition.

The greatest challenge faced by these new private schools will be to avoid consoling themselves with their own superiority over the public schools and resting content with that goodness which consists in being better than the worst. The great opportunity which they offer is that they are amenable to reform. More genuine *regress* can be made by a few good men in a handful of such schools than by hiring a thousand Dr. Arnolds at the federal Department of Education. If these brave new schools can realize firmly that bigotry is no substitute for learning, and if they can regain the vision of their ancestors by turning back to the ancient wisdom, then and only then is there hope that the South may survive the twentieth century with some of her principles intact.

IV

A MIRROR FOR ARTISTS

Southern Literature
Here and Now

GEORGE GARRETT

> Without any censorship in the West, fashionable trends of thought are carefully separated from those that are not fashionable. Nothing is forbidden, but what is not fashionable will hardly ever find its way into periodicals or books or be heard in colleges. Legally, your researchers are free, but they are conditioned by the fashion of the day. There is no open violence such as in the East; however, a selection dictated by fashion and the need to match mass standards frequently prevents independent-minded people from giving their contribution to public life. There is a dangerous tendency to form a herd, shutting off successful development.
>
> —Alexander Solzhenitsyn,
> address at Harvard University's commencement, 1978

IN THE following discussion it will be more than a contention, it will be more a matter of firm and unquestioned assumption that in this particular observation, as in so many others, Alexander Solzhenitsyn said what is purely and simply true. Serious consideration of a wide range of serious subjects, including both the general subject of this book and of this minor part of it, is severely restricted in these times by "fashion," by "mind set," by all the elements of a fairly uniform liberal intellectual consensus (and its consequent intellectual rigidity) in contemporary America which so startled Solzhenitsyn.

It is difficult even to try to describe the contemporary South and its literature without departing from the boundaries of that fashionable consensus. To deviate from the consensus, in public and in print, is an exercise of bad manners which most Southerners would as lief avoid. As Lisa Alther, a Southern novelist now living in Vermont, wrote in the *New York Times Book Review* ("Will the South Rise Again?"): "Most Southerners have strong and cranky opinions yet know that it's not polite to insist on one's own point of view or to dispute someone else's."

As a compromise, I shall do my best not to insist on my own point of view. However, I reserve the right to dispute anyone else's.

1.

Lisa Alther, given a prominent position and an opportunity to ask her perennial question, produced a lively and entertaining article which arrived at no firm or startling conclusions beyond the casual observations that there are still some basic distinctions between the practice of good manners, and the emphasis upon them, in the North and the South; that the Southerner seems naturally to fall into the structure, language, images, and idiom of anecdote when sending his messages and communicating his thoughts and feelings; that, in a strictly literary sense, there have been some Southern writers in our times who are widely acknowledged to have been masterful and profoundly influential literary artists; that there appear to be a good many gifted new writers still coming out of the South, but that "the Southern Renaissance writers are a tough act to follow however inspirational their example." She duly noted the signs of the much-discussed "New South," and she wondered (as have so many others) whether the South can possibly survive this season of transition from old to new, enduring all the apparently homogenizing and standardizing forces of the culture, both good and bad, and yet still somehow or other manage to preserve at least some of the region's distinct and admirable qualities of daily life, qualities which have given rise to some of the distinctly admirable qualities of Southern literature. This is not, as indicated, a new question; and her answers to it (being inevitably and in large part the kind of "answers answerless" which Queen Elizabeth I once so favored) are familiar enough also.

None of which is to fault Lisa Alther. Who, knowingly or unknowingly, has found herself, for whatever reasons, allowed simply to reiterate both questions and answers already often proposed by many others within and outside of the South. Her views are based upon and, indeed, elucidate a great many of these commonly held assumptions about the South, its way of living, and its forms of literary art. These *assumptions* of and behind any critical and intellectual consensus must be at least tested and explored before we can even pretend to move toward any kind of description of things as they may be and of things as they may well come to be in the foreseeable, imaginable future.

Another recent, and more relevant, item is the excellent introduction by Guy Owen and Mary C. Williams to their *Contemporary Southern Poetry: An Anthology* (Louisiana State University Press, 1979). Brief as it is, this essay is riddled with insights and fresh and accurate views of the present state of Southern poetry. Yet here, too, the essay must necessarily begin by discussing (questioning, anyway) the validity of the notion as to whether or not "the region has lost its distinctiveness and has been absorbed into the mainstream of America." Thus one major question troubling most critics of Southern literature is the extent to which the overwhelming weight of our national culture has so far changed the literature of the South. There seems to be no question in anyone's mind that, outwardly and visibly, Southern *life* and styles are being submerged in the American "mainstream." No one who trusts the reports of his senses and the records of his memory can doubt that the South, with its growing cities and its sprawling miles of standard suburbs, has become all too much like most of the other urban and suburban parts in the United States. Same tricky maze of interconnected highways. Same shiny, noisy, busy airports. Same motels and tacky shopping centers and fast food franchises. Same festering and decaying inner cities. Same chain stores with pretty much the same products. And many of the same national and evidently insoluble problems—high taxes and poor services, pollution, crime, the idleness of so many of the ill-educated young and the loneliness of the forgotten and exhausted old, the shrugging indifference of the powers that be, the brutal, yawning impersonality of our bureaucrats, the primitive ignorance and irresponsibility of our politicians. It is as if the worst of the Fugitive nightmares had now come to pass. On any given day in, for example, Atlanta or Richmond or Raleigh or New Orleans or Birmingham or Houston, it would be easy to believe not only that the South thoroughly lost the War, but that since then it has been effaced, ploughed under, and covered with asphalt. Has vanished forever in a total and final Yankee triumph.

Still, most sane Southerners, however much they may be offended by what is new and seems to be wholly alien, however much they suffer nostalgia for what seems to have left so little behind, are willing to admit that there have been at least some improvements, if only technological ones, in the quality of day-to-day living. Even so, much that was admirable, amiable, amenable, honorable, and even beautiful looks to be gone for once and for all. By now there is probably no corner of our South rural and remote enough to have been spared an infectious dose of the products of "today's mass living habits" in America, which Solzhenitsyn cited as "the revolting invasion by publicity, by TV stupor, and by intolerable music."

The long and the short of it is that a great many of our most sensitive and intelligent observers perceive, indeed, now assume, that most of the things which made the South distinct within the larger national culture are going or have already gone. To many thoughtful Southerners it seems a great pity; to others it may seem high time. But it is quite possible that neither the friendly nor the hostile view is more than superficial, that this hasty perception of the present is, at the very least, out of date. It has been well argued, on the strength of some very solid evidence, that, throughout the entire world, the high season of centralization is over and done with. The dominant and characteristic worldwide trend in this last quarter of the twentieth century is toward the breakdown of all large and unwieldy political units; we are already witnessing a breakup so thorough and powerful that it may soon spell out the end of the whole concept of the nation-state as we have known it. (In which case, the South would prove to have *won* the War after all. Finally!) In many places this is taking place amid a context of war and revolutionary upheaval. Here in America it is (so far) more peaceably manifest in what René Dubos has called "regionalism by choice." Each census seems to indicate that Americans are now more and more *choosing* the places where they want to live. It seems not to be merely a matter of climate and comfort; for even though there is, inevitably, a major nomadic movement toward the Sun Belt, there is also a surge of settlers moving into the West and even into upper New England. The phenomenon, as it is developing in America, appears to be based as much upon popular perception of and affinity for a regional "lifestyle" as anything else. It follows that these new settlers will desire to protect and defend the qualities and characteristics which led them to their new homes in the first place; or, in the case of the native born, qualities which led them to choose to remain there. So, in this sense, very powerful forces for conservation, if not strictly and conventionally conservative, seem already at work. The irrepressible anxiety and nostalgia shadowing much contemporary literature and literary criticism can be seen not so much as the last trumpet calls of a lost cause (no matter how much we Southerners, by nature and in art, rejoice in the celebration of forlorn hopes), but instead as the expression of some of the deepest and, yes, even the *latest* trends in the culture.

It may be noteworthy that *each generation* of modern and contemporary Southern writers has responded in much the same way— lamenting the dimming of many bright things and the falling away of familiar certainties. Allowing for the fact that this is a traditional Southern trope (itself probably directly descended from the alliterative poetry of the Anglo-Saxons, who seem to have been happiest and easiest in the elegiac mood long before their own vital culture gave them any serious need to cultivate it), it is mildly strange that much of what the very youngest generation of Southern writers laments and regrets the passing of had to be, in fact, among the crowd of *new things* whose arrival and presence on the scene was roundly deplored by the previous generations. One of the things shared by these generations of Southern writers, masters and apprentices alike, is this very general yet essential sense of loss. Which, in turn, may be taken as an attractive characteristic of the Southern spirit, one which draws others toward the South and one which Southerners, wherever they may end up, by choice or out of necessity, always carry with them. Surely the knowledge that changes, whether for good or ill, always include some losses grows out of the bitter Southern historical experience and is a valuable corrective contribution in a society which not so much seeks to make a virtue of necessity by accepting change as to embrace all change on principle and, wherever possible, to manipulate it to advantage.

To begin, then, it is at least possible to doubt that the South as we know it, with its various people and its diverse culture, is in any danger of vanishing from the scene.

2.

The most formidable fact which the working Southern writer must face (not really a *problem*, mind you, though it may be taken as one by many writers) is the recognition of his coming after at least one generation of Southern master artists. Of all these masters, some still living and a few (like Robert Penn Warren) still vigorously creative and actively influential, none casts a longer shadow than William Faulkner. All of the newer Southern writers—by which I mean to identify all those (and they are many and various) who have produced work since World War II; thus, by the old-fashioned reckoning, at least a generation and a half—have to live with the overwhelming example of William Faulkner and must come to terms not only with his great body of work, but also with his ghost. For his influence and example is now personal as well as artistic, thanks to Joseph Blotner's biography, and to the published selections of his letters, speeches, and interviews. Perhaps, ironically, more so than if he had not so zealously and successfully defended his privacy during his lifetime; that is, the *personal* influence and example, being suspensefully delayed and likewise partaking of the fresh impact of discovery, can be seen as stronger and more immediate, more like "news" than like history. Of course, it is worth remembering that the influence of Faulkner's work, of his purely artistic example, was also long delayed, deferred by the unconscionable length of time that passed before he earned any widespread recognition in establishment literary circles. In fact, his recognition began to occur almost a generation after he had earned it.

The contemporary Southern writer must also, and simultaneously, contend with many other powerful, pervasive influences and examples coming from the worldwide generation of masters. And Southern writers must now seek to find some form of accommodation with the larger, the *national* American literary situation, the "scene," insofar as it exists and infringes upon their capacity to create and to be recognized. There is nothing precisely new about this. William Faulkner and our other masters have always had to make the same kind of accommodation, at least ever since the Civil War and Reconstruction ended (for all practical purposes) for a long time the serious potential of the South as a center of publishing as well as writing.

That particular topic—the relation of the contemporary Southern writer to the larger context—will be treated in a separate section of this essay. But it is useful, here and now, to bear in mind that it is not a truly abstract or separate situation. For example, in addition to the undesirable inner and regional pressure, the *family* feeling, as it were, felt by every Southern writer that his efforts will be measured against the standards of achievement of the masters (thus, inevitably, against those of Faulkner), there is also an outer pressure coming from Northern critics and scholars and book reviewers, a good many of them alien and even indifferent to both the Southern experience and its literary traditions. It is, at the very least, an intellectual convenience for most of these people to maintain the notion that Southern literature began and ended with the prominent masters of the Southern Renaissance; that its greatness began and ended with William Faulkner, against whom every apprentice writer can be judged and found wanting in a way that, say, a Jewish first novel would never be strictly measured against the standards of Bellow or Singer or Malamud.

The Southern writer today must contend with a discouraging double standard when he ventures outside his region and traditions, as venture he still must until (and if) small presses, university presses, and Southern trade publishing and bookselling become, again, a viable alternative.

As to the influence and example of Faulkner, and of the other masters whose present influence differs only in degree and not in kind, everyone is familiar with Flannery O'Connor's often-quoted image of the overwhelming influence of William Faulkner on all subsequent Southern writing: "Nobody wants his mule and wagon stalled on the same track the Dixie Limited is roaring down." Cited by Guy Owen and Mary C. Williams (in slightly different form) in *Contemporary Southern Poetry*, it is used by them to distinguish between the special position of today's Southern poet in comparison with other Southern writers. "One reason many of our poets may feel free to be southern, rather than simply American," they write, "is that they are not competing with predecessors of towering reputations as southern novelists are." Of course, Flannery O'Connor was partly fooling; it would be hard to imagine any way in which William Faulkner's achievement served to inhibit her own artistic development. Her wisecrack was addressed, in part, to the aforementioned Northern literati, who no doubt needed to be reassured that she was writing out of a different experience, creating her own world.

The contemporary Southern writer must be unusually self-conscious about the whole matter of literary influence. For some it may take the form of a flat denial of any influence, as in this comment by Reynolds Price (in *Kite-Flying and Other Irrational Acts*): "I can say, quite accurately, that Faulkner has been no influence, technical or otherwise, on my work. I admire the work of Faulkner that I know—by no means all—but with a cold, distant admiration for a genius whom I know to be grand but who proved irrelevant to my own obsessions, my own ambitions." Another stance, perhaps more credible, is that taken by Shelby Foote in any number of interviews. Foote, who knew Faulkner personally, simply *assumes* the influence of Faulkner on any contemporary Southern writer. But he clearly indicates that the major influences on his own fiction have been other modern masters: Proust, Joyce, and Mann.

Calder Willingham, a wonderful and outrageously comic Southern writer, has taken a much more aggressive and highly exaggerated position. In his *Transition* interview, he calls Faulkner (among other things) a "nitwit," a "half-educated village philosopher," "a total fool and a very bad writer." "If this man is a great writer," he adds, "shrimps whistle Dixie." Willingham contends that the best Southern writer is Erskine Caldwell. I mention Willingham's hyperbolic fooling around because, absurd as it is, it represents the lengths a gifted writer is willing to go to in order to dissociate himself from the reflexive critical dismissal of much of the work of contemporary Southern writers as no more than shabby imitations of the achievements of their predecessors and betters.

It is ironic that there should be pressures on the Southern writer to forfeit—to offer up, as it were—one of the qualities which has served to identify his work and to distinguish it from a great deal of other contemporary American literature: namely, a deep awareness of his own literary traditions and a sense of blood kinship with the past. It remains a part of the knowledge (and spirit) of the Southerner that the experience of the present is continually informed by the living past; that the past cannot be ignored or denied; that the result of acting upon any assumption that the present can somehow be lived in isolation from the past is both a crippling spiritual inhibition of the present experience and a destructive prospect for the future; that, thus, to embrace the present, with all its novelty and flowing sense of change, without being mindful of the past, is a grotesque distortion of reality and a fundamentally self-destructive enterprise. In short, for the Southern writer to deny, ignore, or pretend to be free of his own literary past would, in fact, mean the death of Southern literature.

A good deal of recent criticism and scholarship demonstrates that, despite their unquestionably innovative achievements, the works of the modern masters of Southern letters—and most centrally those of William Faulkner himself—were deep rooted in the traditions and conventions of both the literature and the historical experience of the South. The consistently dazzling virtuosity of Faulkner's style (which is idiosyncratic enough so that it cannot be discreetly imitated) has, as he perhaps intended, served to divert attention from the often classically traditional elements of his fiction. Frequently there is a dramatic opposition between style and substance, creating comedy or a stormy sense of tension. But even as Faulkner was in some ways a profoundly traditional writer, he was also a pioneer. No two of his books employ the same kind of narrative strategy. It is true that the celebrated style, voice, and certain deliberate and habitual personal tropes and techniques (as well as, in many cases, links of subject matter and characters, etc.) bind his works intimately together, but none of his novels is designed in quite the same fashion. He simply did not choose to repeat himself in this way.

It is important to realize the considerable courage involved in Faulkner's artistic strategy. All of the conventional pressures of the times, and especially those emanating from the commercial heart of America's popular culture, are designed to force the artist in the opposite direction. Artists of all kinds are discouraged from the risks of cultivating variety and are strongly encouraged to exploit any limited areas which, by popularity or critical recognition or (rarely) both, have come to be acknowledged as their provenance. In that sense it may be that Faulkner was fortunate to have been spared both popularity and extensive critical recognition until later in his life. Otherwise the pressures to conform might have been, as he ironically indicated in his introduction to the Modern Library edition of *Sanctuary* and more directly stated in the unpublished note on *The Sound and the Fury*, too overwhelming to resist. Even so, it is clear that he was much more interested in pioneering than in settling for one kind of fiction and then developing that to its limits. It was always Faulkner's *intention* to be a discoverer, which means that a part of his complex intention was to open up new vistas and directions for future writers. Whatever his intent—though I do believe it can be properly inferred, from many things in his published speeches, interviews, and letters, that Faulkner was consistently concerned with the art and artists of the future—it is certainly the effect of his example. That example, not precisely his literary "influence," can be at once liberating and inspiring to be contemporary Southern writer.

There are other ways in which Faulkner's work and his life (which become, more and more, inseparable from the work) can be exemplary to the late twentieth century Southern writer. One way, of course, is in his exemplary exercise of what has been called "the conservation of literary material." He was fearless in returning to a subject or situation when he felt it could sustain the force of further exploration. This tactic, of course, breaks both the critical mind set and the rule against treating with anything but apparently new directions and new materials. Just as he broke the habits of our times by continually seeking new *techniques*, new and different ways of *telling* his stories, so he broke the other conventional attitude of at least professing that *the subject matter* is always new and different.

At the very least, then, Faulkner's work offers consolation and direction to the contemporary Southern writer. It offers a challenge as well: the writer is dared to divorce himself from easy habits of thought which are prevalent in the overall culture. Dared, by that towering example, to cultivate his art without regard to present systems of praise or blame and, indeed, without embarrassed or inhibiting reverence for the immediate past, the past which includes the achievement of William Faulkner, of Thomas Wolfe, of all of the Fugitives and other masters. By example, he demonstrates that the Southern past is not dead or disposable and cannot be ignored. It is and remains a resource to be wisely *used*.

Finally, and not least important, the life of William Faulkner offers a model for bedeviled contemporary Southern writers. The world has changed in many ways, some sharp and startling and some very subtle, in the almost twenty years since the death of William Faulkner. As noted, the South has also changed greatly, at least outwardly. The American literary situation is now quite different from that faced by Faulkner and the others of his generation. The whole publishing industry has changed drastically in the last two decades, so greatly altering the status and importance of the serious writer that the writing of poetry and fiction has almost become a different kind of enterprise. However, the situation is, on the whole, no less formidable or difficult for the serious writer.

Faulkner's great courage and patience and unceasing productivity are inspiring. The absence of recognition and reward did not silence him, nor did his belated triumph. Perhaps this was because, very early in his professional career, he came to terms with frustration and neglect, turning them both into positive energy. As indicated in his "unpublished preface" to *The Sound and the Fury*, Faulkner experienced great discouragement with his first three novels. After *Sartoris* was repeatedly turned down: "One day I seemed to shut a door between me and all publishers' addresses and book lists. I said to myself, Now I can write." (I have written elsewhere that Faulkner's statement is something every aspiring writer should have tattooed on his skin, so as never to forget it.)

His career is usefully emblematic in other ways also. There is the relevant fact that, without considerable financial resources, he still managed to survive, to do his work and to maintain a place and a family. He did this in part by writing short stories for the popular magazines, when that was still a possibility, and chiefly by his stints as a salaried screenwriter. His letters show that money was a serious, often urgent problem for him almost up until the very end of his life; he never really had a secure financial base. This may have caused him much anxiety, and there is no denying that the time spent in Hollywood, for instance, was time lost to his real interests and best gifts. Yet neither anxiety nor lost time could deter him. It is hard to imagine a more productive serious writer.

With the exception of a couple of *New Yorker* regulars, no one today could possibly earn more than pocket money by writing short stories. The movie studios no longer produce films on the same grand scale and no longer employ whole stables of writers. (However, it should be noted that the financial rewards are generally now much greater for the working screenwriters. And it is noteworthy that a good number of serious and highly regarded contemporary Southern writers—Calder Willingham, James Dickey, Larry McMurtry, and William Harrison, for instance—have made a mark on and a contribution to the development of that special narrative form.) By and large the Southern poet and fiction writer today earns some or most of his living by working for another kind of institution: the academy. Much has been said, and no doubt remains to be said, both for and against this affiliation, which is a fairly recent national phenomenon; but this is not really the place for that kind of discussion. All that needs to be said here is that if William Faulkner did not find the brutal institutional world of the film studio completely stultifying, then the working Southern writer can be allowed to hope that exposure to and labor for the academy (which is, after all, ostensibly dedicated to the preservation and dissemination of our best cultural myths and artifacts) is not necessarily a negative experience.

Here, also, the contemporary Southern writer can find many examples among the Agrarians, who in fact did so much to make a place in the academy possible for the poet and the novelist. Donald Davidson, John Crowe Ransom, Allen Tate, Caroline Gordon, Robert Penn Warren, Andrew Lytle, and others demonstrated that it is possible to maintain a serious literary career while actively associated with institutional education. Not only that: they also proved that it is, likewise, possible to make a major contribution within the context of the institution, as a teacher-scholar. Just as Faulkner managed to write some memorable and artistic screenplays, against the odds and even against his own expectations.

The real significance of all this, however, lies not in the possible influences of academic institutions on contemporary writers or vice versa. Rather, it is important that the contemporary Southern writer who has rarely, until very recently indeed, come out of a situation which allowed for much leisure to cultivate fine (and usually unprofitable) arts can now do so, earning and paying his own way. Ever since the Civil War and until very recently, the South has been *actually* as well as statistically poor. Yet serious poets and novelists, black and white alike, have flourished in that society and are still flourishing. The results are (though utterly unprovable, still and all undeniable) a literary art which is, as it has always been in theory and practice, close to the lives and the common experience of Southern life and history. It is a literary art which may or may not be difficult or obscure but which, in any case, is only rarely elitist. It is a literary art which is both democratic and populist in spirit and which is very seldom (except in occasional lapses into imitation of national intellectual fashions) created from a stance of haughty alienation from the quotidian world and the concerns of others. There is often hatred and anger in Southern literature, but one seldom sees the more usual contemporary contempt for all who are stupid or ignorant or unwashed or invincibly ordinary. Faulkner could find and celebrate the humanity (and the divinity) in the idiot, the pervert, the criminal—not, as in more fashionable contemporary literature, as anti-heroes or any such, but as fully delineated characters. There are plenty of villains in Southern stories, and, because the South remains a predominantly Christian culture, evil, sin, and folly are hardly ever absent from the Southern vision. But the Southern writer has not set himself up as judge and overseer of a hostile and absurd universe. In fact, even the minor alienation of the artist (such a popular subject in our national culture and throughout contemporary European writing) has seldom figured very importantly in Southern writing. Tennessee Williams, Carson McCullers, and Truman Capote have all written minor works on this theme, and the major "portrait of the artist" by a Southerner is to be found in the work of Thomas Wolfe. But the artist Wolfe depicts, himself, though misunderstood and often ignored or rejected by others, is an artist with a communal and social spirit and function, anxious to be part of the community and to serve it.

3.

Recently John Leonard, former editor of the *New York Times Book Review* and still chief cultural correspondent for the daily *New York Times*, and Harvey Shapiro, Leonard's successor as editor of the *Times Book Review*, an enormously influential publication (the more so in the absence of any serious regional competition), spoke, on separate occasions, to staff and students at the Bennington Workshops. Although each was very gently, very gingerly critical of the other (Leonard: "I found the sixties a more interesting decade than Harvey did"), they were largely in agreement about the goals, ways, and means of the *Review*. Both insisted that it is at least as much a part of a newspaper, therefore concerned with "news," as it is a popular organ of literary criticism. As John Leonard put it, "I am as much a reporter as I am a literary critic."

This explanation seems simple and straightforward enough, yet it camouflages some complex problems. For one thing, the insistent claim that the book-reviewing function is merely a part of the larger function of the press brings us quickly back to the special situation of the press in America today. Returns us to the thoughtful and coherent criticism of Solzhenitsyn's Harvard speech, in which he called the press "the greatest power within the Western countries, more powerful than the legislature, the executive, and the judiciary," adding, "There are generally accepted patterns of judgment and there may be common corporate interests, the same effect being not competition but unification. Enormous freedom exists for the press, but not for the readership, because newspapers mostly give emphasis to those opinions that do not too openly contradict their own and the general trend."

It needs to be noted that contemporary journalistic theory, denying the possibility of any truly "objective" reportage, allows that all good reporting is, in a sense, "advocacy journalism." Thus, though journalism may (or may not) seek to be fair, it nevertheless takes moral and political and social stands and choices. To the extent that the *New York Times Book Review*, and the reviews of books in the daily *New York Times*, are considered to be journalism rather than criticism, they are licensed to practice advocacy and to take the opportunity to make moral, political, or social points. Which can be very dangerous (for the writer, in any case) when the critic starts from a certain stereotypical hostility toward all things Southern.

Leonard, speaking at Bennington College on July 28, 1979, put it another way, but in no way contradicted Solzhenitsyn's impression and judgment. "There is something peculiar about the New York literary community," Leonard said, "and it might as well be spelled out." While he was quite emphatic that there is no organized conspiracy among the New York *literati*—"There is no conspiracy. There is no literary Mafia"—he nevertheless allowed that there is "an undeniable coziness" among critics and reviewers in New York," and he acknowledged that, as a reviewer, he regularly depends upon "a whole network of signals from people I have come to trust." In short, then, there may not be any "conspiracy" among the critics and reviewers of New York; but there is strong evidence of precisely the kind of consensus which Solzhenitsyn saw not only as stifling any "new ideas," but also as eliminating the kind of serious debate which must accompany political and social free choice.

Second, the emphasis on the *New York Times Book Review* as being more a part of a newspaper than anything else ties it closely to the editorial positions of the *New York Times*. Which, like the city it serves, views itself sometimes as a national center and sometimes as only one region among others. The city is losing business and industry and tax base; even if the Census Bureau is allowed to count illegal aliens, the city is losing population. Statistics continue to show an alarming rate of increase in violent crimes committed in New York City. The independent Citizens Crime Commission, in a six-month study, reported that violent crime is "more serious and widespread than statistics indicate and is worsening." The city is now compelled to depend on federal money (i.e., tax money raised in other regions) to provide its essential services. In all the practical areas, except as a headquarters for mass communications and as a cultural center, New York's power and influence are steadily declining. Even in the area of culture the city must depend upon extensive federal support to maintain its apparent cultural preeminence.

In the business of commercial publishing, such as it is, New York remains the center it became early in this century, largely overcoming nineteenth-century competition from Boston and Philadelphia. Even so, the publication of poetry, short fiction, and serious novels by university presses and small independent presses, found nationwide, is beginning to prove that these firms can do as well with literature as can the large trade publishers. The situation is already changing, which breeds a certain testy defensiveness on the part of the self-interested custodians of "official" culture. For example, in the "Letters" section of the *New York Times Book Review* (January 6, 1980, p. 27), the Southern poet and novelist Guy Owen politely questioned the statement by James Atlas, in a piece about Thomas Wolfe, that Alfred Kazin is "the only well-known defender of Wolfe." Owen mentioned the significant work of Louis Rubin, C. Hugh Holman, and Richard Walser. To which the *Times's* Atlas replied: "I wrote that Alfred Kazin's was 'virtually the only sympathetic criticism' Wolfe has received since his death. Of course there have been other critics who admired him, but I would dispute Professor Owen's claim that the three he cites are 'well known.'" Translated, that can only mean: *One Kazin, our Kazin, is worth three of yours. We determine who may be called well known and who may not be.*

This is what Southern writers have been up against for more than one hundred years, but it is exaggerated and exacerbated now that New York is falling into decline and knows it. Under the circumstances, it is only reasonable that those who profit most from the status quo should strive to protect their enlightened self-interest. Unquestionably, the salaries of the professional book reviewers, earning them far more than all but a small handful of the serious poets and novelists they review, make them, together with the employees of commercial publishing houses, among the very few who actually *profit* directly from contemporary literature. They have a considerable inducement towards the preservation of the status quo, if possible.

I do not wish to deal with the speculative subjects of integrity and corruption, the presence or absence of either—except to say that one day, in some form or other, they will have to be dealt with seriously, even as a purely literary matter. Except to say, therefore, that a thorough discussion of integrity and corruption, at the center of the American literary establishment, would prove to be neither digressive nor irrelevant. And except to argue that the commercial literary culture, being part and parcel of the overall commercial culture, the *whole* society, offers as much (or as little) evidence of integrity as the latter and manages to maintain roughly the same levels of personal and institutional corruption.

4.

Closely coupled with practical considerations (and corollary considerations of self-interest and self-service) are many elements of a social if not ideological consensus. Most of it has, in fact, proved to be subsumable under the rubric of "radical chic," an epithet created by a Southern writer, Tom Wolfe, to satirize the complex duplicities and hypocrisies of the New York artistic and intellectual elite. Wolfe was one of the first and is certainly the most successful writer to see contemporary New York City, itself as a region susceptible to the kinds of satire that used to be reserved for other regions. That his stance is both Southern and traditional may not yet be so widely recognized because of the dazzling flash and fire of his prose style, and because his usual mode has been ironic and satirical. But his most recent book, *The Right Stuff*, points up values he presents positively, as do such well-known articles as "The Last American Hero" (about Southern stock-car driver Junior Johnson) or "The Truest Sport: Jousting With Sam & Charlie" (dealing with Navy pilots during the Vietnam war). Perhaps Wolfe's most explicit and detailed picture of the prevailing "liberal" intellectual consensus, and its (deliberate) separation from the thoughts and feelings and perceptions of other Americans, is to be found in "The Intelligent Coed's Guide to America" (in his *Mauve Gloves & Madmen, Clutter & Vine*), in which he deals with the style and substance of "the literary notables of the United States" who are busy "giving lectures at the colleges and universities of America's heartland, which runs from Fort Lee, New Jersey, on the east to the Hollywood Freeway on the west." "Giving lectures," he adds, "is one of the lucrative dividends of being a noted writer in America." One of his chief points is that what these intellectuals think and say, and even prefer to believe, *is not true*: it flies in the face of the evidence, of all the facts. By and large, he suggests, these people know this very well; but it is comfortable and profitable and companionable to maintain the myths as a consensus of opinion. Here is his one-paragraph summation of the standard lecture colleges and universities were paying these "literary notables" for:

Sixty families control one half the private wealth of America, and two hundred corporations own two thirds of the means of production. "A small group of nameless, faceless men" who avoid publicity the way a werewolf avoids the dawn now dominates American life. In America a man's home is not his castle but merely "a gigantic listening device with a mortgage"—a reference to eavesdropping by the FBI and the CIA. America's foreign policy has been and continues to be based upon war, assassination, bribery, genocide, and the sabotage of democratic governments. "The new McCarthyism" (Joe's, not Gene's) is already upon us. Following a brief charade of free speech, the "gagging of the press" has resumed. Racism in America has not diminished; it is merely more subtle now. The gulf between rich and poor widens daily, creating "permanent ghetto-colonial populations." The decline in economic growth is causing a crisis in capitalism, which will lead shortly to authoritarian rule and to a new America in which everyone waits, in horror, for the knock on the door in the dead of the night, the descent of the knout on the nape of the neck—

Speaking of Solzhenitsyn's arrival and tour of the nation in 1975, Wolfe writes that "the literary world in general ignored him completely." He argues that they could not bear the public exposure and subsequent dissipation of certain deeply cherished sociopolitical assumptions:

In the huge unseen coffin that Solzhenitsyn towed behind him were not only the souls of the Zeks who died in the Archipelago. No, the heartless bastard had also chucked in one of the lost great visions: the intellectual as the Stainless Steel Socialist glistening against the bone heap of capitalism in its final, brutal, fascist phase. There was a bone heap, all right, and it was grisly beyond belief, but socialism had created it.

The Southern intellectual tradition has not been especially hospitable to the theory and practice of modern corporate capitalism. But neither have many Southerners rushed to embrace the rigid, bureaucratic schemes of modern corporate socialism. Populist or elitist (and some even socialist), of whatever political persuasion, Southerners have tended toward unity in the defense of individual civil liberty. And, in general, Southerners take intellectual integrity very seriously; thus intellectual hypocrisy is seen as particularly despicable. (A certain gentle *social* hypocrisy, on the other hand, may be a form of good manners.) One of Wolfe's chief and regular targets for satire has been the hypocrisy of the New York intellectual-literary establishment. Which, taken together with their constant search for more signs and tokens of personal status, their desire for ever more privilege and honor, and their bad manners and deep streak of lightly disguised vulgarity, is a large and vulnerable target indeed.

Since the beginnng of his journalistic career, Wolfe has been satirizing the bad manners of New Yorkers (and once he even dared to ridicule *The New Yorker* itself). Probably his most devastating single piece on the subject, "Tom Wolfe's New Book of Etiquette" (in *The Pump House Gang*), distinguishes two forms in which, in New York, "the entire Book of Etiquette is being rewritten." He defines these two forms as *"the rationalization of politesse;* i.e., the adapting of social etiquette to purely business ends," and *"nostalgie de la boue;* i.e., the adoption by the upper orders, for special effect, of the customs of the lower orders." It is all illustrated with lively examples.

Because it was done in fun and with accuracy, if exaggeration, most critics and reviewers seem to have missed the darker indictment in Wolfe's satire. Most often he has been treated as a bright, eccentric, and amusing dealer in trivia, a pedant of the superficial. Such an assessment, equating manners with triviality, tends to confirm Wolfe's thesis and is certainly at odds with Southern assumptions about manners. Lisa Alther was right: manners *are* more important in the Southern tradition. They mean something. In a theoretical sense, good manners are conceived of as a mean between brute savagery (barbarism) and frivolous foppery (foolish oversophistication). In a practical, literary sense, good manners represent the

mean between the utterly idiosyncratic (mannerism) and the tedi-
ously conventional (the cliché and the stereotype). In both life and
art, the Southern emphasis upon manners and amenities derives
chiefly from an assumed, a *given* view of the nature of Man, and
thus from a view of the quality and nature of Man's history. The primarily Protestant, and certainly Christian, base of the Southern
social structure—and thus, also, of the social fabric of Southern
life—begins with the assumption and acceptance of the universal
equality of original sin. This is one area, perhaps the only one, and at
the anagogical level, where Southern assumptions are unabashedly
egalitarian. (The Southerner is more or less democratic in *secular*
spirit. But not exactly egalitarian.) All men are immortal souls,
equally fractured by sin, equally and mysteriously loved by a loving
God. Equally liable to enjoy grace and salvation, chiefly by and
through faith. That faith may or may not manifest itself in good
works. Therefore, for the Southerner, there is an unspoken and unquestioned religious, and often theological, basis for the importance
of good manners. Manners represent a formal obligation to one's
neighbor (who is always Everyman) and the ritual recognition of the
love of God and for the presence of the Holy Ghost in all of one's
fellow creatures. Therefore an act of bad manners may well be, to
the Southerner, an act of violence. A violation of the code of manners may well be taken as at least *meaning* the same thing as a fist
in the face or a blade between the ribs.

It is a cliché of intellectual criticism of Southern literature and society to say that both are permeated by violence. It is a cliché of the
intellectual establishment to assume that violence derives from social causes and is therefore reparable. The Southerner is baffled by
this assumption. At his deepest level of knowing, the Southerner
expects this world—filled as it is with fallen fellow creatures, creatures who are, to a greater or lesser extent, depraved—*expects* the
world to be a violent place, as brutal and savage as conditions will
allow. The secular-liberal view believes that violence, insofar as it is
really present in the world at all, derives from social conditions. The
Southern, more fundamentally Christian view is that conditions
can only serve to check or to release the natural and inevitable ener-
gies of violence. Thus—as a part of those social conditions—formal
manners become urgently important. Under certain circumstances
a shrug, a raised eyebrow, a rude tone of voice can become clear acts
of violence.

The very least that can be said, then, is that Tom Wolfe's satirical
assault on both the intellectual hypocrisy and the bad manners of

the New York scene, under the label of "radical chic," is just about as violent an attack as he could make, short of tossing around a case of fragmentation grenades.

"Celebrity," which is so closely associated with "radical chic" in Wolfe's definition, is usually frowned on by Southerners. Perhaps because it can be just as easily derived from notoriety as from good report, fame which is dependent upon celebrity is usually seen as false. For instance, the North Carolina novelist and poet Fred Chappell, in a review of *Contemporary Southern Poetry,* notes with pleasure the fact that the better-known Southern poets, "the Big Reputations," do not, in truth, stand out as obviously and inherently superior to the other poets included in the anthology: "the big guns make no grander bangs than the smaller ones." Taking James Dickey as an example of an unquestionably well known contemporary Southern poet, Chappell arrives at a skeptical conclusion, questioning not Dickey's serious gifts but the source of his wide *celebrity*: "Crowded in with his peers, Dickey is simply an equal among equals, and one begins to realize how much his personal flamboyance has contributed to his national acclaim." Chappell's observation is accurate both in terms of the anthology and in the larger sense of the literary scene the anthology represents.

The South has a wonderful and wonderfully various crop of contemporary writers. The reason for this are many and complex, but not the least of them is the example of the earlier generation of masters (and many of these teachers as well) of the Southern Renaissance. Thus, ironically, there is a full precedent for the *concept* of the master artist. It is a concept which teases and troubles the contemporary writer until (and if), like Fred Chappell, the artist finds an occasion to perceive the richness, variety, and complexity of the whole literary scene. So the writer has the model of mastery, of extraordinary artistic adventure by an exemplary few. And the scholar accepts the image, knowing it to be an oversimplification and indeed a distortion of history, yet knowing also that it is the only way to imagine and understand the literary past. The critic accepts the notion of a few masters, surrounded by a crowd of apprentices and journeymen, because it makes public criticism, as it is understood, possible. The masters of the earlier generation become more than models of excellence; they become also, paradoxically, standards of measurement against which the newer work of contemporaries is to be compared. Teachers have found the concept extremely helpful ever since modern and then contemporary literature became a part of the institutional educational curriculum. Within the boundaries of classroom times and academic calendars, it is only feasible to deal with certain significant, representative and *teachable* examples.

Southern writers, scholars, critics, and teachers are all, in one way or another, supportive of the creation of contemporary literature. Yet each is necessarily also at least a tacit supporter of a system of artificial celebrity which no longer describes a real condition in the literary world. If it ever did. Unfortunately, this outmoded concept coincides with the commercial and self-serving aims of publishers and the whole periphery of professional intellectuals around them. Which, in turn, is an evidently inextricable element of the national economy.

5.

Among the nationally oriented anthologies published during the last decade, Edward Field's *A Geography of Poets* offers more work by Southern poets than any other of its general kind. I count 39 of the 228 poets represented in this anthology as Southerners by birth or lifetime affiliation. A much more typical representation is to be found in *The American Poetry Anthology*, edited by Daniel Halpern, which presents work by only two Southern poets out of 75 in the anthology. (Actually there are 76 poets listed, but at least one of them is a completely fictional creation.)

Field, in the honest and revealing innocence of his introduction to *A Geography of Poets*, seems to feel that his own discovery of any number of reasonably intelligent and gifted and well-read poets out in America's provinces and hinterlands roughly coincides with their own arrival on the literary scene. Thus our history and traditions are seen as merely coincident with his. This is what all Southern writers have had to contend with (and *against*) at least since the mid-nineteenth century.

James Atlas, an editor of the *New York Times Book Review*, has published in the *New York Times Magazine* (February 3, 1980) an extensive article on "New Voices in American Poetry" in which only four Southern poets are mentioned by name: the late Randall Jarrell and the living Donald Justice, in reference to the bygone attitudes of the 1950s; Robert Penn Warren, as one of the "few older poets" still creating; and Charles Wright, not as a Southerner at all, but as a master of the school identified as the "New Surrealism." There is no indication, in this influential popular article, that any other Southern poets or writers might be an active part of the contemporary scene.

The South itself, even including the literary South, is another matter. Though many of our individual writers may be neglected and ignored, our magazines and institutions are not being left to their own fates and devices. Just as Northern industries have moved and are continuing to move into the South in search of various things (including the prospect of cheap and reliable labor), just as many Northerners are continuing to move to the South to live and to work—and thus *to earn their livings* within the economy and culture of the South—just as members of the Northern professions and services are following close behind this social event, in numbers and variety like the high heydays of Reconstruction, so a surprising number of the Northern literati, members in good standing of their literary establishment, have recently come to the South also. They have come to teach literature and writing at our colleges and universities, to become publishers at our university presses and, indeed, to edit many of our quarterlies and literary magazines. While the "nationalization" of many Southern magazines and presses has resulted in perhaps slightly more "visibility" for these institutions, it has, at the same time, deprived many good Southern writers of opportunities to publish their works, even as it considerably expands the publishing prospects and possibilities for Northern writers. It is, thus, in a literary sense at least, a classic example of colonialism.

This example is reinforced by the ongoing case of the National Endowment for the Arts. Not at all unusual is the picture presented by the 1979–80 Fellowships for Creative Writers ($10,000 each) awarded by the Literature Program of the National Endowment for the Arts. Of the 275 awards given, 33 went to writers listed as living in (or visiting) Southern states. Two Southern states, Arkansas and Alabama, were completely ignored. No Southern state received as many grants as, for example, California, Colorado, Connecticut, Massachusetts, or Vermont. New York (and chiefly, overwhelmingly, New York City), by receiving 78 of the grants, was a little more than twice as lucky and successful as all of the Southern states combined.

The Poetry in the Schools Program, though partially supported by the National Endowment for the Arts, is under the immediate supervision of local and state arts councils. This program presents another sort of problem for the Southern writer, an especially difficult one for the young or beginning writer. The program brings poets and writers into the public schools to teach and to read; it pays an adequate honorarium for the service, enabling a writer to earn a living at his craft and without losing all of his time and energy in the process. It also enables the often-neglected public school students to have some encounters with contemporary literature and the people who create it. On the whole a laudable idea. And yet . . . troubles began with the question of who should qualify, who should be legitimately "certified" as a poet worthy of being brought into the program. A difficult question, especially in the case of the new young writers for whom the program is most efficiently intended. Most of the state and local arts councils, ready and willing to defer to the honest judgment and expertise of others, choose to depend on official listings in *A Directory of American Fiction Writers* and *A Directory of American Poets* (together with revisions and supplements to both) published by Poets & Writers, Inc., a federally supported, tax-exempt organization based firmly in New York City. From the beginning until the time of this writing there have been a number of strong, probably valid complaints about the organization and its policies. Primarily the complaints have been that the outlying regions and states are underrepresented and underlisted, and that it is extremely difficult for a local or regional writer to win listing in the directories. On the other hand, a few large urban centers, most particularly New York City, are both inaccurately overrepresented and overlisted. For the writer in New York City, for example, it is very easy to gain listing, even with a minimal publication record. The full "truth" of all this remains to be determined, but it is certainly perceived as true by many (probably most) Southern writers. One undeniable result of the listing system is that many Southern states have not been able to fill the vacancies in their Poetry in the Schools Programs with local writers, and it has been necessary for them to turn to the Northern states for candidates. Thus a surprising number of New York City poets have enjoyed warmer (and well paid) winters working in Southern public schools.

Of course, abuses can be corrected and commonplace corruption can be exposed, but there is not much that can be done about the *attitudes* which permit both abuse and corruption at the expense of Southern writers and their culture. Not, at least, until they somehow feel independent and free and secure enough in their own good sense and judgment not to need any alien approval.

Finally, the very basis and strength of so much Southern literature, its *language*—its own version, alive and lively, of the English language—is itself under attack. Robert Bly, a prominent and polemical (many would say, pontifical) figure in the national literary establishment, is quoted in the Atlas article as using the lingo of "radical chic" to attack both our language and our tradition: "We have to get rid of the alien English element. We're a colony of England, and you can't speak the language of your conqueror." Bly may not see the irony of that in terms of our own American history, but it is clear, from his record as an editor and critic, that he has been mostly indifferent to Southern writing. Although he has devoted a good deal of time and attention to attacking the achievement of James Dickey, otherwise he seems, like so many other establishment editors and critics, largely unaware of the presence of any contemporary Southern literature. When that presence becomes (somehow) undeniable—as, for instance, when Walker Percy won the National Book Award for *The Moviegoer* and a good many years later Mary Lee Settle was awarded the same prize for *Blood Tie*—their outrage often lapses into shrill vulgarity. In both cases the writers were initially ridiculed by prominent reviewers for being previously "unknown" and thus apparently unworthy.

A perhaps even more outrageous example of what has to be called the vulgarity of ignorance was the failure to award any prizes to Shelby Foote's *The Civil War: A Narrative*. This trilogy, vast in scope and subject, occupying the complete attention of one of our most gifted novelists for a quarter-century, may yet, when it is at last read by the critics, be recognized as one of the very few truly great works by an American in this century. Like a good deal of the best Southern literature, it has not been completely ignored. But, on the other hand, it has yet to be really recognized.

6.

We have seen (I hope) some of the ways in which the contemporary Southern writer is beleaguered and isolated—by his religion in a defiantly secular society; by tradition in a society seeking to define itself as if it were without roots and traditions (at least as far as this nation and this continent are concerned); by their own highly developed idiom and dialect of and in a language which is at least fundamentally different from and often only a generation or two familiar to other American writers elsewhere; by a history which is at once rich and tragic and yet is (even as far as the facts are concerned, and never mind interpretation and any deeper understanding) unknown to others except within the terms of common misapprehensions and crude stereotypes. The South was different by being the most cosmopolitan and pluralistic part of this nation until the Civil War and then, following the great waves of immigration into the North, different by the label, if not the fact, of being uniquely homogenized, separate from the economic life of the rest of the nation by being dirt poor for a long, long time while the rest of the nation richly flourished. Now it is different because it is affluent and blooming while, for a multitude of reasons (a Southerner might say, a multitude of sins and errors), much of the rest of the nation, most especially the Northeast, is in swift and shabby decline. The South has been exploited and ignored, in a literary sense, by outsiders whose power (at least for the time being) is real enough, whose contempt and hostility are open and unembarrassed, whose indifference to the life and arts of the South is matched only by the weight of their ignorance about both. But what remain to be seen—what are, finally, far more important—are the actions and reactions of Southern writers here and now.

These actions and reactions depend on where these writers are and where they stand. Those mostly of an older generation who have been officially, nationally recognized, who have been awarded some place in the literary pantheon—I think, for instance, of Eudora Welty, Peter Taylor, William Styron, Reynolds Price, Robert Penn Warren, and Walker Percy—have certainly brought honor and distinction to Southern letters, and no less of both to themselves. But in a simple and serious sense they have been restricted, if not severely limited, by the very terms of the recognition afforded them. None of these people is apt to give any real criticism of the flaws and inequities of the literary status quo. (The exception is the rare occasion when one or more may rise up in defense of another when a perceived injustice has been committed: for example, when Styron's *The Confessions of Nat Turner* [1967] was savaged by various unhappy black writers and critics, or when some critics failed to respond warmly enough to Reynold Price's novel *The Surface of the Earth* [1975] and Eudora Welty came strongly and publicly to his defense.) By and large, their position is what it has to be: that the status quo may have flaws, but that it is generally fair and equitable and that ultimately (look what happened to William Faulkner!) right, if not justice, is done. How else can the imagination perceive it? They are part of the literary establishment, and there is nothing to challenge their happy assessment of it—indeed, no particular incentive (quite the contrary) to growl and bite the hand that feeds them.

These people are exemplary to the younger Southern writers in perhaps the best way, by the example of their work. But the examples of their lives and careers can hardly be of much value to the neophyte. And though some of them, Warren and Price and Welty, for example, have earned reputations as excellent teachers, none has been of much practical help or assistance to younger or less fortunate writers. There is no reason why it would occur to them to be so. In the absence of any serious threat to the status quo, there is no pressure toward a communal feeling.

There are those, like Willie Morris and Larry King and Tom Wicker and Marshal Frady, who have gone North and have actively joined the establishment, establishing their own impeccable liberal credentials by denouncing Southern life (often confirming stereotypical liberal suppositions in doing so) while managing to preserve something of the Southern style for themselves. This is, in effect, the ironic contemporary equivalent of the gesture called "pulling wool" or "pully woolly" (in some parts of the South), whereby certain sly black men ingratiated themselves with their oppressors by acting out with gusto and enthusiasm the part already assigned to them. This example is not likely to be followed by many younger Southern writers, if only because there is no room for more than a very few "house Southerners" in the North at any one time. Moreover, the influence of some of these Southerners-in-residence *can be* pernicious in the sense that, since they are mostly journalists (who would feel the need of coopting a Southern poet or a novelist?) and since they almost always say precisely what is expected of them, they are regarded as experts and are influential not so much in passing judgment on Southern actions and events as in enforcing conventional judgments already passed by others. Of course, it can be justly argued that these writers are subtly "working from within the System" even as they honestly criticize and call attention to the many faults and flaws of the South that they profess (as all of us do) to love. And it may be that in their new and rapidly developing field of creative writing, contemporary journalism, they are excellent models for young Southerners. Certainly in journalism and nonfiction if one were today to take a different tack and approach than these Southerners-in-exile, one would not likely go far or succeed as well.

Unless, of course, one took the opposite approach, the strategy of head-on attack. Like Tom Wolfe and, to a certain extent, Truman Capote, and sometimes James Dickey, who, given an occasion, has been known to thumb his nose, figuratively, at Yankee expectations. Wolfe, Capote, and Dickey have enjoyed considerable success (in Northern terms) by and through satire, irony, sarcasm, and deft attack on many of the clichés that the Northern establishment holds dearest. But it should be noted that Wolfe and Capote are not perceived as primarily Southern; that is, it does not yet seem to have occurred to the critics that the terms of the satire and attack rendered (differently, it is true) by Wolfe and Capote are conventionally Southern. Talent and virtuosity disguise the traditional stances of these writers. As examples for others they are, of course, limited. If you want to attack the enemy on his own ground and live to tell the tale, you have to be extremely gifted and equally clever.

What is left is something else, no less exciting for taking place somewhere else, far from the fading cultural centers, and probably far more valuable and lasting in the long run. There is some kind of explosion of talent and passionate interest going on in the South right now. There are literally dozens of good writers (perhaps it is not an age for *great* writers; we should be thankful, I believe, that so many are around who are very, very good), and they are scattered all over the South. They are in every part and in every state. No anthology of prose or poetry can begin to represent them or contain them. Though they belong to no school (and that quirky refusal to be part of an organized school or movement is characteristic of contemporary Southern writers ever since the Agrarians *had*, for a time, their school), there *is* a community of spirit which is noticeable and almost unique. (There is, of course, a sense of community elsewhere, within the context and confines of one school and another; but those groups are organized hierarchically, whereas the loose affiliation of Southern writers is generally egalitarian, as it has to be.)

The community of spirit of contemporary Southern letters extends elsewhere, to writers born and raised in the South who have gone away in body if not in spirit. It also extends itself fully and warmly to all of the other writers I have mentioned as being, one way and another, outside this large and (in the wide world) largely anonymous community. Throughout the South today good writers who have published fiction, poetry, and nonfiction (it is characteristic of many Southern writers that they do all three, evidently as it pleases and suits them) are teaching a large crop of good and eager students, mostly young, but also including adults, white and black, and often involving people from social groups which have not had, until now, any real voice in our literature.

This development of teaching modern and contemporary literature and creative writing in Southern colleges and universities, with working writers as faculty members, has grown most strongly in the past two decades, although it has its roots in earlier Southern traditions and attitudes. Many of the contemporary Southern writers were at least exposed to the teaching of earlier masters; and there were not only the well-known Fugitives, but also other teachers of great influence and distinction like William Blackburn of Duke and Jesse Lee Rader of Chapel Hill, George Williams of Rice, A. K. Davis and John Coleman of the University of Virginia. Even before the Iowa Writers' Workshop began, these people and others in the South were teaching writing to young students. Often they did so under the guise of courses in rhetoric and composition; under whatever title, they taught and inspired any number of Southern poets and fiction writers. Their story, an important one in modern literary history, has been largely ignored and remains untold, but their influence is evident.

Insofar as the teaching of the craft of writing is concerned, the general attitude of the contemporary Southern writer seems to be chiefly positive and to be (again) special for being so. The most extensive discussion of this subject, *Craft So Hard to Learn: Conversations with Poets and Novelists About the Teaching of Writing*, edited by John Graham and this author, indicates what amounts to an almost uniformly positive attitude held by the Southern writers, each otherwise distinctly different from the others. Represented therein are William Peden, Fred Chappell, Henry Taylor, Michael Mewshaw, James Seay, James Whitehead, Sylvia Wilkinson, James Dickey, and William Harrison. All agree that a writer cannot be "made" by the experience of creative writing courses, though all likewise agree that the experience can be very helpful in developing the skills of the writer with natural talent. But all these writers insist that there are positive values for students who study the craft of writing and of close reading. They become better readers and a possible future audience, to be sure; but there is also the effect of the experience on the awakening imagination. As Fred Chappell puts it, "I have seen persons come alive to themselves in writing classes in a way they never have done before." The results of all this activity are beginning to be evident in the magazines and anthologies, in collections of poems and stories by new writers, in first novels. Even as literacy is steadily and dangerously declining in the United States (and the South is not immune to the general trend), there is a whole new generation of Southern students coming along. They seem eager to learn reading and writing, and they are lucky enough to have good writers to work with, writers who teach by example as much as by any precept.

The two great dangers of formal study of the craft of writing (and both of these are strongly evident in the more prominent programs *outside* the South) are the imposition upon beginning talent of the rules and rigidity of a single school of writing and the development of an uneasy, self-conscious relationship with the tradition; that is, either too slavishly following traditional examples or, on the contrary, seeking to ignore and escape tradition. Somehow the most recent generation of Southern writers seems to have escaped both dangers. In Fred Chappell's thorough and thoughtful review of *Contemporary Southern Poetry*, he makes note of various changes which seem to have taken place in Southern writing during the generation since the Fugitives. At the same time, he recognizes that the masters of the earlier generation would not be incapable of appreciating what is done now, though they might never have dreamed of doing the same thing:

Gone with the wind are the gentle strategies of our elders and betters: tenuous literary allusion, velvet irony, historical immanence, latinate diction, veiled satire and the reverence for Europe. One has the impression, looking at the differences in the work, that the Fugitives might look upon the present lot of poets as a herd of wild-eyed sans culottes, but of course they were too wise and tolerant ever to be shocked.

Clearly, from Chappell's tone, the respect and tolerance work both ways. The tradition endures many outward and visible changes.

If one allows oneself even the least whiff of optimism, it becomes hard not to believe that something good, perhaps something quite wonderful for the future literature of the South is going to come from all this reservoir of talent, all this energy and desire. While it is too early to say what that future may be, it is certainly not too early to say that all signs indicate that Southern literature, far from being on its last legs and far from representing a falling off from earlier and better days, seems very much alive. Having come to honorable terms with its own past, it seems almost certain to grow into a future worth waiting for, worth witnessing.

Listen and Remember

DAVID B. SENTELLE

SURVIVAL OF THE SOUTH is essential. The South must not die. I do not merely believe this; I know it. I learned it in a country song. Not the first time I heard the song, or the second, or the third. It was just a simple little country song about an old filling station, John's Place, where good old boys sat around and talked, and picked and sang; where the good old boy in charge, a guy named John, employed the young of the community to let them earn a little and, while they were at it, learn a little about life, and work, and music. There was nothing unusual about the song. It would never sell a million copies or make anybody's top forty.

It wasn't until the fourth time I heard it, or maybe the fifth, that I began to wonder why I was listening to this song so many times if it was indeed such an ordinary, unremarkable sort. And it wasn't until I had listened and wondered about it a few more times that I began really to understand why. Much later still I learned from it the importance of the South's survival. Joe Allen wrote "John's" and George Hamilton IV sang it, each with the solid sort of sincerity and realism that only two good ole Southern boys, who had spent a lot of hours in just such a place as John's with just such company as his, could sing and write. Though I had never met Joe Allen and though I was, I think, three thousand miles and a good-sized ocean away from George when I first heard the record, I had spent enough time in the same sort of circumstances to settle into a warm, fraternal embrace of shared recollection from the very first line I heard George sing.

It was a little like the experience of running into a total stranger in a beachfront tavern and finding out after only a little conversation that he not only went to college with your favorite cousin but he used to go out with the same good-looking redhead she once paired you with. Yes, and he even took her to the same restaurant. It was a lot more like getting together with an old best friend you had not seen since high school, and you and he telling each other all about the funny, wonderful things you did together; not only reminding each other of details you had forgotten but each of you remembering for yourselves details that you hadn't really forgotten, but hadn't really remembered in a long, long time.

That song and that insight into my own affection for it first let me realize what it is that makes me love not only George Hamilton IV's singing and that particular song, but country music in general. It is that phenomenon of shared recollection. There is some pleasure in solitary musings on the older contents of your dimmest memory, but there is greater pleasure in sharing with another from your differing perspectives the deep memories you own together. The greater the overlap of your experience, the more articulate your companion in his recollection, the greater the expansion of your satisfaction in his company.

This is true even if the experience recollected is not the same one. Witness the tender, infinite, passionate love of one drunken bum for another. They do not drink to soothe the same consciences, or to alternately fuel and douse the same smoldering fires of the past, but each knows in the main what the other is about. (In case one doesn't, they tell each other over and over.) In the end, although each would fight the world for a bottle of wine, once he has won the prize he readily shares it with his friend.

Just so, although I know that the singer is not crying about the same love that I lost, or the same parent that I mourn, or the same old home that I remember, still the sense, the feeling, the remembrance is so much the same that when he pours out his tale I listen and remember. Not only do I remember, but country music listeners up and down and across the Southland do the same. There are qualities, experiences, lifestyles that are uniquely and generally Southern. We remain an identifiable region, while the Northeast, the Midwest, and the West Coast become increasingly indistinguishable for anything other than climate. Obviously there *are* shared traits that mark us.

Jimmy Carter running for president was conspicuously a Southerner. Ford was in no conspicuous sense a Midwesterner, or Nixon a Westerner. It is no coincidence that Carter, whatever he was as a president, as a man is a lover of country music. He has an identity which other politicians lack. He thrives on the art that marks that identity, and so do Southerners of all classes and strata.

This country music, so generally written, played, and appreciated by Southerners, has become the music of our region precisely because a few of our number can, through it, relate the events that have happened to us all. Country singers express the emotions and the actions that these events have evoked in us all, and they invite the rest of us to share in the old wine of common recollection. When a particular country song becomes unusually beloved, it may be because it is well written, original and well performed; but more than likely, it is also an unusually moving expression of what the Southerners who love it were feeling, consciously or unconsciously, all the time.

If the South loves country music because it sings of experiences that are Southern, how can we explain the fact that increasingly the non-South also loves country music? Why do New Yorkers, Chicagoans, and Californians make pilgrimages to Nashville? How have Johnny Cash, Buck Owens, and Mel Tillis commanded national television audiences? How does George Hamilton IV make his triumphal ambassadorial tours of Canada, South Africa, Ireland, and England? In short, how can the song of the South become so much the song of the whole Anglo-Saxon world? Why, the same way it became the South's—the same only more so. Think again for a moment of the reunited high school classmates. Suppose instead of just remembering with you that both of you used to really give hell to Mrs. Edwards in twelfth-grade English, and that you all had a great time the night you and he and Billy Joe tied a mule in the first stall of the women teachers' lounge, suppose he also remembers and tells you (and your wife, and her mother, and your five kids) that inside that mound of oh-too-solid flesh in which you now appear there beats the heart of a hundred-and-sixty-pound scatback who once ran ninety yards from scrimmage in the last five seconds of the state championship game to score the winning touchdown? (Which was, by the way, your third six-pointer of the night.) Yes, and after the game was over, you caught the very devil for keeping the head cheerleader out until 3:00 A.M.

Don't tell me you wouldn't relish that reunion with an old friend. You might just make your wife and kids hush and listen to him a little longer. It wouldn't even matter if the story wasn't exactly the way it happened, so long as it was somewhere close. You would still remember it while he told it, and you would cherish that memory.

Of such is the popularity of the South's music in the Anglo-Saxon world. And of such is the resultant necessity for the continued existence of the South.

Some writers may tell the Anglo-Saxon that his is a dull and uninspiring tribe. He may hear from some media that he is cold, exploitative, and unlovable. No wonder he likes to listen to the singer who knew him as he used to be; a singer who knew him when he was on his own field, before he moved to New York, or London, or Sydney, and blended in with the mass of humanity. By way of comparison, historians tell us that Roman emperors employed Greek orators to come around and tell annually the stories of the greatest triumphs of the current Caesar and his cohorts. Without exception, the Caesars loved to listen—not because the battles were new to them, not because Caesar wasn't there, but precisely because he was. He was there then, and he is here now. Today he may appear to be a fat, pampered politician in a clean toga, but there was a time when he was there. He was a randy, sweaty, battle-seasoned soldier out there at the head of his troops, able to stand and fight with the best of them. "Listen to that Greek," Caesar would say to his court; to himself he would say, "I remember."

Just so the Anglo-Saxon. Some may say his religion is cold, formal, out of touch with God and man. What? His religion? His people produced the most fiery evangelists of the Protestant world. They produced Catholicism so fervent as to thrust into the flame first the hand that had signed a recantation. In the South, that kind of fire and ice still burns and cracks the souls of churches. Churches are still the most ubiquitous feature of any Southern county or town— churches with preachers who still thunder forth the condemnation of the evil deeds of their very hearers. Southern pulpits are not places for the espousal of sociological theory or for the denunciation of far-off wars; Southern sermons are personalized, toe-treading, meddlesome indictments of the misdeeds of the congregation at hand. Even the best-educated Southern pastors often mention sin. Little wonder that Southerners still hold at the core of their souls consciences that are still personal, not dissipated into those vaguely clucking "social consciences" that are always declaring "there ought to be a law" or that the government should do something about whatever problem arises. Much of what is Southern grows out of the kind of religion that once inspired the whole Anglo-Saxon race to battle their own kin, conquer oceans, and take their gospel and their rich heritage to heathen lands. In the South, Johnny Cash, Arthur Smith, and the Carter Sisters still sing about that kind of religion.

Or has the Anglo-Saxon heard that he doesn't know how to work? Has he heard that the once-proud WASP is now a post-capitalistic drone, lying around the board rooms of the hive while black and Spanish-surnamed bees buzz out to bring him back the honey? The South knows better. Comic strips may caricature the Southerner as a lazy, flea-bitten moonshiner whose wife must make such meager crops as can hold bodies to souls until the next welfare check arrives. Television may immortalize these caricatures with impunity while the F.C.C. and social mores forbid the slightest hint of categorizing any other ethnic group. But in truth, Southerners are a hard-working people. Laziness can't plow the same red clay that bricks are made of. Laziness can't bend a back from dark to dark again, to sucker tobacco or pull corn or even (as the stereotype goes) to pick cotton. Southerners can. They not only can, they do. They always have, and most of them plan to keep right on doing so. Even where industry has moved in, even where the city has covered the fields, the Southerner has remained a part-time farmer or at least a heavy gardener. Why? To make a little extra when the tobacco comes in, or to save a little on vegetables? Yes, that too—Southerners are too Scotch not to be thrifty. But mainly it's because he loves it. He loves exertion, the satisfaction that a man can feel when his axe bites through the last root that holds the stump in the ground where he means to plant his tomatoes. He loves the feel of the earth finally yielding to his spade. And if he doesn't especially love the weeding and the suckering and the other tedious, piddling necessities of husbandry, he at least loves the way his body and mind feel when at last he can lie down after he gets those things behind him. A feeling that cannot be entirely duplicated by athletic effort, though part of the current popularity of jogging comes from the partial satisfaction of the innate need for hard, goal-reaching exertion. The Southerner still knows how to exert productively, and the South will sing about it. Just listen to the worksongs of Merle Haggard and Merle Travis and the singing brakeman himself, Jimmie Rodgers.

Do some call the Anglo-Saxon stodgy, cautious, afraid to live life at its ragged edge? They have never seen the rambling boys of the South, and they have never heard the road songs of Hank Snow, or Don Williams, or Lester Flatt and Earl Scruggs. These fellows came out of the South. When you've grown up in Southern churches and learned—really learned—the eternal consequences of irresponsibility, you fully appreciate the danger of what you are doing when you break bad. No matter how your mouth may reject the teachings of your saintly mother, your soul still knows the lessons that you had burned into you on her lap at the old camp revivals. When you know—really know—that you are on the road to hell, you want to make sure that the trip is worthwhile, because you know that getting there is all the fun. If other Anglos have forgotten, let them listen to the South. We will sing it for them.

Perhaps most insultingly, some tell the Anglos that they are no lovers. They say the men lack the passion of Latins, the abandon of blacks. They say that the women are frigid and castrating. In the South, great love affairs are not gone with the wind. Southerners can still love; they love and hurt, love and cry, love and regret, love and remember. All that and they sing about it, too. Southern affairs are like Southern hell-raising: either by actual or contemplated adultery, the lovers are risking perdition. You don't take that kind of risk without strong feeling, but if you do find yourself in that kind of fix, you make it worthwhile. You don't dare the devil over something shallow or cold or small. If you have forgotten that, then just listen to the Southerners sing. Listen to men like George Jones, Don Gibson, and the incomparable Hank Williams; or listen to women like Kitty Wells, Loretta Lynn, and Tammy Wynette.

Most falsely of all, some say the Anglo-Saxon lacks roots. They claim an African can feel the dark, rich soil of his homeland in the marrow of his bones. They say that Latins and Poles can feel their ancestry pulsing in their veins, but that an Anglo's family tree only hangs on the wall or guarantees membership in the D.A.R. The South knows better. That's the other part of the Southerners' love of work. The Southerner loves to work the land; therefore he loves the land; therefore he stays close to it. He keeps it and himself in the family. Southerners have seen, often lived on, the land where their grandparents grew up. We know them; we remember our ancestors. Just let us sing about it. Let Eddie Arnold sing about the land. Let Doc Watson sing about his family. Hear Roy Acuff tell about his mountain home.

So, you may say, this is indeed the charm of country music. It cries out to the Anglo-Saxon about his half-forgotten memories. How then are we to explain Charley Pride, the black pride of country music? And what of Ray Charles and his success with Don Gibson and Hank Williams songs? Or what of Johnny Rodriguez and Freddy Fender, or John Denver and Fred Rose? Again, I say, it is shared recollection. Even conceding that Rodriguez and Fender are part of a separate question (that is, how "'n Western" became an appendage of country music, which, like how "'n roll" was amputated from "rock," is a topic for another essay on another day), the general answer remains the same. The South remembers and sings about its memories. The world listens.

After all, nobody ever said that blacks lack soul, or Latins passion, or Jews a sense of time. And if they can feed the hungers of their spirits on the yield of Nashville's soil, then surely this commerce can only enrich the common humanity of them all. But still, the main appeal of the music of the South, like the main support of any social good, is found among those who benefit most from it. In this case, they are the long-historied, little-loved descendants of the people who built half the civilized world—the Anglo-Saxons.

To others, the South is important; to the Anglo-Saxon, I say again, the South is essential. Nashville grows the only proper food for their spirits (with literary apologies to Austin, Memphis, Bakersfield, and all the other geographic locations that also turn out good varieties of the same or related victuals). Just as the Greek glory could not have endured nearly so long without blind Homer to sing its greatness, just as the Roman emperors could not have maintained half so long a bridge between republic and decay without their aforementioned orators, so shall not the culture that Britain built live long without its gritty bards to remind it of the quality of individuals who did, do, and shall comprise it, and maintain it and pass it along.

Even when the progeny of the British Empire has endured its last, whether after Churchill's thousand years or less, it still shall be essential that the South and its music shall have been. One of the rare great moments of television occurred in the outstanding British program, "The Six Wives of Henry the Eighth." Catherine of Aragon's spiritual advisor observed that the queen's adherence to the Catholic faith, whether successful or not, had been essential, even if it should bring down her life and her society. He declared that she was like a captain of a ship who turns it into the waves, rather than run before the storm and be destroyed without a trace. Either way, the ship and its people will be lost; but with the courage of the captain, those who later find the bits of spar and mast and keel will know that there were people there.

When future generations shall find among the ruins of an English past the bits and pieces of the music of the South, they will know that there were people here—people to say, "Oh you of future generations, we who did what we did, have shown that you can do what you do design, because we yet sing of our common humanity."

Some may say that the success of country music springs from its appeal to people of the South and elsewhere who lack the taste and training to respond to finer music; others, who take the time to consider the quality of the genre, have become instead apologists for the art. Indeed, some serious students of poetry have attributed the success of country music to the accomplished poetry of such lyricists as Kris Kristofferson and the immortal Hank Williams. Serious music critics have pointed to the instrumental virtuosity of Roy Clark and Earl Scruggs, the vocal perfection of Jim Reeves and Tennessee Ernie Ford, or the general musicological excellence of Eddie Arnold and the unique Willie Nelson. But we totally unserious good ole boys know better. We know that country music is not only popular but irreplaceable—simply because, in a thousand John's Places through and beyond the South, a Joe Allen can write, a George Hamilton can sing, and a million good ole boys can listen and remember.

V
REMARKS ON THE
SOUTHERN RELIGION

A Note on the Origin
of Southern Ways

Thomas H. Landess

AS SOUTHERNERS we are so used to certain slanders that we no longer even bother to answer them. They are like old bruises turned yellow: the pain is so slight now and so familiar that it is almost a pleasure. Some of us still grow angry and write letters to the TV networks, but most of us smile and nod our heads, not so much in agreement with the charges as in acknowledgment that we are still listening. I think it is good of us not to have organized a Southern Anti-Defamation League. Such restraint is a testimony to our manners in an era of radical rudeness.

But there are some slanders that need answering in order to isolate our true vices as well as to affirm our virtues. No need to waste time curing sins of which we are not guilty; better to address ourselves to the real ones, which, God knows, are sometimes almost as bad as the Yankees tell us.

One of our faults, according to the Solemn Remonstrance of the Northern Elect, is a tendency to be "puritanical"; and whenever the question is raised of our religious life, the word "Puritan" is likely to be used. In one sense only the charge is true. An elderly relative of mine was fond of saying that she did not go to church because there were too many sinners in attendance there. When we ventured to suggest that no one was guiltless, she became indignant. *She*, it seems, was no sinner, at least not according to her creed. After all, there were only three sins: smoking, drinking, and that other one, which she could neither name nor discuss without turning a deep shade of red. She had never committed the first two, and the third, which she had once been forced into as the result of a brief marriage, was forty years behind her and had been no sin after all because she had never taken the slightest pleasure in it.

This kind of puritanism is still to be found in our region as part of the evangelical bent of the Southern church. But such an attitude is not solely characteristic of American Puritanism; one finds it as a strong element in Ulster Scotch Presbyterianism, in Irish Catholicism, and in other world religions, non-Christian as well as Christian. Besides, even if this Southern tendency is an inheritance of the Pilgrim Fathers—and I seriously doubt such a theory—it is still no more than a doctrine wrenched away from the larger body of Puritan philosophy.

But Southern religion is considerably more complicated than our critics would like us to believe, and its essential nature cannot be dismissed by any phrase or sentence or paragraph. What that nature is I would not presume to say, but its importance to the way in which Southerners have behaved over the past two hundred years of the Republic cannot be overemphasized. Indeed, I would suggest that what is regarded as quintessentially "Southern" grows in large measure out of a certain kind of regional orthodoxy which, in modern America, is a rare phenomenon, if not without parallel.

Out of a belief in religious pluralism most American Christians have been too prone to underestimate the importance of orthodoxy, too ready to dismiss heresy as harmless or irrelevant, as something which should be tolerated with casual good humor. For this reason trinitarian heresies abound in modern America. An exclusive emphasis on God the Father, that is, on the Mind of God, has led one segment of modern Christendom to emphasize thought and discourse to the neglect of ethics and feeling. Such people tend to believe that when you've explained a problem intellectually you've solved it. And when the world fails to behave according to abstract precept, they either ignore such realities or else rationalize them with endless revisions which further complicate the problem. Surely the Puritans and their spiritual heirs fall into this category.

An excessive focus on God the Son leads men off into another kind of heresy, one that places an undue stress on action apart from thought or feeling. The Second Person of the Trinity reveals God Incarnate acting out in history what the Father would be if He were us. Too exclusive a preoccupation with this aspect of God's nature leads men to say, "Give your life to Jesus. Never mind who He is." Or else, the results can be a benevolent dedication to destructive causes or a cold and efficient commitment to works of genuine charity.

An exclusive concern with God the Holy Spirit results often enough in an excessive emphasis on the emotional aspect of religious life and has led to revivalism, quasi-mysticism, and some of

the more exotic forms of corporate worship, which have no significant theological content and fail to alter the existence of those who
participate in them, except, perhaps, to infect them with a twinge of
sadness and frustration that such experiences cannot be sustained
daily, hourly in their ordinary lives.

Most aberrations in contemporary Christian thought and behavior grow out of one of these trinitarian heresies, and as a nation we
abound with them. In contrast to the rest of the country, however,
Southerners have always been more trinitarian in their religious
outlook, which is to say they have been more orthodox. I am not
suggesting that the South is a paradigm of modern Christendom.
Our deepest thinkers have always been disturbed by our pluralism,
which at best has been ineffectual and at worst divisive. The failure
of the region to produce a single outstanding theologian, while
boasting any number of literary artists and political thinkers, should
give us some pause. Yet it would be erroneous to say that Southerners have no concern for theology or that they are less religious
because they have produced no St. Thomas Aquinas.

We will retain enough of our emphasis on God the Father to unite
in common cause against Modernism. More than any other Americans, we are suspicious of heterodoxy. If our theology is sparse and
simplistic, it is by no means heretical. For example, Southern Baptists more than any other denomination in the country expect their
clergy and laymen to affirm the ultimate truth of the gospels, including the historicity of the important miracles. There are times
today when one suspects that no one on Manhattan believes in the
virgin birth or understands the genuine importance of such a belief.
If a Southern Baptist preacher has any doubts on the subject, he had
best keep them to himself. And the same is true to some degree of
clergymen from other denominations: it was a Southerner a few
years ago who formally brought charges against fellow Episcopal
Bishop James Pike.

Of course no one will deny a concern with the Holy Spirit in
Southern evangelical churches. If sophisticated Christian congregations in the East and Midwest are rediscovering the importance of
feeling in their corporate worship, Southerners have been aware of
this dimension from the beginning and have never quite forgotten it.
The tent-house evangelist has been both the scandal and the glory of
Southern Protestantism from the beginning of regional self-consciousness. The so-called charismatic movement may well be novel
and exotic to the congregations of Manhattan; it is ancient history
to Tupelo, Mississippi, and Milledgeville, Georgia.

As for God the Son, He is continually stressed not only in the reaffirmation of the miracles of His birth and resurrection, but also in a Southern tendency to believe in His personhood and to use His name frequently in everyday conversations. Preachers speak of Him as if He were a close friend, someone known to every member of the congregation as the incarnation of the way they all should behave and never quite do.

Because of this familiar Presence (at times too easily familiar), Southerners have always paid some corporate attention to ethics, exemplary behavior as a mode of serving and worshipping God. Perhaps the best example of such an attitude is to be found in Robert E. Lee's famous statement, "Duty is the sublimest word in the English language." Such a sentiment is typical of low-church Episcopalianism as practiced in the Virginia of his time, and Lee himself, though the South's most paradigmatic nineteenth-century figure, was by no means exceptional in his religious attitudes. His sentiments are echoed in the letters of countless ordinary citizens as well as in those of public figures and are by no means narrowly sectarian.

Thus, a "good Christian" is someone who behaves well, and the phrase is still more likely to be used in the South than elsewhere in the nation. Indeed the attention to personal conduct that characterizes the South has considerably strengthened communal feeling over the years, though in ways that make many people uncomfortable. Typically, one is always under scrutiny in Southern towns and cities. Virtue is measured in terms of objective behavior as well as in properly orthodox sentiment, and vice is noted as well, though not in the same way that it was noted in seventeenth-century Salem. God the Son, after all, does not persecute witches.

This strong sense of the Second Person of the Trinity is the most important characteristic of the South's religious outlook. What, then, have been the political and cultural consequences of this religious attitude? In order to answer this question we might profitably examine those aspects of Southern life which are most characteristically "Southern," the things about us that are both the pride and despair of our regional identity. Among these would surely be our identification with the land, our politics, and our literature.

Southerners have a sense of place in a way that sets them apart from other Americans. New Englanders, Easterners, even Midwesterners have always believed in abstract America, the land of the free and the home of the brave, with liberty and justice for all. Southerners have been more inclined to love its rocks and rills, its woods and templed hills, and more accurately, certain rocks and woods, the ones they see and move among and know are real. Abstractions, however pretty, are to most Southerners no more than vague and in-accurate rumors of the truth, a questionable report on the nature of God the Father.

As initial evidence of this difference I would offer the perennial reluctance of people in the South to celebrate the signing of the Dec-laration of Independence, a holiday which until fairly recent times has been characterized elsewhere in the nation by picnic oratory and editorial bombast. On the Fourth of July Southerners have tended to lie around and eat, or in a few urban areas to fire off a few rockets and Roman candles. It is unlikely that many of them believe in the sentiments expressed in the Declaration of Independence, not so much because they still harbor good feelings about slavery, but be-cause they don't see any evidence of men being equal in the flesh-and-blood world.

Yes, it would be nice if they were, but they aren't. And yes, we ought to do what we can to make sure that less fortunate folks can have a better chance in life; but can such goals really be attained through changes in language? Better to pass the hat or gather a group of the church ladies or even—and here the ice gets pretty thin—give to the United Fund. Yankees, on the other hand, too often believe that all political and social ills can be cured by an amendment to the United States Constitution or a ruling by the Supreme Court. For Southerners, social justice is neither so easy nor so impersonal. At best it is something to be sought as a sense of duty in a world of imperfect people.

For this reason Southern elections are likely to be run less on is-sues and more on *ad hominem* arguments. For Southerners know that *argumentum ad hominem* is never a logical fallacy in an elec-tion campaign and that no one can be held strictly accountable for his campaign rhetoric, only for his character. Thus they will elect a man whose oratory is an embarrassment to them and whose intel-ligence seems questionable, provided they know him to be a man of personal integrity. For they still tend to regard politics as something to be carried on among people who know one another, however foolish such an idea may be in a nation of over 200 million people. It is God the Son who represents the family in the councils of the land. God the Father remains at home, brooding over the headlines in His newspaper, which tell of the perennial failures of mankind. He knows in His infinite wisdom that almost nothing can be done, but He sends the Son anyway, as a testimony to His good will and His agreeable nature.

The Son goes to the town council, or the state legislature, or the

United States Senate knowing that he will be crucified. He is particularly well versed on crucifixions as the result of the War, which He knows was not Armageddon but one of the many just causes in history that are defeated by superior forces and confused logic.

When He wins a victory He knows that it is only limited and temporary, something the opposition will in time undo or mitigate to some significant degree, not because they are devils but because they are people, and people are finally unregenerate.

When He suffers defeat He may be disappointed, even angry; but what, after all, is one defeat among so many? The Great Victory is always made up of a string of defeats, the more the better. Or so He tells the Father in His letters home, which are preserved in the family album to instruct future generations in the fine art of losing like a gentleman.

When God the Son encounters graft or corruption He is better able to handle it than most. For example, a few years ago when scandal touched the White House, He was less angry with the President of the United States than was the rest of the nation because He expected less from the man in that office, given the true lessons of history. In fact, the Son looked with greater disfavor on the president's accusers, with their smug puritanical faces and their presumption of their own radical innocence. The Son believed in His heart of hearts that the accusers had done worse things than they were attributing to the president, that the president himself had undoubtedly done worse things than these. Far from believing in the president's innocence, the Son believed in the guilt of them all. During this period He, too, would have preferred that the president make a clean breast of it. He approves of public acknowledgments of sin as a means of purging the soul, but He does not believe that media priests in electronic booths are licensed to hear confessions. They are among the many false prophets who no longer even profess His name when they are carrying on their crusades against social ills. If such people believe in sin at all, they believe in it as ideological transgression, and ideology is a heresy of those who believe only in the Father.

Indeed, Southerners have been relatively immune to the tyranny of ideas in an age characterized by the emergence of one ideology after another. Nazism and communism, the two dominant political schemata of the twentieth century, have had some currency in the Northeast and even in the urban areas of the Midwest. In the South the Communist party had no following, and during the 1930s, when the German-American Bund was holding huge rallies in Madison Square Garden, there was not a single active chapter in a Southern state. Not one.

In some measure this reluctance to join the larger movements of the age results from the fact that Southerners do not believe they have to join anything in order to have a sense of belonging, to derive some personal satisfaction from an emotional identification with a larger group of their own kind. They belong, after all, to the family, which has the advantage over "the Folk," or "the Proletariat," or "the Party" in that the family is composed of flesh-and-blood people, whom you know well and who know you and who, because they are so complicated, defy ideological classification.

When the Agrarians wrote *I'll Take My Stand* in 1930, they shared the assumption that the region was an extension of the family and that in a sense everyone could know everyone else through connections and friends of friends. In the past fifty years the South as well as the nation has grown alarmingly in population; yet Southerners still have the feeling that they can meet strangers from other parts of the region and discover who they are in ten minutes of conversation. And during such encounters, even if they don't discover friends or acquaintances in common, they can know a great deal about strangers by recognizing signs that place them within certain branches of the larger family.

In such a world there is an ease, a grace, a comfort that other Americans neither understand nor share. There is a communal spirit that moves in the blood mysteriously, almost providentially to touch the heart and stir the memory. Any old lady in any small Southern town is your grandmother or great aunt or distant cousin Maude—one of the three for sure.

Of course, such a recognition is not always pleasant and heart-warming; it can be a warning and an anathema. We recognize in one another the sins of the blood as well as the virtues. If we are all proud of our familial triumphs, we are likewise humble in the remembrance of our shared and inherited sins. In being members of the same tribe or clan we share with one another the secret of our own depravity, our certain knowledge of what it was that the Son died to save us from.

This knowledge, as many critics have recognized, is what has made Southern literature over the past fifty years the most significant in recent American history. Our writers have somehow set themselves apart from those of other regions by their capacity to deal with the enormous depravities that man is capable of, those special and imaginative sins that mark us all beyond self-redemption. I don't mean to suggest that Southern writers are exploiters of the sensational in the way that stringers for the *National Enquirer* are. In fact, they are subtle and delicate in their work, the way

Mozart would be if he were writing the score for the Charles Manson murders.

They simply know where the soul really lives, the depths to which it sinks in self-revelry. Allen Tate has pointed out the irony inherent in the fact that Eastern critics once scoffed at William Faulkner's "A Rose for Emily" as utterly beyond credulity. Who could believe that an aged woman would sleep with the corpse of her dead lover for the last years of her life? Then, after the story's publication, authorities discovered just such a case—not in Mississippi, but in New York City. In fact, no such thing had ever been uncovered in Faulkner's home town of Oxford; but he had guessed at the potential depravity in the proud spurned hearts of old ladies. And both Tate and Faulkner have written subtly and movingly about lynchings, a sin which Eastern writers would like to view as somehow beyond the pale of their own community, despite the fact that more blacks were murdered by New York mobs in a few hours than were lynched in the entire history of most Southern states.

But Southern writers have placed the blame where it belongs, on the home folks—not because these writers hate their region, but because they understand its humanity, the innate wickedness which it shares with every other place on the planet Earth. In one sense the power of Southern fiction lies in the very fact that it is not about the South but merely takes place there. Thus it has a fine particularity that gives flesh and bone to its universal soul. In that respect it is analogous to the created order itself. We delight in its accidental variety and are spiritually moved by its substantial revelation of the Divine. As it is with great literature, so it is with people. Understanding this truth, who would believe that Faulkner in his greatest work is saying anything of importance about Mississippi or the South that he isn't saying about Philadelphia and the East? Just as in "A Rose for Emily" he is not merely rendering the pride and madness of certain old ladies, but ours as well. We all sleep with the corpses of our dead lovers. Faulkner knew that about us before he ever began to concoct his tale of horror.

To boil the matter down to an essential proposition, the best of Southern literature is characterized by its ontological orthodoxy. For the most part Southern writers believe somehow, some way, in the Incarnation and in all that such a miraculous event implies. The flesh—the concrete particulars of time and place—are therefore important, good, and hence sacred. That's why few Southern stories of lynchings occur at no time and in no place, as in the case of "The Lottery" by Shirley Jackson, the rendition of an action which could not have occurred in Mississippi. In that story, as you may recall, without anyone really knowing why, members of a village conduct an annual lottery in order to choose one among them to be stoned to death by the rest. In the final scene a woman is duly chosen, whereupon those of her own family, including her small child, with relative unconcern join the rest in the ritual execution.

But, as I said, none of this occurs in Mississippi. In the first place, if such a practice were to persist, say, in Yazoo City, any number of old maid aunts would be able to tell you *precisely* why it was done. Their facts might be in error, but they would have an explanation. And in the second place, no one in that part of the country would participate in organized cruelties that cut so easily across family lines. Other kinds of cruelties might be (indeed, are) perfectly acceptable in Mississippi; but where the South is still the South, the family remains its most important institution.

As a matter of fact, it is the family that has given Southern writers their true subject matter, for where else do you learn about the remarkable virtuosity of sin except from your own flesh and blood? Such conduct as Miss Emily's, were it to occur in Mississippi (and, come to think of it, maybe it did) would be a family scandal, to be hidden at all costs from the eyes of outsiders and then whispered about at reunions for the next hundred years. Sooner or later such tales find their way into print, with names and addresses altered in order to protect the writer from the wrath of his kinsmen, who, despite his protests, never quite trust his loyalty again.

Yet, what else is he to do? He must write about the things he knows, and what he knows best is the family, which includes the distant as well as the near, the dead as well as the living. When he writes, he is involved in a communal act, for all the aunts and cousins who accuse him of treason have been his accomplices in repeating the old gossip—and they know it, which is why they are so hard on him. Perhaps in response to their disapproving stares William Faulkner once said: "If a writer has to rob his mother, he will not hesitate; 'Ode on a Grecian Urn' is worth any number of old ladies."

Of course he didn't really mean it: with a few exceptions old ladies come off well in his fiction. But something of his attitude is essential to the good poet or novelist: he must be willing to tell all, whatever the costs to his region, his public preoccupations, his personal pride.

And Southern writers tell all because, with their familial consciousness, they know all and know it so well that they do not easily fall victim to ideological distortion. For example, the family never completely exonerates its errant members just because they are economically deprived. To do so would be to remove from all the kinship their dignity as free human beings and creatures of God. But neither is the sinner cast out completely. Rather, he is claimed the way the executed black is claimed at the end of *Go Down, Moses,* not because he is redeemably good but because he is redeemably bad and in some way an extension of the family itself, a little bit of every member, black and white, executed in some impersonal Northern death house as partial atonement for us all.

And Allen Tate, at the end of his poem "The Swimmers," also claims for the community the dead black who has been lynched by local night-riders, claims him not only as a victim of corporate malice but also as kinsman to every man, black or white, who suffers the pain and indignity of being human.

Indeed, the tendency to *claim kinship* is primarily what distinguishes Southern poetry and fiction from the more ideological strains of modern literature. Shirley Jackson, Theodore Dreiser, Sinclair Lewis, and others tend to *disclaim* some or most of their characters, to define themselves (and by implication their readers) as different, superior, "saved" in some limited secular sense from the aberrations of the aliens who inhabit their fictional world like pasteboard demons. On the other hand, Southern writers have claimed for themselves, their families, and their region the largest household of flesh-and-blood monsters in all of modern literature: idiots, rapists, murderers, sodomites, fanatics, sadists, hypocrites, lynchers, child molesters, maimers, necrophiliacs—virtually every human depravity known to the police dockets or to Krafft-Ebing, and they're all ours, they invariably suggest, and more to the point, *they are all us.*

The source of such familial recognition is surely the Christocentric vision of the world, imperfect, ill-understood, but something still vaguely akin to Christianity. For though Southern writers are often theologically confused or ostensibly heterodox, or even skeptical, they all seem bound together by a kind of "orthodoxy of the blood" which makes them less susceptible to the temptation of falsifying the fallen world. It is not, after all, a mere abstraction to talk about the brotherhood of man under the Fatherhood of God if you acknowledge in such a statement that there is more than a little of Cain in every brother. Any other meaning is the worst kind of theological or literary sentimentality.

Finally, then, it is the concrete world with its transcendent implications that Southerners believe in and bear witness to in their

daily lives. In politics, in social arrangements, even in their literature there is always the implicit presence of God the Son, both as
the crucified Jesus and as Christ the King.

The crucified Jesus is most obvious in the continuing defeats that
have beset the region, whether economic, social, or political. We
have had a fine instinct for disaster since the days when we believed
we could overcome Modernity on the field of battle. More than the
War itself, Reconstruction taught us the essential lesson of life, the
one that everyone eventually learns. But as a community we absorbed that lesson more quickly and thoroughly than the rest of the
nation, and when we are not too defensive or greedy, it gives our
lives the touch of grace we need in order to endure the perpetual
mockery of the Gross National Product, the persistence of hatred,
the implacability of nature.

Christ the King, who embodies all we aspire to be as a people, provides us with a better paradigm than the Average American or the
Economic Man. Not that we often heed the model. Flannery O'Connor has suggested that no longer can any segment of the nation be
termed "Christ-centered," and she was surely correct. But she believed that the South, unlike the rest of the nation, was still "Christ-
haunted," and therein lay the capacity of Southerners to recognize
the present abnormality of everybody in the world, including themselves. Such a capacity is often enough a curse rather than a blessing. It makes us stupid, improvident, and hopelessly reactionary, a
people whose perverse past is so full of contradictions that the rest
of the nation cannot abide us without undertaking significant al-
terations in the nature of our being.

In the past few decades the image of God the Son has diminished
to some degree and God the Father has begun to assert Himself in a
new Southern self-consciousness and a new attention to our history
and its philosophical implications. Hegel has suggested that when
philosophy paints its gray in gray a shape of life has grown old, that
at this stage in history it cannot be rejuvenated but only understood.
Such may be the case with the continuing dialogue on the meaning
of the South. The gray owl of Minerva may indeed have spread its
wings at twilight.

But then Hegel did not believe in resurrections, only in the upward spiral of history with progress, the cold immutable God of the
universe. On the other hand, we still have some expectation of the
true grace of God and the descent of the Holy Spirit on our dream
of community. To be sure, a few of us believe He will come down
from New York, Chicago, and Detroit, His pockets full of money in

search of better air and non-unionized labor. But the number of believers in this kind of millennium has been drastically reduced in the past twenty years. Most of us now regard such an advent as the coming of the Angel of Death, and we are beginning to consider what can be done to avoid such a fate.

As for the rest of us, we figure we will get along until that other millennium, the one that occurs beyond time when all our sins will be revealed for what they are—the accidental flaws of mortality which are sloughed off in the resurrection of the body. We believe in that resurrection because we believe in the body itself, not as the ultimate revelation of our existence but as the place where truth begins to have meaning. In that respect we are still peculiarly though not perfectly Christians, which probably makes us unique among Americans. And it is in that uniqueness that we find our patience, our uneasy pride, and our enduring sense of belonging to one another in the mysterious and substantial Body of Christ.

Solzhenitsyn as Southerner

MARION MONTGOMERY

> The dragon is by the side of the road, watching those who pass. Beware lest he devour you. We go to the Father of Souls, but it is necessary to pass by the dragon.
>
> —St. Cyril of Jerusalem,
> quoted as epigraph to
> *A Good Man Is Hard to Find* by Flannery O'Connor

> I have been in the dragon's belly, in the red burning belly of the dragon. He wasn't able to digest me. He threw me up. I have come to you as a witness to what it's like there, in the dragon's belly.
>
> —Alexander Solzhenitsyn,
> to the AFL-CIO in New York City, July 9, 1975

1.

WHEN ALEXANDER SOLZHENITSYN was forced into exile in the West in February, 1974, I was waiting the release of my new novel *Fugitive*, living (as I still do) in a small Georgia town in a sparsely populated county. Our citizens here, my neighbors, were largely unaware of either dramatic event, though I knew that my novel would be of passing interest since its setting was so local as to memorialize some community history and landmarks. What effect Solzhenitsyn's exile would have on local consciousness was doubtful. I don't know how many of my neighbors, even now, would recognize his name. Certainly a house-to-house poll made in the swift, efficient modernist mode would show him a stranger here, though were I to spend a morning at the barber shop or a few evenings on front porches talking about him, my neighbors would very soon recognize the sense in which Solzhenitsyn is our cousin. Such discovery of old relationships, though, requires the manners and pace of an older day. Aeneas, an unknown exile in Italy, discovered his old kinsman Evander and claimed Evander's aid because of blood ties and family honor: "We are bound together . . . by the old ancestral kinship and by your broad fame." And even under the pressure of defeat by the Rutulians, Aeneas lingers with Evander to restore a relationship through ceremony stronger than the moment's crisis.

Such might be my own importuning words to the famous Solzhenitsyn, but that he might, as a strong exile himself, help me recall my neighbors to ancestral virtues now heavily besieged by the forces of modernism. Here in Oglethorpe County we are increasingly tempted to believe that some new Rome of a strange foreign devising might be built overnight, on principles of "need" determined by a house-to-house survey of our present appetites and then interpreted in Washington, D.C., or its branch offices, the social science departments of various universities. I fear tarpaper cities built on the rubble of older ways; I fear that uninhibited appetite is the end our natural hungers bring us to when unordered by ceremony. I notice, for instance, that the considerable advertising campaign in support of the 1980 census attempted to imbue a color-the-slot document with mystical powers: depending upon the citizen's conscientious execution of the document and his faith in it as revealing his own essence, a general national revival is in the offing. That modern Sybil, the Computer, will be giving us the necessary signals. If, as Solzhenitsyn was to say with shocking effect at Harvard, the West is increasingly given to operating "according to the letter of the law," at "the extreme limit of legal frames" in pursuit of "more things and a still better life" in the materialistic sense of those terms, it is also given to valuing the individual and his community as abstract facts, mystically interpreted by statistical priests. Our perfect response to the census will result, we are told, in a just and equitable distribution of goods and services by the Federal Father, and then we shall all be progressively happy.

I have watched Solzhenitsyn with fascination and with ironic pleasure, knowing that we both hold certain principles as central to the meaning of individual and community life, however much distorted and obscured those principles by the forces of modernism. I have listened to him with thanksgiving, pleased at the larger and larger audience attracted to him in places where those principles seem more thoroughly clouded and obscured than they are here in

Crawford, Georgia. So, whether or not particular of my neighbors at once recognize in Solzhenitsyn the kinships I see between them is not my concern. What is of concern is whether we here will continue to bear witness to those common principles. I have every confidence in Solzhenitsyn's steadfastness; but I am less certain about my community's, given the insidious and unspectacular invasions by that modernist spirit that I attempted to expose in my Fugitive-Agrarian novel. For in the South as in the nation there has been a subtle shifting of spiritual and political values to materialistic ends, as witnessed by the promotionalism surrounding our current census. Still, those kinships are strong enough at the moment to promise recovery. And I know that as Solzhenitsyn works his work in the larger arena of Western and American consciousness, we do the same here in Oglethorpe County—enough of us to keep the principles alive.

We Southerners in particular, then, welcome this displaced person from the East, whose enemies are our enemies—the man whom *Time* magazine calls "Russia's greatest living writer." That description is *Time's* apology to its readers for presenting an essay (February 18, 1980) which it calls as "grim" as Solzhenitsyn's Harvard commencement address of 1978, an essay of "Advice to the West, in an 'Hour of Extremity.'" The apology is necessary, *Time* feels, since "Many Americans will find Solzhenitsyn's views too harsh, his vision too chilling." Still, if popular comedians, actors, singers have been media-elevated to the rank of spiritual and political leaders, their random views certified by media exposure and validated by their "art," who is *Time* to deny Solzhenitsyn a hearing? For he, too, has become both popular artist and evening newsfare, no less than were Jane Fonda or Joan Baez and a host of international statesmen née popular entertainers of the 1960s. Solzhenitsyn's reputation as fiction writer requires *Time* to give his views "wide attention," though the reader is warned to proceed at his own risk. (In its review of *From Under the Rubble*, a Russian version of *I'll Take My Stand*, *Time* was even more cautionary on November 25, 1974: "In the West, the essays may buttress the conviction of Solzhenitsyn's critics that he is a mystical reactionary who places too much faith in the values of the Orthodox Church and Old Russia.")

My own *Fugitive* I shall set aside here, after observing briefly that it grew out of a long devotion to Fugitive-Agrarian arguments, putting them to the test as they engage an accelerating modernism in this Southern ground, that insidious undermining that threatens the spirit I treasure here in Crawford. It explores the ground of a local experience out of which (in a phrase from *I'll Take My Stand*) a "genuine humanism" must grow, as opposed to that intellectually derived and largely academic and ultimately rootless "New Humanism" which the Agrarians found inadequate to rescue the life of man in community. The salient Agrarian passage is in their "Introduction: A Statement of Principles": Genuine humanism "was not an abstract moral 'check' derived from the classics—it was not soft material poured in from the top. It was deeply founded in the way of life itself—in its tables, chairs, portraits, festivals, laws, marriage customs." The drama I projected was of a would-be Agrarian's attempt to regain this genuine humanism. My protagonist, who comes by his principles through the academy (he is a Vanderbilt graduate), receives his comeuppance when he attempts to pour those valid principles "in from the top." I tried to dramatize the weakness of such misguided attempts and thereby imply the firmer ground necessary: the intimate experience of the world out of which intellectual principle emerges, our daily struggle in what Eric Voegelin calls the "In-Between."

For that is the ground where principle must take root and grow into one's life. Principle is seldom to be recovered or established by the forced spectacle that was so widespread in the 1960s, the daily confrontations between largely ignorant factions given to conflicting dreams of some instant Eden. It grows slowly in a struggle of spirit in oneself as it reaches outward to the world through the bonds of community. I might put that struggle in scholastic terms, to which such kindred spirits as St. Thomas or T. S. Eliot and Donald Davidson, Solzhenitsyn and my unlettered neighbors in Crawford would and do subscribe. For, though they may not share the terms, these diverse people share an understanding of the things the terms name out of experience. As St. Thomas expresses the point: "Although the knowledge which is most characteristic of the human soul occurs in the mode of *ratio*, nevertheless there is in it a sort of participation in the simple knowledge which is proper to higher beings, of whom it is therefore said that they possess the faculty of spiritual being." Thus reason (*ratio*) is to be distinguished from the understanding (*intellectus*) in the old scholastic distinction. One possessed of that distinction may not command the terms, but he is already forearmed against the distortions of his soul which separate the two modes of knowledge in that soul. In our age the separation has occurred widely, elevating reason to an absolute in whose name "soft material is poured in from the top" through federal formulae. Accompanying such external imposition of abstract order is the elevation of feeling (the *understanding* divorced from *reason*) whereby occur radical denials and destructions of our sense of reality through vague collective social passions. In sum, we are being structured as a people through formulastically executed sentimentalities.

As a young man, T. S. Eliot was concerned with a "dissociation of sensibility" in English letters, a separation of thought and feeling which he declared to have occurred at about the time of Dryden and Milton. But that dissociation has been more general in our history than its literary symptoms reveal. It may be said to begin in the Renaissance, leading to the conspicuous antipathy of the nineteenth century toward the eighteenth—the struggle between an age of "reason" and an age of "romanticism." But the struggle is not accounted for simply by reference to the dominance of one position at a particular time in the course of history. The antipathy of thought to feeling is fundamental in human nature, and the struggle occurs for each when he attempts to come to terms with creation. Excesses of thought or of feeling may give a particular color to a calendar segment of history, giving an age its name (ours seems to be the Age of Alienation). But the struggle against dissociation knows no date: it is the ambiguous sign in the individual soul of that fortunate curse called Original Sin, an inheritance from that "Fortunate Fall."

Whatever one's calendar reads for the particular person in time, his understanding calls him to an open surrender beyond himself. It is a call to see the self in a perspective of creation that acknowledges the Cause of creation, what Solzhenitsyn speaks of as "a Supreme Complete Entity." The Agrarians, characterizing the Southern address to this Cause, speak of "the God of nature," an openness toward Whom helps distinguish the Southern mode of being, with its garrulous hospitality and celebrated manners. On the other hand, the individual's *ratio* is that consolidating inclination of the soul that attempts closure, that is tempted (when untempered by the understanding) to elevate the self by separation from the rest of creation through alienating Pride. Donald Davidson, seeing us "still Yankee, still Rebel," recognizes this difference in the more reserved manners and cautious hospitality of our New England cousin, who is more given to the *ratio* than we. But he knows a kinship, nevertheless, which rests on fundamental grounding of both Yankee and Rebel in our common human nature.

The Southerner's fascination with and fear of Pride and his sense of the relation of *intellectus* and *ratio* as faculties of the soul are still very much evident. As our literature shows, it affects our sense of drama to the degree that we are suspicious of deterministic ideas, seeing the dramatic center to be the individual will as it wrestles with dissociation of reason and understanding. Thus the Southerner tends to be suspicious of social programs that ignore the complexities of the real social world, in which for him Original Sin is an important complication. He is suspicious of abstract programs which would reform a community by pouring solution to human problems "in from the top." In the 1960s such a Southerner watched with distress the rival attempts of a secularized activist left and a seemingly establishment right to gain dominion. If only (he might be heard to say) if only those mobs in the Chicago streets and those in conference at the 1968 Democratic National Convention would sit down and read *I'll Take My Stand*.

Another sign of the Southerner's attitude toward the complementary roles of reason and understanding is to be found in his strong sense of the family as the viable social structure, his sense that the family is bound together as individuals in a particular place and in a manner beyond the power of reason alone to comprehend. Accompanying this attitude is his address to nature as an existence in which one discovers the presence of the God of nature. The Nashville Agrarians took their stand upon historical ground heavy with these concerns. One might say that theirs was an "ecological" concern, but a concern built upon a spiritual base. But theirs is not simply "Southern" ground: it is more ancient than American history and more universal than the North American continent, to be recognized wherever man is in tune with his portion of the world. Here is that knowledge expressed by Heraclitus, who speaks of a vision of the creatures of nature through which one finds himself "listening to the essence of things"; by William Wordsworth, who through such a vision "sees into the life of things." It is in the biblical injunction to "Be still, and know that I am God." It is in the plaintive lyric of a country singer, "Don't you hear that lonesome whippoorwill / So sad he cannot fly; / The moon has gone behind a cloud; / I'm so lonesome I could cry." (Such "lonesomeness" is not answered at last by another person, but only by another Being. The relation between country music and country religion has been almost destroyed by its commercialism now, one of the insidious accomplishments of the enemy of spirit.)

Southern spokesmen have often failed to articulate this Southern position, which pervades the "Southern life" they attempt to maintain. Or rather, they have not articulated it in a mode persuasive to its "Northern" opponents, particularly during the South's most spectacularly beleaguered history—the period from about 1850 to the publication of *I'll Take My Stand*. Some of the reasons they fail to do so are brilliantly presented by Richard Weaver in his *Southern Tradition at Bay* and in several of his essays. But the failure was a relative one. That is, the Southerner did not attempt his defense of principles in the strict mode of the *ratio*, and those in whose souls the *intellectus* had atrophied could hear little of what he had to say. Flannery O'Connor puts the difference succinctly when she says, "The Southerner knows he can do more justice to reality by telling a story than he can by discussing problems or proposing abstractions." It is "his way of reasoning and dealing with experience." The consequences of those differing modes she also assesses caustically: "I have found that anything that comes out of the South is going to be called grotesque by the Northern reader, unless it is grotesque, in which case it is going to be called realistic." The flowering of letters in the South in this century is directly out of the Southerner's concern to do justice to the complexity of reality, and that literature has in it a stand taken against the "Northern" inclination to value abstraction as reality, a species of gnosticism. For, again to quote that perceptive defender of the Southern vision, Flannery O'Connor, "a view taken in the light of the absolute will include a good deal more than one taken in the light provided by a house-to-house survey." And so she declares herself, as artist, to be "a realist of distances," through which vision she sees the transcendent in the immanent; as writer she dramatizes an active presence of the transcendent in the imminent action.

2.

Art, the Southerner believes (even when he does not call himself an artist), serves transcendent vision through its faithfulness to proximate nature. He is likely to see "science" as reducing nature to fact, which is then mystified by statistical exegesis. Thus storytelling becomes for the Southerner his homage to the largeness of reality, as well as a means of resisting deformations of reality by abstractionism. Indeed, storytelling becomes one of the modes of his worship of the God of reality through which he sustains a piety toward creation, and most particularly toward that special creature of God's creation, man. Through story he bears testimony on behalf of reality, whether in the courthouse or on its lawn in the shade of trees, or on his front porch, or in his multitudinous churches so given to dramatic revivals of the spirit. It is in the light of the absolute that he holds fill-in-the-blank questionnaires suspect. What he is and has been he finds better served through such documents as Ben Robertson's *Red Hills and Cotton,* Horace Kephart's *Our Southern Highlanders,* Andrew Lytle's *A Wake for the Living.* In Faulkner's *Go Down, Moses* and *The Hamlet* and *Absalom, Absalom!* In Tate's "Ode to the Confederate Dead" and Davidson's "Lee in the Mountains." In Warren's *All the King's Men* and O'Connor's *Wise Blood* and "A Good Man Is Hard to Find."

I think it is safe to say that, although such works have sometimes received generous attention at the hands of critics, they have not often been wisely understood in their implications about man's spiritual place in the world. Miss O'Connor puts the matter more fiercely: "No matter how favorable all the critics in New York City may be, they are an unreliable lot, as incapable now as on the day they were born of interpreting Southern literature to the world." For they see Southern writers almost invariably as "unhappy combinations of Poe and Erskine Caldwell," especially when the grotesque is involved. Why has that vision Miss O'Connor defends failed to reach those critics and, through them, the popular American spirit? Because the Southern writer has been seen as separate from his vision? Seen as a reporter of social facts? Or separate because art is understood as trading in the grotesque, to titillate the popular spirit rather than to celebrate reality? Miss O'Connor certainly felt those to be some of the reasons, insisting that in truth the grotesque character's "fanaticism is a reproach, not merely an eccentricity"—that "the freak can be sensed as a figure for our essential displacement" from reality in whom is revealed the drama of a struggle to regain his proper spiritual estate. Only in the disparity between his passion for reality which fuels his fanaticism and our age's general separation from complex reality does he attain "some depth in literature."

Miss O'Connor's "all the critics in New York City" is figurative, as a careful reading of her words in context shows. For though such critics as she describes tend to congregate in certain places—New York City, for instance—she is speaking rather of a quality of mind than of all persons in a particular place. She is talking about a quality which one of the Fugitive poets characterizes as making one a "Yankee of the spirit." (Hence my putting "North" or "Northern" in quotation marks to suggest the distinction.) The "Southern" quality of mind tends to be most general in the South, though I know and value many "Southern" Yankees. The importance of this distinction will, I trust, emerge with increasing clarity as we proceed to focus upon Solzhenitsyn as "Southerner." In the light of this distinction, one surely sees Solzhenitsyn's Ivan Denisovich as a "Southern" grotesque character. But we must also observe in Ivan a depth not found in Erskine Caldwell's Jeeter Lester. All Southern writers are not Southern in the same sense, any more than all Soviet writers are Russian in the sense Solzhenitsyn distinguishes.

In Solzhenitsyn we have a Fugitive-Agrarian risen out of the most spectacularly suppressive regime of modern history, a regime which undertook a "Reconstruction" whose horrors can be better appreciated by Southerners than by most other Americans. For we endured the prelude to such modern reconstructions of reality as we see raised to an ultimate horror in the twentieth century. And though now exiled by the Soviet Reconstruction, Solzhenitsyn speaks as one deeply anchored in place. From "*what* soil should one fight the vices of one's country?" he asks in "The Smatterers." It is a plaintive cry of one whose native soil stains him in an unforgettable way. "I live," he says, "in constant awareness of my desire to return to Russia, and I know I will go back." We might recall Granny Millard's handful of Sartoris soil she carries with her as she flees the invader in Faulkner's *Unvanquished*. Or, less poignantly put than Granny's action or Solzhenitsyn's words, though no less particularly tested by necessity, we remember Flannery O'Connor's remark that "The Southern writer apparently feels the need of expatriation less than other writers in this country. Moreover, when he does leave and stay gone, he does so at great peril to that balance between principle and fact, between judgment and observation, which is so necessary to maintain."

Of that "Northern" spirit (as we might label it) which denies Solzhenitsyn his roots, he says, "Spiritually all intellectuals nowadays belong to a diaspora. Nowhere are we complete strangers. And nowhere do we feel quite at home." He attacks that Sovietist spirit for its deliberate and systematic destruction of "men of the soil" so that they might be replaced by those "people of the air, who have lost all their roots in everyday existence." In distinguishing between "men of the soil" and "people of the air," he is making a separation which Allen Tate makes between men who are regional and those who are merely provincial. As Tate puts it in his essay "The New Provincialism," at about the time Solzhenitsyn was discovering his true country in the Gulag (1945): "Regionalism is . . . limited in space but not in time. The provincial attitude is limited in time but not in space. . . . Provincialism is that state of mind in which regional men lose their origin in the past and its continuity into the present, and begin every day as if there had been no yesterday. . . . From now on we are committed to seeing *with*, not *through* the eye: we, as provincials who do not live anywhere." But we must recover our sight, says Solzhenitsyn, who speaks with a voice dedicated to and convinced of an ultimate emergence of the regional man over the provincial. That is the most healthful burden of his prophecy, without which his vision would be "grim," "harsh," and "chilling" indeed.

As I watched a provincial man, Walter Cronkite, interviewing this regional Russian soon after his exile, I had already been gathering myself for sometime to explore the ground out of which Fugitive-Agrarian principles had grown, under the working title of "The Prophetic Poet and the Popular Spirit of the Age." One might say that my study is an exploration of a remark Stark Young makes near the end of *I'll Take My Stand*: "Though the South . . . is our subject, we must remember that we are concerned first with a quality itself, not as our own but as found everywhere; and that we defend certain qualities not because they belong to the South, but because the South belongs to them." They are qualities, I contend, more easily discovered to us in a community at a particular time when that community is anchored in a particular place. Life, we discover as regional men—as "men of the soil"—is enlarged by our participation in common humanity in the neighborhood of hills and valleys and by streams we know with the Psalmist's certainty. The enemy to this view is that provincial spirit which would gather all men up into an aimless drift, a journey whose only end is the journeying. The community of which I speak shows us to be members one of another in a mysterious and fundamental way that binds forebears and descendants within a life much larger than the provincialist can see. For when existence has been secularized by Hegelian thought in the provincialist mind, it sees only *with*, not *through*, the eye.

When history is secularized, whether by Hegel or Marx or the New Humanists, "humanity" becomes a shibboleth whereby all existence may be manipulated: the reality of human life is (to use Eric Voegelin's term) "deconstructed" by whatever self-proclaimed lords of existence have declared the world a mechanism in need of repair. Now the first deconstruction necessary to the manipulation of being is the reduction of regional man to provincial man, under a range of catchy terms such as "progress" or "humanity." Those manipulations do not necessarily reveal themselves as Leninist or Stalinist purges. But though less spectacular than mass purges, they may yet be more fatally destructive of one's life through gradual, almost imperceptible shifts. We react sharply to the suddenness of one's being shot by dictate or killed in a highway accident, but not

to a gradual attrition of spirit in us. That is a truth extremely difficult to make heard in the popular spirit of our age, precisely because
spirit has been so gradually displaced from reality. Such is the point
Flannery O'Connor makes through her grotesque characters, for as
she says, "to the hard of hearing you shout, and for the almost blind
you draw large and startling figures." Hers, then, is the same understanding of this hour of our spiritual extremity that Solzhenitsyn
recognizes when he reminds us that the tsar executed about seventeen persons a year, but that in Stalin's purge 40,000 persons were
shot each month, and that "15 million peasants were sent off to ex-
termination" by Lenin. His impassioned call is itself more persuasive than his facts, for we have been so buffeted by facts, so immured
of spirit by statistics, that his comparison registers less upon us than
his burning personal, accusing presence. He is as uncomfortable to
behold as Miss O'Connor's Haze Motes in *Wise Blood*.

Those twelve Southerners of *I'll Take My Stand* understood community to be much larger than its secular, geographical manifestation. For them, the sense of place incorporated history in relation to
the timeless, so that the local community of a Harmony Grove,
even when it changes its name to Commerce, carries in it a sense of
the eternal. Through local particularity—*these* individuals of *these*
families of *this* community—a sense of the spirit abiding in nature
is acknowledged. C. Vann Woodward, at the meeting of the Southern Historical Association in Atlanta in 1979, remarking the effect
on the South of the Civil War, reminds his brethren that "The South
did lose it, and one consequence was that the old planter influence
was diminished, cut back, and the new group of industrialists and
capitalists, typified by Henry Grady, took on a new role of leadership." I have pointed out elsewhere the interesting correspondence
between Henry Grady's New York speech after the war, in which he
warns the North that the South will bury it with its own industrial
spirit, and Nikita Khrushchev's New York address to the West in
which he asserted "we are going to bury you." (It is this same New
South spirit that in fact led a town near Crawford to change its name
from Harmony Grove to Commerce.) But though historians pronounce
the South now given to a deracinating industrialism, Professor John
Shelton Reed points out the South's continuing attachment to local
over world affairs and its continuing attachment to organized religion. A Yankee, he says, may ask you what you do, but a Southerner still asks you where you are from. I have heard Andrew Lytle
argue that the most telling form of the Southerner's address to a
new acquaintance is, "Where do you bury?" In Lytle's inclusive

sense of "you," not only the individual and his immediate family are incorporated in a family body, but his "people" as well. In such language resides that Southern sense of place as a window upon the eternal.

The Agrarians understood and believed in these customs to which the South belonged, and still belongs. Finding them dangerously threatened by the industrial spirit, they celebrated customs as essentially Southern, in the context of recent American history. They talked of "the South" as a "minority section" besieged by an "American industrial ideal." They saw such Southerners as Henry Grady as scalawags. Yet they were quite careful to make clear that an agrarian society such as they valued "is hardly one that has no use at all for industries, for professional vocations, for scholars and artists, and for the life of the cities." Their concern was that life be anchored in nature itself. Now this is not the same concern as Henry David Thoreau's. For Thoreau, an independent individual must be freed of community by his attachment to nature. Nevertheless, the Agrarian position was often attacked as if it were the same as Thoreau's, as if it were radically separatist. Since the 1960s Thoreau's influence has grown, but his is not an influence that will serve to strengthen community as the Agrarians sought to do.

The most immediate resistence to the Nashville Agrarians took the tack of distorting their position into a form of reactionary romanticism, whether of the Thoreauvian variety or of some vague throwback to an imaginary feudal dark age. These Agrarians, it was suggested, were merely a benighted remnant who attempted to advance long-since discredited views of man and society; they wanted to "turn back the clock" largely because of their Bible Belt mentality (This was a favorite phrase in Ralph McGill's annual attacks on their position in the *Atlanta Constitution*, McGill being the Henry Grady of the post–World War II South.) From our perspective in 1980, however, such arguments sound as shallow as Mrs. Lucynell Crater's provincial insistence to the drifter Mr. Shiftlet (in "The Life You Save May Be Your Own") that the "monks of old" just "wasn't as advanced as we are." The Agrarians said in 1930 that "modern man has lost his sense of vocation," that "The act of labor as one of the happy functions of human life has been in effect abandoned, and is practiced solely for its rewards." We know now that those observations are more intensely true than when spoken fifty years ago; we look back on the tumult of the 1960s with new eyes through *I'll Take My Stand* and better understand that recent painful decade.

The young in the 1960s were struggling, though most of them blindly, to escape those provincial reductions of life against which the Agrarians took a stand. But they found few of their elders who understood the causes of their discomfort any better than they did, few who could point them toward a sounder recovery than their confused actions promised. With no West to "light out to," they became deracinated Huck Finns, shrewd in their perception of society's failures, but unwise in the pursuit of remedy. John F. Kennedy's "New Frontier" of space explorations hardly served their hunger. One could watch the first steps taken on the moon over and over, but not smell the dust stirred. Vicarious participation in such events cannot satisfy the desire to participate in reality. It is an indictment of our intellectual community that many of those young people were cast wandering, becoming "people of the air." That phrase seems particularly suited to the so-called flower children, those frail orchids in the modernist jungle. Some of them turned, in desperation and with violent consequences, to such of their elders as Herbert Marcuse. For where could they learn of *I'll Take My Stand* or of Richard Weaver's *Ideas Have Consequences*, of Josef Pieper's *Leisure: The Basis of Culture* or his *In Tune with the World*?

Those young minds—many of them—would certainly have understood and responded to the Agrarian attack upon a rampant industrialism to which they gave a devil name, the Establishment; that was their attempt to name some Antichrist. They might have realized also that the Agrarian attack was upon both the secular left and the secular right and been rescued, in some degree, from recklessness. For it was the *secularist* aspect of industrialism that the Agrarian attacked, the reductions of both man and nature to efficient and material causes in the interest of product. The Twelve Southerners saw such products as the dead end of applied scientism and they said so. Hence they found little sympathy in either political camp. Nor did they find much support among those intellectuals increasingly encamped in the academy, those mediators of an optimism about the new god, Progress. By 1930 that new god had long since been established as worshipful in the American mind, and the God of nature as understood by regional man had been cast out by what the Agrarians called "the American or dominant" spirit. And here the academy's influence in this displacement needs some brief consideration as a primary agent in our spiritual displacement.

3.

Near the turn of the century Charles W. Eliot, having rescued Harvard University from its old role in American life as the formal support of mind in relation to spirit, bid farewell to that school which he had succeeded in tailoring to the service of the state through his long tenure. He addressed Harvard's Summer School of Theology on the subject of the "Religion of the Future." The new religion, he said, "will not be based on authority, either spiritual or temporal," since "the tendency towards liberty is progressive." There was to be "no worship, express or implied, of dead ancestors, teachers, or rulers." It would not be "propitiatory, sacrificial, or expiatory." Above all, it must not "perpetuate the Hebrew anthropomorphic representations of God." It would be dedicated to "service to others," and its contributions would be to "the common good." What, in such requirements, could Karl Marx object to? For either President Eliot or Marx, here was suitable ground upon which to build the future. The common good was now to be defined, whether in the name of Marx or Eliot, by a modernist spirit which understood man as a recent accident of an anciently accidental natural world, still genially referred to as "nature." Man by accident was somehow suited to elevate himself over nature as nature's god. President Eliot called for the reduction of regional man to provincial man; his sermon was a prophetic charge to educational institutions, a charge received and advanced since the 1909 address until it now permeates the American academy. But the American academy, in modeling itself on Eliot's Harvard, has effected a displacement of man from reality. Thus, although Stalin's precipitous handling of the "Kulak Problem" registers upon us more spectacularly, the subtle displacement of regional man through "education" has been as destructive. Indeed, one suspects that it has been even more persuasively destructive of our nation than Reconstruction was to the South. The crises of the cities in the past two decades seems evidence to the point, about which problem a vast library now exists.

The Agrarian symposium ran head-on into that "American spirit" which Charles Eliot had conjured, a spirit as much at home on the political right as on the left. Solzhenitsyn was also to encounter that spirit at Harvard in his commencement address. In the reaction to his address, as in the reaction to *I'll Take My Stand*, we discover that "Agrarian conservatism" is a creature apart. The Vanderbilt spokesman asserted that "the first principle of good labor is that it must be effective." But, they added, "the second principle is that it must be enjoyed." Labor must be enjoyed in and of itself, as one enjoys raising nature by art through an ordinate respect for both the reality of nature and of one's own gifts. The industrialism they saw as enemy to labor is "the economic organization of the collective American society," through which labor and pleasure have been effectively disjoined. Through that separation, harmony between community and nature became progressively dissonant. The good seen in labor, by either the laborer or his director, was translated into a final product, which in turn was translated by abstraction into dollar "value," in which figure *joy* was at best fractional. (The recent history of the American dollar on the world market is an ironic commentary on this point.) *Good* was lost to *goods*, and *goods* to abstract reckoning. Thus the spiritual struggle of one to answer his "calling" in nature, to find his proper labor within the range of his gifts, was shifted to an economic struggle, primarily a wordly and worldwide struggle. And that struggle came to center on the distribution of goods, in consequence of which (for the individual) labor became increasingly divorced from leisure, rather than being intimately related to leisure as it must be for one's spiritual health. Divided man is left in two worlds, the world of 9 to 5 and the world of his ersatz leisure. But he can find satisfaction in neither.

Industrialism's goods, from the Agrarian perspective, are seen as nature manipulated by abstraction for abstract ends. The holy texts of this new religion of nature, to be submitted to exegesis by both political left and right, are statistics. Thus an authorized text could be established upon which was founded an orthodoxy, President Eliot's "Religion of the Future." What followed was a Reformation, the breaking away of secularized labor from secularized capital. "But nature industrialized," the Agrarians had warned in their preface, when "transformed into cities and artificial habitations, manufactured into commodities, is no longer nature but a highly simplified picture of nature." Through such pictures "we receive the illusion of having power over nature, and lose our sense of nature as something mysterious and contingent." The God of nature under these conditions becomes "merely an amiable expression, a superfluity, and the philosophical understanding ordinarily carried in the religious experience is not there for us to have." *God* as an amiable expression soon loses all meaning; profanity ceases to be profane. The order of language, whether in court or conversation, begins a rapid decay; oaths speak less and less to the integrity of persons or community (though one is still well advised to choose words carefully in many Southern communities.) As Miss O'Connor's Haze Motes discovers to his increasing frustration, blasphemy is impossible without belief, even as pornography is impossible where physical unions are reduced from a sacrament to merely a civil ceremony. Shiftlet, in "The Life You Save May Be Your Own," remarks of his civil marriage to the idiot child Lucynell Crater, "That was just something a woman in an office did, nothing but paper work and blood tests."

To state our point from another perspective, the Agrarians were characterizing industrialism as that aspect of the provincial mind which, since Eric Voegelin, has been spoken of increasingly as secular gnosticism. This modern gnostic attitude toward nature holds that man's mind is the first cause of creation. Put in a Marxist form, as Voegelin shows by quoting Marx, "Nature as it develops in human history . . . as it develops through industry . . . is true *anthropological* nature." Now that conclusion is only a step down from the pre-Marxian position that God, rather than nature, is anthropological. Once God has been officially pronounced anthropological, as was done in the eighteenth century, one does with the term "God" whatever he will, using it amiably (as Ralph Waldo Emerson tends to do) or exiling it from the language altogether (as the more rigidly deterministic positions require). But when the same conclusion as to the cause of nature is reached, whether by Emerson or Marx, nature itself becomes merely prime matter for the exercise of one's will. There are no longer any strings attaching nature to a reality conceived as larger than man's consciousness; there are certainly no strings attaching nature to the God of nature.

Marx is observing, we note once more, an attitude toward nature which is compatible to gnostic capitalism no less than to gnostic communism. While the structure he would build upon this view of nature differs from the capitalist structure, it is not radically different, because the first principle of man's relation to nature in each is the same. That is the point Solzhenitsyn made at Harvard in 1978. But in order for either Marxist or capitalistic structure to be erected on that first principle, "reality must be destroyed" in the popular mind, as Voegelin says. "This is the great concern of gnosis," since gnosis "desires dominion over being" above all else. Such is the elevation of knowledge over nature by the *ratio*, and it leads to destructive separations within the individual soul. As Flannery O'Connor says, "Judgment will be separated from vision, nature from grace, reason from imagination." The most significant aberration in this deconstructed nature is man himself. From a regional amplitude he is reduced to provincial estate, to be exploited by the lords of gnostic power.

4.

In his Harvard commencement address, Solzhenitsyn took up the argument against the gnostic attitude toward creation. In that speech he quotes Marx as saying that "Communism is naturalized humanism," and adds: "One does see the same stones in the foundations of

a despiritualized humanism and of any type of socialism: endless materialism; freedom from religion and religious responsibility . . . ;
concentration on social structures, with a seemingly scientific approach. . . . Such is the logic of materialistic development." The
words were almost as direct an attack on President Eliot's Harvard
as Solzhenitsyn might have made had he known in advance the prescription for "The Religion of the Future." Now the Agrarians included in their own indictment of the modern secularist world both
the communist and the New Humanist. They, too, saw the same
stones in the foundations of capitalism. These several factions, sup-
porting a common philosophy, were focused for them in the term
"industrialism." In particular, they characterized a species of socialist entrepreneurs, the "Optimists," those advocates of gnosticism
who "rely on the benevolence of capital, or the militancy of labor, to
bring about a fairer division of the spoils. . . . And sometimes they
expect to find super-engineers, in the shape of Boards of Control,
who will adapt production to consumption and regulate prices and
guarantee business against fluctuations: they are the Sovietists."
They are also, we have pointed out, such "super-engineers" as President Eliot had geared Harvard to manufacture for the state, though
the Agrarians in 1930 were looking primarily at the experiment un-
derway in Russia, and at the many "Sovietists" who were rising to
activist roles in American society, particularly in industrial centers,
rather than in the academy. (We remember that Warren had suggested calling the symposium "Tracts against Communism.") Nevertheless, their words are prophetic of the social and economic
engineers who were even then entering the federal bureaucracy and
who would do so in swelling numbers after the election of that son
of Harvard, F.D.R. Charles Eliot's inaugural address as president
of Harvard in 1869 had laid out a program for the education of just
such engineers. During his tenure he restructured not only the
educational philosophy and its pragmatic program at Harvard, but,
through Harvard's influence, all higher education in this country.
(His most generally remembered contribution is the elective system, through which mind is adjusted to pragmatic prospects by a
tailored program of courses.) Thus he effectively undercut all that
remained of the old ideal of a liberal education, though that ideal
still has a struggling existence in many private and a few public
schools.

Well aware of such destructions of higher learning, the Agrarians
warned that the decay of human values, of "true humanism," would
continue apace, whether under federal auspices through boards of

control or by corporations through their boards of directors. In either instance the first job of such engineers is to restructure the attitude toward nature held by the popular spirit. From that restructuring follows a redistribution of the spoils of nature, whether by the hands of Astors, Rockefellers, and Goulds or by the hands of their counterparts, the managers of the socialist state. The point is worth emphasizing: whether the laws for the control of nature are advocated by the industrial right or the industrial left, those laws are derived from the same principle. The blueprints of laissez-faire capitalism or state socialism, or that totalitarian amalgam of the two, communism, are strikingly similar when the controlling vision has lost sight of the relation between nature and nature's God. But if man's final end is the consumption of goods, whatever the mechanism advocated, the "quality of life" thus championed must inevitably be determined at the level of a merely biological function. However glowingly it is advertised in the name of the common good, the "good life" is still defined from a presumption that man is a self-refined animal and nothing more. Gone from one's labor is any sense of a calling, and gone from the laborer's "director" is any sense of stewardship under the grace of a Supreme Complete Entity.

Most tellingly, those losses are reflected in the reduction of mystery from ceremony, whether at the family's supper or the community's feast. The bonding of community to a transcendent mystery dissolves, along with its bonding to history. Thus we should observe with equal misgiving the Soviet's rewriting of history and our own rewriting of it. The pernicious docu-dramas of popular television and the manipulation of historical dates, initially for the convenience of federal labor schedules, are alike symptoms of a pervasive disease in the spirit. When Washington's or Lincoln's birthday is shifted to the proximity of Sunday, by an act of Congress, those historical men begin to lose their anchors in history and to float as vague figures, more nearly disembodied gods than fathers, upon whom the rhetoric of a false worship may be the more easily focused. When manipulations of the reality of our history become an acceptable means of artificially induced ceremony, we end up with such radical deconstructions of community as I recently witnessed just across the county line. A historian of my acquaintance, whose field (ironically) is local history, engineered a Mardi Gras Ball in a dominantly Protestant neighborhood to raise funds for preserving the neighborhood. The "Fat Tuesday" dance was held on a Saturday night at the YWCA gym—a week and a half after Ash Wednesday. Such perversions of history, trading on nostalgia—that remnant of feeling out of a decaying spiritual hunger—make it evident that it would be better for people to tear down a neighborhood already lost and begin all over again. Genuine humanism emerges from our deportment in nature toward family and community history. It is revealed in our intimate relations to "tables, chairs, portraits, festivals, laws, marriage customs," as the Agrarian "Preface" puts it. Such a humanism requires that we value our history in nature with a piety that does not pervert community or its history for either sentimental or pragmatic ends.

Industrialism as we have been defining it—an attitude of the gnostic mind toward creation—leads men to lose that joy which is the effect of festival rightly taken. As Josef Pieper puts it, "Underlying all festival joy kindled by a specific circumstance (whether family supper, community gathering, or a legitimate Mardi Gras) there has to be an absolutely universal affirmation extending to the world as a whole, to the reality of things and the existence of man himself. . . . *To celebrate a festival means: to live out, for some special occasion and in an uncommon manner, the universal assent to the world as a whole.*" But a festival "without gods is a nonconcept, is inconceivable." However much Southern festival may have lacked the support of a theological foundation such as Pieper brings to his argument (*In Tune with the World*), a festival joy is nevertheless the center of that Southern life the Agrarian defends. It is at the heart of Southern manners. It is in the ceremony of family reunions (see Eudora Welty's *Losing Battles*). It is in our regular church gatherings, but especially at those all-day gatherings to which people from California or New York return home, away from the place they stay to the place they live. It is in those more solemn gatherings with which we bury one of our own. It is in our storytelling on quiet summer evenings on the front porch, or when we draw about the kitchen or parlor fire on fall and winter evenings. For the Southerner knows, through an understanding beyond the reach of the *ratio*, that (in Pieper's words) "Existence as we know it . . . does not just 'adjoin' the realm of Eternity; it is entirely permeated by it," whether we are at labor or at festive rest.

The gnostic address to existence, on the other hand, chooses as its absolute authority the *ratio*, denying the more fundamental truths about existence which the understanding must certify. By an act of will it chooses, through its gnosis as instrument, to disembody the self, to separate mind from nature in the interest of a dominance over nature, as it has already separated itself from the transcendent. And thus gnosticism comes to occupy a place which is no place, being neither in the natural nor in the spiritual world. But the gnostic must so deport himself, for otherwise he would be forced to abandon his insatiable hunger for power over being. John Milton cast the gnostic's motto in memorable, seductive verse. It is the battle cry of the New Prometheus who, since the Renaissance, would commandeer both theoretical and applied science: "The mind is its own place, and in itself / Can make a heaven of hell, a hell of heaven." But Milton puts those words in the mouth of that great angel fallen from brightness, who, having denied reality, must at last lament the hell within him. He is doomed henceforth, as storytellers have it, to walk up and down, to and fro in the land, in an agony of placelessness, as the eternal tester, the canvasser of souls and salesman of emptiness.

5.

The Southerner's suspicion of the traveling salesman is a commonplace in our folklore. It is a theme sufficiently present in our art to warrant a scholarly monograph. Mrs. Lucynell Crater's suspicion of Shiftlet in O'Connor's "The Life You Save May Be Your Own" initially has to do with the question of what he has to peddle. "What you carry in that tin box?" she asks in response to Shiftlet's testing question, "What is a man?" (There are certain touches in the story, incidentally, that suggest Miss O'Connor is mischievously reducing the story of Job to its modern ironic equivalent. Shiftlet is a wandering spirit presenting himself as a carpenter, though he is of the company of Job's Adversary rather than of Christ. And Mrs. Crater is hardly so just and upright as Job.) Salesmen are held suspect by the Agrarians as well, and they find advertising "along with its twin, personal salesmanship" a disturbing development out of industrialism. "Advertising means to persuade the consumers to want exactly what the applied sciences are able to furnish them. . . . It is the great effort of a false economy of life to approve itself."

The grounds of the Southerner's suspicions, however, are deeper than those exhibited by such writers as Sinclair Lewis in *Babbitt*, just as the Agrarian understanding of the nature of community differs from Lewis's version in *Main Street*. Lewis finds the difficulty of a Babbitt or Sauk Centre in their smallness and localness; the corrective perhaps lies in an enlargement, as is suggested by Lewis's own troubled journey eastward to New York and beyond. Advertising's effort to sell a false economy is not so simple as an attempt to sell a new soap or cereal to the unsuspecting. It is exhibited in its falseness in those attempts to move new federal programs; the advertising budgets of federal agencies have reached outrageous proportions since 1930. One finds the same procedures in the pages of *Pravda* as in the *New York Times*. The consumer pays the cost of wooing himself to a suspect cause in one way or another, whether through the open market, his income tax, or through his labor in some Soviet factory or commune.

What profits it to lose one's soul in winning the world? Solzhenitsyn asks that question of a startled West, a question put in the arena of politics but at a level more radically disturbing than economics or sociology or political science is usually willing to address. In 1980 he insists that the West is losing (if it has not already lost) another world war, this time "without a battle," through a "spiritual impotence that comes from living a life of ease." In 1974 he had come to us insisting that "the problems of the West are not political. They are psychological and moral. When dissatisfaction with government is expressed, it should be understood not in terms of political failure but in terms of weakened religious and ethical foundations of modern society." The only salvation for East or West, therefore, "lies in a moral and religious rebirth." That such a diagnosis touches a hunger in the popular spirit is at least suggested by the 1976 election, in which, whatever the degree of naiveté in the candidate or the voters, an obscure rural figure with a "born-again" message was elevated to the presidency. (Not without unfortunate consequences, however. For the *intellectus* requires its complement, the *ratio*, without whose aid one stumbles toward recovery as if by instinct, guided only by "wise blood.") Those economists who approach the market in this present time of inflationary disaster through their applied science are more and more acknowledging the truth of Solzhenitsyn's judgment and increasingly warning that it is our "faith" which must overcome the panic reflected in the roller-coaster movements on Wall Street or the fluctuation of gold and silver on the world market.

Neither side of that division within the body of industry—labor or capital—is easily persuaded of the necessity of recovering spiritual being as the solution to social disorder, particularly since the residual faith of a whole people had been effectively shifted from the transcendent Cause of being to rest in an applied science that promises a multiplicity of temporary ends. Thus the Agrarians had to overcome difficulties larger than geographical divergences of "North" and "South." For when one's understanding does not support his reason in an encounter with the Agrarian position, whether he be of the secular right or left, one easily confuses the position with the hypothetical socialist position. Agrarianism must constantly extricate itself from that distortion. The confusion is understandable in part, given the celebrated "agrarian reforms" practiced in Russia, China, even in the shah's Iran, and widely advocated as the solution to all problems in the Third World. Within the context of American history and closer to home, however, that confusion is worse confounded by the ambiguous presence of populism in the Southern mind. The Nashville position touches upon populism here as that phenomenon has emerged in the past hundred years from that increasingly beleaguered yeoman spirit which is deeply rooted in our Anglo-Saxon history. It would appear, however, that populism has been marginally effective in the national arena to the degree that it has been able to ride unmatched horses. For the populism that has grown out of an ancient English inheritance has increasingly revealed itself as *statist*, while advancing itself in the name of those regionalist ("conservative") principles which the Agrarians defended. Jimmy Carter would seem to have been successful largely through his pragmatic skill in riding these antithetical positions at a time of confused spiritual crisis in the national soul.

Since the Agrarian symposium, a host of Southern politicians not unlike Carter have maintained their base of local power largely through socialist programs, in spite of their national cartoon images as arch-conservatives. These politicians have argued in Congress for programs based on "conservative" principles—in the name of tradition, of the individual's birthright, of family and community. But beneath the surface of that posture has lain an egalitarianism which helps maintain local power but which gnaws at our regionalist principles like a cutworm at a tomato plant. That specimen of our political bestiary, then, the Southern conservative congressman, has too often succeeded in accumulating power not simply through conservative—"conservationist"—principles which he embraces publicly once he has gotten to Washington, while voting otherwise; that step is also consequent upon egalitarian reductionism at the local level. He has confused political issues to a degree that his conservative cousins outside the South, though allied with him on many issues, have felt uncomfortable in that alliance. One may appreciate the existential circumstances that tempt him to such strategy: it grows out of a forced unconditional surrender of the South in 1865 and the severe effects of Reconstruction. Yet we must recognize in such strategy the compromising of those abiding principles the Agrarians were recalling to us, and the considerable damage done to those principles through such strategy.

The Agrarians were also aware of the confusing and often mis-
leading emphasis in the dominant American mind upon that "peculiar institution," slavery. They resisted the growing insistence that
slavery was *the* cause of their late unpleasantness with the North,
memorialized under the dates 1861–65. In consequence, they often
found themselves unjustly labeled "racist." Slavery has been a highly
visible cause in the political arena since the 1800s, as the whole nation is acutely aware because of current social concerns. But if we
are to recover an equilibrium in a community of black and white,
quiet minds must begin to consider whether racial problems are
more symptomatic than pathological, a concern too easily raised by
passion beyond the guides of understanding and reason. Consider
this peculiar circumstance: the "Southern system" in which the
"little man," downtrodden by the rich and powerful (as an argument
goes), maintains his "Jim Crow" institutions, whether under the
leadership of Tom Watson or Gene Talmadge or Senator Bilbo. But
equally, though less spectacularly, confusing are the obligations of
Herman Talmadge to the remnants of the rural woolhatters, who
have provided him the necessary popular vote, and to the industrialists, the corporations with seats of power in Atlanta. In such confusion one must insist, along with Solzhenitsyn, that such political
contradictions have cause in spiritual confusions about our relation
to each other, to our place in nature, and to nature's God.

Beyond question, the Southern Agrarian ground has in it the ba-
cilli of a spiritual anthrax which breaks out in public as foot-in-
mouth disease again and again. Money-lined raincoats are a recent
symbol. Less recently, we remember the story of a folk politician
who, when caught lining his pockets, insisted with vehement conviction, "Yes! I stole it! But I stole it for *you!*" We acknowledge the
ground as contaminated, then, but it is contaminated as all lost
Edens are—by a failure that is spiritual, not geographical or social
or economic or political. Yet we necessarily return to that ground
which is a literal, geographical place: it is the ground upon which we
must build, for there is no other. But we may stand more knowing of
dangers hidden in it, so that our spiritual and moral failures will not
allow us to abandon the valuable principles from which we have
fallen. There are still among us strong souls who insist that an always threatening failure requires that we regain those ceremonies
through which alone lost innocence is ameliorated in community.
Those ceremonies above all require that one resist a reduction of
community, of family, to numbers in an egalitarian manipulation of
souls to socialist or capitalist ends, especially when the manipulation is put in the name of "Southern" or "States' Rights." They hold

most firmly that community does not exist simply *now*, the point of time at which gnostic expediency is always attempting to obscure the reality of man's place in nature—always attempting to impose provincialism upon regional man. For this sense of community implies that the present moment bears in it the fruits of yesterday (not brought, or seldom brought, to full harvest) and the seed of tomorrow (flawed by the old loss we credit to Adam). Despite the imperfections (or more truly *because* of them) we hold to a truth inherited from our fathers and everywhere certified by present realities—a truth that reality itself refutes the reductionism in egalitarian shibboleths, those secular versions of lions and sheep and jackals in millennial Edens. Nature itself involves hierarchy, we observe; it is therefore a principle to be honored as the structure of reality, a structure particularly reflected in any viable community. That does not mean, of course, that such truth does not carry with it the threat of spiritual destruction by prideful usurpation of authority in the structure of public office. Original sin is a principle Willie Stark insists upon most persuasively in *All the King's Men*.

6.

The hierarchic principle of reality which we see in nature and in community exists in an anagogic dimension for the Southerner. St. Paul speaks of that dimension through a metaphor, (significantly) to citizens of a corrupt Rome: "For as we have many members in one body, and all members have not the same office: So we, being many, are one body in Christ, and every one members one of another." The most immediate manifestation of St. Paul's hierarchic principle, to the Southerner, is in his family. And because the family is the earthly structure through which the individual discovers his ordinate membership in a nature and state whose head is Christ, family structure is overridingly important. C. S. Lewis distinguishes the family from the collection of bodies to which modernism would reduce it, in words tellingly to my point:

A row of identically dressed and identically trained soldiers set side by side, or a number of citizens listed as voters in a constituency, are not members of anything in the Pauline sense. . . . How true membership as a body differs from inclusion in a collective may be seen in the structure of a family. The grandfather, the parents, the grownup son, the child, the dog, and the cat are true members (in the organic sense) precisely because they are not members or units of a homogeneous class. They are not interchangeable. . . . The mother is not simply a different person from the daughter, she is a different kind of person. The father and grandfather are almost as different as the cat and dog. If you subtract any one member you have not simply reduced the family in number, you have inflicted an injury on its structure.

Even so, in the Southern understanding of family (as indeed in Lewis's own) a member is never subtracted, whether by death or by his own chosen expatriation. When he strikes out for the West, or even when he serves at the county or state prison farm, his participation in the family body continues, though he may appear removed to the world's eye. Even death does not remove a member's presence, though that presence may be ignored. (The organic nature of the Southern family is spoken to beautifully by Ben Robertson in *Red Hills and Cotton*.)

   This fundamental stone in community, the family, has to be torn down if the gnostic value of the individual as a unity of a "homogeneous class" is to be established. The varied assaults of modernism on the family have been a conspicuous labor of the past two centuries, reaching disastrous proportions since World War II. For the organic structure of the family stands against those attempts to restructure human nature so that the individual may be displaced from his sustaining community membership and then artificially reassembled as a component of an abstract, rationalistic structure. The Southern family still contends with a perversion of family membership as affected by the natural rights doctrine that rose ominously in the eighteenth century; in its most destructive guise, it reduces man to the status of animal, as the term "animal" had already been reduced from its implications of naming the *creatura* of God. The holiness of existence, because it is God's creation, was thus exorcised from all nature; being was thus opened to the conquest of mind, and the strongest mind was justified in doing its own thing with nature. One might study at length, I believe, the destructive consequences of this displacement in the confused lives of estranged children, particularly the spectacular phenomenon of children's eruptions from the family in the 1960s. In "doing their own thing" so many of them were but imitating on a small scale the gnostic attitude of the powerful "Establishment" they took themselves to be opposing. Thus the family as we describe it here—the locus within which the individual discovers his bond with nature, with community, and with the God of nature and community—was eroded from within as it had been systematically deconstructed from without.

The Agrarian arguments, though blanketed and dampened by the advocates of the prevailing American way, smoldered but were not extinguished. They began to break into flame again in the very popular fiction of Flannery O'Connor and in the essays of Richard Weaver. Then came Alexander Solzhenitsyn, bearing his witness to a strikingly similar life, grown out of a common ground. His experiences were given magnitude by a political history larger than the personal, including the accelerated decline of the West and the ascendance to power of the Soviet world; his prophecy could hardly be ignored. A Misfit rejecting the prevailing way of East and West, a disturbing displaced person pointing out to us the same stones in the foundations of both, he insisted that the fundamental crisis in modernism is spiritual. "Among enlightened people," he said with cutting irony in New York City (and how Miss O'Connor would have treasured the irony of place), "it is considered rather awkward to use seriously such words as 'good' and 'evil.' . . . But if we are to be deprived of the concepts of good and evil, what will be left? Nothing but the manipulation of one another." The protest he encourages is "a protest of our souls against those who tell us to forget the concepts of good and evil." For their evil counsel denies the nature of reality precisely so that the world may be made into an arena within which we manipulate each other, without the shadowing presence of conscience upon our manipulative acts.

Initially Solzhenitsyn was attempting to rally the West to an opposition to communism. Increasingly he has discovered a West so like his East in its spiritual decay, in its rejection of spiritual (as opposed to so-called social) conscience, that he engages us more and more as if a Southern evangelist at a summer revival. It was as embarrassing to some people, enlightened from a concern with good and evil, to have Solzhenitsyn deliver that Harvard commencement address as it might have been had Billy Graham delivered it, or Miss O'Connor's Haze Motes. For he raised fundamental questions about the quality of spiritual life in the materialistic West, and not a few of his listeners have come to agree with the woman in Haze Motes's audience: "He's nuts."

7.

So the Southerner may watch with concern the "Northern" reaction to the presence among us of that fearless, blunt man, but with some amusement as well. For Southern humor is one of the modes whereby the Southerner is enabled to endure the mystery of evil. Particularly, he watches the drama of encounter between the "American or prevailing way" of life and the indomitable Solzhenitsyn. He will appreciate in particular Walter Cronkite, the Captain Kangaroo of the American way, in the presence of this strange prophet from the East. He will appreciate, as Solzhenitsyn's distress of the moment could not allow him to do, Cronkite's seeming bafflement over the Russian's outrage at being forced from his native ground. Why was this strange man not rather delighted by prospects of a new life in the enlightened West? Of course, one may also be moved to anger rather than amusement at a recent interview between Cronkite and a Sovietist, one Vitali Kobysh, a fellow journalist, official of the Central Committee of the Communist Party in Moscow, and quite possibly a KGB operator. This time Kobysh did the interviewing. According to Kobysh's version of the interview, to the question of why Cronkite would agree that "the Soviet Union menaces someone, that our people are preparing for war," Cronkite answered, "If you watched my program every evening for several years you must know that I never agreed with that and do not agree." (Lost in the response, of course, is the distinction between faith in a possible illusion and facts of reality, something Reed Irvine's "Accuracy-in-Media" repeatedly shows to be a common failure of our media.) Furthermore, Cronkite is said to have responded, "An honest person cannot believe that [the Soviets menace anyone or prepare for war], and I am positive that the overwhelming majority of Americans do not believe it. But they are thoroughly muddled. They are being scared on all sides." By whom? asked Kobysh. "By those who for various reasons consider it useful," Uncle Walter is reported as responding. Whether Kobysh's account of the interview is accurate I do not know, but Cronkite has not corrected the interview as printed in two Soviet magazines. Cronkite's administrative assistant reported to Reed Irvine that neither the tapes of the interview nor their transcription could be found, adding, "It's like Watergate." Perhaps though, Uncle Walter has laid the groundwork necessary so that some year soon he may be a commencement speaker at Harvard. If so, we Southerners will listen to the report of his address on our evening news with some amusement, but with some anger as well.

For a little while longer may we afford to be amused by the general circus displays of the spiritual displacement of our national spirit; we do not at the moment face the stark horrors of repression that Solzhenitsyn, Ginsberg, Sakharov, and the like have experienced. However, it is important that, as we wait and watch, we remember and keep alive the careful distinction Solzhenitsyn draws between the Russian spirit and the communist ideologist, a distinction with analogy in our separation of the regional man from the provincial man. "It pains us," says Solzhenitsyn, "that the West heedlessly confuses the words Russian and Russia with Soviet and U.S.S.R. To apply the former words to the latter concepts is tantamount to acknowledging a murderer's right to the clothes and identification papers of his victim." (It is the same pain I sometimes feel on hearing Jimmy Carter explained as a typical Southerner.) But leisure for amusement in such confusions is almost over; it is increasingly clear that Western gnosticism is more insidious and subtle but equally destructive, and its symptoms break out more violently at every hand in this new decade. Khrushchev's declaration to America was "We will bury you!" That bluff challenge, delivered as he pounded his shoe on the podium, has itself been buried under a new approach to the competition between Eastern and Western gnosticism. Solzhenitsyn observes, "Now they don't say 'We are going to bury you' anymore, now they say 'Detente.'" It is a senator from Georgia, Sam Nunn, who sees in the SALT II negotiations the very Soviet strategy that Solzhenitsyn warns against; but it is also a president from Georgia who only too late began to suspect the possibility of Soviet subterfuge. That irony indicates a division in the South too troubling to be very amusing.

What a Southerner of my persuasion fears is that our national spirit more and more breathes within a world whose thermostat and filters are set by gnostic intellectuals; a climate in which there are more destructive contaminants than the Southern intelligence and will may detect; certainly more than the Midwest Research Institute can measure, given its emission standards with respect to "quality." Only after forty years have we become aware at last of the dangers to the human body of breathing the air of asbestos plants; how long before we discover the effect upon spirit of those filaments of modernism taken in more gradually and revealed more slowly in the popular spirit? But these are the more fatal contaminants of being in the light of the transcendent vision upon which Agrarian position is founded, ultimately more dangerous than the radiation level at Three Mile Island. If we watch a program of managed evening news night after night as if it were a bedtime story, accepting Uncle Walter's comfortable words that "that's the way it is," we may wake some morning to a strangely altered world.

And so we Southerners make welcome this outlandish Russian, who speaks so effectively against "the American or prevailing way" of life, recalling us to known but forgotten truths about man and his place in the world. We value his personal testimony, which our grandfathers would understand and which we trust our children may come to understand: "I have been in the dragon's belly, in the red burning belly of the dragon. He wasn't able to digest me. He threw me up. I have come to you as a witness to what it's like there, in the dragon's belly." He affirms and defends certain qualities of life not becaue they belong to the Russia he loves, but because the Russia he loves belongs to them. Without those qualities, life becomes meaningless. If we lose them, we shall wake to find only a dream world in which our bonds with illusion leave us in an ultimate horror of spiritual emptiness, the desperate moment like Haze Motes experiences: "There are all kinds of truth, your truth, and somebody else's, but behind all of them, there's only one truth and that is that there's no truth. . . . Where you come from is gone, where you thought you were going to never was there, and where you are is no good unless you can get away from it." That is a dark morning of the regional man as he discovers himself transformed almost completely into the provincial man. He will live nowhere, only stay in random place. He will be citizen of a boundless state larger and more empty than can be described by "Southern" or "Northern" or "American" or "Russian" or "Soviet"—the state Milton's fallen spirit attempts to celebrate: "The mind is its own place, and in itself / Can make a heaven of hell, a hell of heaven." In those words lie the death of family, community, country—the death of the whole person, and of those workings of the spirit through such persons joined in a community of which we should properly be members.

The Enduring Faith

CLEANTH BROOKS

A RELIGION should offer a view of ultimate reality. Man's conception of reality implies, of course, his essential goals and values, and determines his proper behavior in this life as well as his relation to ultimate reality itself.

Yet a great deal of what calls itself religion today in America does not do this. It often sees its primary task as that of ameliorating the human lot—providing counseling in human relations, or improving the circumstances of the poor and oppressed, or in a dozen other admirable humanistic enterprises. Please take note of precisely what I am saying here: I am not saying that such enterprises are beneath the notice of Christianity, and certainly I am not saying that they are not praiseworthy. I am simply saying that they are not in themselves religious but are finally humanistic, and that one does not necessarily have to be a religious person to take part in them. I am also saying that none of these in itself defines Christianity or religion in general. Yet the present widespread confusion on this point, especially among the intellectuals, accounts in great part for the erosion of religion in America today.

Religion, in short, finally rests upon some sort of theological basis—a particular view of the nature of man and of ultimate reality. In the South, from the beginning, the trouble with religion has been weakness in the realm of theology. In the Old South, the religion of the upper levels of society—typically the church of the planters— was prevailingly secular and social. The planters took their theology for granted; they simply didn't think much about it. Good manners and the civilized decencies pretty well got them through without much worry about theological niceties. The religion of the plain people, particularly in the back country and on the frontier, was emotional and evangelical in character. Again, it did not involve much speculation on theological issues. Those folks, since they took the Scriptures very literally, could confine their doctrinal debates largely to the specific interpretations of specific proof texts.

I want to make it perfectly clear, however, that I do not deny that a particular theological position is clearly implied in the preaching of the fundamentalist sects. Nor am I interested in disparaging what these sects have accomplished. They could be and often were a stabilizing force in what was often a lawless society.

Yet the concessions that I have just made do not appreciably alter my earlier remarks about the weakness of theology in the South. Religion has lacked a coherent intellectual structure sufficient to undergird the expression of the believers' experience. The result has been that religious views in the region have been often narrow, warped, or truncated. Such has been the situation typically in the fundamentalist sects. At the other end of the scale, expressions of religion have been in scarcely better state: they have tended to be vapid, banal, and sometimes shallowly optimistic. Such are the typical weaknesses of the liberal "main-line" denominations.

Worst of all—and what I shall say applies to the whole scale, from top to bottom—such characteristic thinness in theology makes religion in the South vulnerable to the secular culture that is all around it. Years ago one of our intellectuals coined the phrase "the acids of modernity"; it is a useful one. The acids vary in corrosive quality: some, like acetic acid, are relatively mild; others have all the destructive malignancy of the sulphuric or nitric varieties. The corrosive forces vary from such counseling on sex, love, marriage, and social manners as is poured forth in the newspapers every day for the instruction of millions, to the vitriolic blasts of the dedicated aggressive atheist. But most important of all as a debilitating force is simply the pressure exercised by the culture as a whole—through its advertising, its typical sales pitches, its movies, its magazines, its popular literature, its very habits of daily life.

Most of this secularism is not consciously anti-Christian, and most of those on whom it impinges are not even aware that its effects are anti-Christian and anti-religious—these are precisely the factors that make this all-encompassing secularism so powerful a corrosive force. Only those who are theologically informed and whose theology is basically sound have a chance to retain anything like an orthodox position.

The denominations in the South that pride themselves on their college-bred learning are vulnerable simply because they have too frequently gone out to meet the enemy with open arms and receptive feelings. Having adopted the very terminology of our secularism, they lack the weapons to combat it; having themselves accepted what are essentially secularist goals, they have no real reason to oppose it.

Those denominations which have played down intellectual concerns are in a way less vulnerable. As long as they can avoid much contact with the modern secular world because they exist in out-of-the-way pockets of cultural backwardness, they may for a time hold out. But the movie screen, the color television set, and the jet plane are powerful missionaries of the world of progress and secular culture. In short, how long can the fundamentalist sects continue to evade the modern world? And as soon as they themselves become permeated with its habits, customs, ideas, folkways, and ideals, how long can their orthodoxy remain unaffected? I doubt that it can, though I must admit that the fundamentalist sects keep stubbornly alive. They have happily adapted the radio sermon and the television revival service to their own purposes. In doing so, are they—innocent as doves but instinctively wise as serpents?—effectively fighting the secularist devil with his own fire? Or are they rashly preparing for the erosion of their own worldview? I wonder. In any case, I think their theology is inadequate, nor can I wholeheartedly approve of their characteristic expressions of it. I want to see culture and religion moving in closer harmony with each other. I believe it is undesirable to reject modern culture in its entirety. If true religion has much to give our contemporary culture, contemporary culture has some important things to give religion.

This perhaps too-extended preamble may explain why I mean to stress theology in what follows. But I am not a professional theologian. You will not expect me to be profound. What I shall have to say will necessarily be very simple and elementary. Yet I am convinced that the beliefs I shall mention are absolutely fundamental to orthodox Christianity.

I remarked in my first sentence that the basic function of a religion is to provide a true account of mankind and its relation to ultimate reality. Orthodox Christianity depicts man as a limited, mortal being, a creature eventually doomed to die. Yet Man alone among animals can be said to have been fashioned in the image of God, the Creator himself. That surely means that Man is not completely at the mercy of his needs and animal appetites, but is able to rise above them. He can make choices and, difficult though it may be, can sometimes even abide by them. Since he possesses a memory and can also anticipate the future, he is not condemned to live in a virtual present, but can relive the past and have some foretaste of what is to come. Thus Man possesses a perspective on his life that is denied to the beasts. The realm of history lies open to him. The other creatures have no history; there is no history of field mice, for example, or of mountain lions. What was once called natural history we today call science. Though Man is immersed in the sea of nature and cannot sustain his life apart from nature, like a good swimmer he can keep his head above nature's sea. He has intimations of an eternal reality and of a God who transcends the world of constant cyclic change.

Yet Man's consciousness is finally a precious bane. If he can choose his actions, his choices may prove to be bad, even perilous ones. If his consciousness allows him to savor more fully the richness of the natural world and the poignance of his own history, his self-consciousness also ushers in the possibilities of doubt and anxiety, of a sense of failure and the anguish of remorse. Though Man's consciousness can give him intimations of godlike immortality, he must never forget that he is mortal.

Yet Man is tempted to aspire to godhood—to hope that somehow, by eating of the tree of knowledge, he may become a kind of god himself. This, of course, is the whole point of the story in Genesis that recounts the fall of Man. Modern man, who has recently been eating the fruits of various trees of knowledge in quantities unavailable to earlier generations, is peculiarly susceptible to the temptation to godhood. More and more he chafes under the implications that he is a mere creature. Some of his new knowledge has made it possible for him to control nature as he has never before been able to control it. He can manipulate it—may even dare to remake it. He is almost ready to sign a new declaration of independence—this time independence from God—and so displace God as the creator of nature and the lord of history, becoming the lord of history himself and, in the process, assuming the role of the engineer who controls and directs natural processes.

In short, Western Man has become a utopian and is preparing to bring in the millennium by his own efforts. Eric Voegelin, surely one of the most learned men of our time, in a series of books published during the last three decades, has located in this growing millennial confidence the mainspring of all our revolutions in the West, from the English Civil War in the seventeenth century on to the French Revolution in the eighteenth, and down to the upheavals more recently occasioned by fascism and communism. But Voegelin does not confine the millennialist expression to violent revolutionary parties. He also finds it, in less violent form, in the United States itself.

I think Voegelin is correct in his conclusion, and that he can be proved to be so. In fact, other people have of late been making essentially the same point. If Voegelin *is* correct, then Christianity in the United States will eventually be altered out of all recognition. Some aspects of the change are already evident. Whether or not God is dead, as has often been proclaimed, He has for much of the population lost His transcendence. Man has come up in the scale.

Clearly the doctrine of original sin has been largely discarded. Man is less and less regarded as a sinful creature. He makes mistakes, of course, but he is essentially good-hearted and really means well—is naturally good, just badly educated. Therefore, even though he does make mistakes, one shouldn't say that he is *sinful*. If he can only be properly educated and if his environment can be effectively modified, mankind may cease to make mistakes. Then we shall approach that utopia that T. S. Eliot once mockingly described as a "system so perfect that no one will need to be good."

Reinhold Niebuhr has also (and just as sardonically) described what is involved in a Christianity that has been warped toward that millennialist pole. It preaches that "A God without wrath [will bring] men without sin into a kingdom without judgment through the ministrations of a Christ without a Cross."

Why do I mention these matters? Because I want to suggest the tendencies at work in liberal Protestantism and today perhaps at certain levels in Roman Catholicism. Even if true, however, what is the relevance of all this to the South, my particular area of concern on this occasion? It is just this: Though the South has been touched by these modernist movements, it has remained in its religion, as in much else, the most conservative section of the United States.

I want to move on now to consider the importance of a basic worldview, not only with regard to the more conservative view of the South, but also with regard to the more progressive ideas held by the rest of the country.

In 1952 Eric Voegelin touched upon this issue in *The New Science of Politics*. I am thinking especially of his chapter entitled "Gnostic Revolution—The Puritan Case." In it, Voegelin discusses the Gnostic millennialist tendencies of the sixteenth- and seventeenth-century English Puritans. As he shows, the more extreme Puritans clearly were arguing for a "Gnostic Totalitarianism." In his next chapter Voegelin glances at "the America that was founded by [these] very Puritans." His use of the term "Gnostic" will cause the average American citizen to throw up his hands in bewilderment. What possible value is there in raking up the bones of old theological heresies? The American is not interested in doctrinal niceties, but in practical consequences.

Yet since one's actions, domestic, national, and international, are predicated on some notion of what is real and what is not, on what *can* be done by human beings in the realm of human affairs and what cannot, a distorted view of reality could have serious consequences in every field. Voegelin sees such a distorted view of reality as explaining our international politics at the end of World War II. He points out that we settled for a Soviet army on the Elbe while disarming Germany. (We very quickly found that we had to rehabilitate Germany as a makeweight.) We watched the Communist takeover of China while dismantling Japan's military establishment. (Again, we quickly found that we had to rehabilitate Japan, and are now finding it in our own national interest to do something of the same for China.) Voegelin adds that these mistakes "cannot be explained by ignorance and stupidity. The policies were pursued as a matter of principle, on the basis of Gnostic dream assumptions about the nature of man, about a mysterious evolution of mankind toward peace and world order. . . ."

Evidence as to our distorted sense of reality can, however, be gathered from an entirely different quarter. Christopher Lasch, in his brilliant *Culture of Narcissism*, expresses in telling fashion the way in which, for many contemporary Americans, "reality takes on the appearance of illusion":

As the workings of the modern economy and the modern social order become increasingly inaccessible to everyday intelligence, art and philosophy abdicate the task of explaining them to the allegedly objective sciences of society, which themselves have retreated from the effort to master reality into the classification of trivia. Reality thus presents itself, to laymen and "scientists" alike, as an impenetrable network of social relations—as "role playing," the "presentation of self in everyday life." To the performing self, the only reality is the identity he can construct out of materials furnished by advertising and mass culture, themes of popular film and fiction, and fragments torn from a vast range of cultural traditions, all of them equally contemporaneous to the contemporary mind.

"Gnosticism" is not in Lasch's vocabulary. He has no interest in tracing our present disorders back to ancient heresies; he himself regards religion as an illusion. But he indicates in his own terms that many of us are living in a kind of dream world, and in his book he points out the disastrous consequences of that fact in every area of present-day American civilization.

To return to Voegelin's analysis. He associates the New England Puritans with the Gnostic dream world, and he acknowledges the subsequent effects of this distorted view of reality on America at large. But he does not pursue in detail the development of these Gnostic ideas. After all, his book is modestly subtitled: "An Introductory Essay."

The matter in question, however, has been thoroughly explored in a recently published book by Sacvan Bercovitch. *The American Jeremiad* has received high praise, and deservedly so. I cite it here because, to my knowledge, it presents the most convincing account yet of the origins of the so-called American Dream and accounts for the millennialist elements that have, from the beginning, been inextricably incorporated in it. In what follows, I shall have to be somewhat unfair to Professor Bercovitch by reducing his book to summary form. Bercovitch's thesis is this: The New England Puritans regarded their exodus to Massachusetts as a mission into the Wilderness. He begins thus by following Perry Miller's thesis. These Puritans were going to establish on the American shore the kind of church and society that God Himself had ordained in the Scriptures. They would build the New Jerusalem in this very world of time— the eternal city in the world of the here-and-now. Bercovitch points out that their fellow Puritans back in England reproached them for this sacrilegious identification of the New Jerusalem with an earthly state. St. Augustine had long before made a careful distinction between the city of Man and the City of God, which was to be the spiritual model for our temporal societies yet which actually existed and could only exist in the realm of eternity. If the City of God could indeed be set up on this earth, then time itself would have come to an end and eternity would have been ushered in.

Yet the New England Puritans made the bold identification of the church-state that they set about building in New England with the City of God itself. Thus, they truly expected to bring about the millennium.

In time, of course, the specifically Christian elements withered away, and the whole scheme became secularized. Yet, as Bercovitch convincingly shows, the millennial expectations in New England persisted. Moreover, gradually the millennial hope was extended beyond New England to America at large. America truly understood was to be seen as the great hope of the world. We Americans had shaken off the old and wicked past. We represented the future; we were the bright morning star. In the process of fulfilling our own millennial dream, we would realize the hopes of all mankind and set forth the glowing future for the human race. Ever since, as Bercovitch persuasively shows, such has been the basic character of the American Dream. One remembers how many American political addresses have taken their coloring, if not their main thesis, from this confident declaration of America's meaning and promise.

The most interesting thing about Bercovitch's book is that, in his account of the growth of millennialism in the United States, he flatly excepts the whole of the South. In a long footnote to the preface, he quotes from William R. Taylor's *Cavalier and Yankee* the statement that "Those Southern spokesmen . . . who advocated anti- or pre-capitalist forms of life explicitly dissociated their religion from the values of the nation at large." In the same note, he also quotes Louis Hartz's statement that the South was "an alien child in a liberal family" and C. Vann Woodward's reference to the South's "un-American experience."

The only other reference to the South that I have found in Bercovitch's book takes the same line. He is discussing Herman Melville's lengthy and difficult poem, *Clarel*. Bercovitch tells us that one of the characters, Ungar, "is everything which the symbol of America is not"; the first adjective that Bercovitch uses to describe Ungar is "Southern."

The fact that the basis of the concept of America is an abstraction is so unusual that it renders the American case almost unique. Here again the South differs from the rest of the country. Some years ago, when Vann Woodward concerned himself with this problem in "The Search for Southern Identity," he reviewed the various bases of the Southern character that have been proposed in the past: a characteristic kind of economy, that is, agrarianism; race consciousness, that is, the South's characteristic attitude toward the Negro; and myths of the past, such as the myth of its Cavalier origins, of the gracious plantation society, and of the always kindly slaveholding patriarch. All these myths had been deflated or were destined to be so—or, as history had shown, had proved to be accounts of the South which were only partially true. Did the modern Southerner, then, have nothing on which to base his special identity? Was he in fact not special at all? Just another American?

Vann Woodward readily allows the Southerner his special identity, but he bases it upon what he calls "the collective experience of the Southern people"—"their unique historic experience as Ameri-

cans." To be explicit: contrary to other Americans, the collective experience of Southerners includes decades of scarcity and poverty
rather than of abundance; of guilt rather than of innocence; of frustration and defeat rather than of unfailing victory and success. Such
a regional experience has made Southerners skeptical with regard to
the myths which undergird American nationalism. The Southerners' historic experience has given them a better grasp on reality, a
heightened suspicion of all utopian schemes, and an antidote to
moral complacency. In fact, Woodward points out, their historic experience tends to associate them with Europe and the rest of the
world. It is the *other* Americans who turn out to be a peculiar people in the world's history.

In the essay from which I have been quoting, Woodward does not
directly raise the issue of religion, nor, for his purposes, need he do
so. Yet, having in mind my present topic, I think it proper to point
out that the Southern worldview as described by Woodward is much
closer to Christian orthodoxy than is the typical American religion.
In fact, Woodward does quote Will Herberg as pronouncing that "by
every realistic criterion, the American Way of Life is the operative
faith of the American people." European observers have noted that
"the different religions in America resemble each other more than
they do their European counterparts."

I want here, however, to return to Woodward's assertion that the
Southerner's sense of a special identity derives from the South's special historic experience, rather than from an idea such as that of a
utopian society to be achieved in the future. On this general point I
would like to quote a recent observation made by a non-Southerner,
Richard Goodwin. Goodwin has been deeply involved in politics and
government almost from the time he graduated from the Harvard
Law School. (He has, incidentally, served as a speechwriter for characters as diverse as John F. Kennedy and Lyndon Johnson.) In his
book entitled *The American Condition* (1974), he makes several interesting observations about our American society, one of which is
very pertinent to the circumstances I have been discussing: America is the creation of an idea and has been sustained by a continual
effort to realize that idea. Thus, in his own terms, he makes the
point stressed by Bercovitch. Goodwin puts his thesis concisely in
the following passage:

The special nature of our society and its purpose—even its moral mission—
have dominated the idea of America far more than have tradition, cultural
heritage, common language, or territory. To be French or British, Chinese or

Egyptian, is to be part of a cluster of events and beliefs transmitted across centuries. The American idea could not be formed from such continuity. The wilderness had sheltered no Roman legions, no Peter and Constantine, no Renaissance or Elizabethan age. . . . The two basic constituents of nationhood—population and territory—[in our case] constantly grew, and changed in composition.

Accordingly we were forced to find our unity and continuity in a continuing idea. We did so.

We were the land of opportunity and freedom. We were William Bradford's "City on a Hill." Jefferson's "chosen country," Lincoln's "favored land." . . . This national idea differed from that of other nations in a crucial quality. It had to be constantly renewed, always contemporary.

One is tempted to describe this crucial difference in another (though, I believe, not contradictory) way: unlike the national conception of other countries, the American conception had a future reference. In it inhered the notion of continuing progress and millennial achievement to come.

The American South does not, of course, have the centuries-old historic experience of an England or a France. Nevertheless, the Southerner's consciousness of his special identity is not based on an abstract idea. Rather, it resembles the Englishman's or the Frenchman's in being based upon a "unique historical experience."

Certain differences between the Southerners and other Americans have been noted by others, and by no means just chauvinistic natives of the region. Nearly a hundred and fifty years ago, Alexis de Tocqueville found the Southerner culturally different from his fellow Americans. Henry James, that sharp-eyed observer of manners and morals, was thoroughly aware of the special character of the Southern mind. In *The Bostonians* James introduces a Southerner, Basil Ransom by name, to the Bostonian world of post-transcendentalism, good works, social improvement, and the early feminists. In Boston and New York, Ransom has to challenge almost everything he hears and sees. He is not, to be sure, the bull let loose in the china shop; he is too courteous to act with frank rudeness. But he can be forthright, and in the course of things he does manage to break a good deal of crockery. When Verena Tarrant, the charming New England girl who is the charismatic proponent of women's rights, tells Ransom that since he opposes "our movement, you won't want to hear of the suffering of women," Ransom sharply replies: "The suffering of women is the suffering of all humanity. Do you think any movement is going to stop that—or all the lectures from now to doomsday? We are born to suffer—and to bear it, like decent people." This remark, I grant, smacks more of Roman Stoicism than of St. Thomas Aquinas. But in any case, Ransom is clearly opposed to any utopian optimism.

Coming nearer to our own time, Thornton Wilder, that acutely sensitive dramatic artist, who loved Europe and knew it so well, also found the South more than faintly European. He wrote that the Southern states constitute an exception to the abstract quality of the national character. Wilder describes them as "enclaves or residual areas of European feeling. They were cut off, or resolutely cut themselves off, from the advancing tide of the country's modes of consciousness. Place, environment, relations, repetitions are the breath of their being."

Some years ago, in the course of a panel discussion with some of my Roman Catholic friends, I objected to certain sweeping generalizations that they were making about American beliefs and attitudes. My part of the country, I insisted, was not like that. They laughingly agreed: the South—basically Protestant though it was—was still a part of Europe.

Though I may seem to have allowed myself to wander far away from my announced topic, religion in the South, I am satisfied that I have not in fact done so. For if the American way of life now constitutes "the operative faith of the American people," and if the doctrine of progress with its millennial ingredients has become a firm article in that faith, then the Christian faith as once delivered to the saints has suffered radical alteration.

The South's historic resistance to utopian schemes and its skepticism about human perfectibility consequently have some significance. I believe that they point to a residual Christian orthodoxy, but I do not mean to end on a note of complacency and of self-congratulation.

All is not well. Southerners have tried for too long to live on their religious instincts alone. I call attention again to our general weakness in theology and to the pressing need to define and articulate our beliefs. The evangelicals, in their preoccupation with soul-saving, need to look more deeply into what they mean to save men from, and to examine more carefully what their souls are being saved for. Salvation and true blessedness need sharper definition. On the other hand, the urban "main-line" churches and their more liberal leaders need to rethink some of the implications of the all-but-set-aside doctrine of Original Sin and the newer and more fashionable current aspects of spiritual pride.

Even if the South is deemed still relatively free from the Gnostic heresy and millennialism, it is by no means immune to the doctrine of automatic progress and other invitations to enter Utopia. The slogans and procedures of the teachers' colleges are loud in the land. The old sense of history is probably being—perhaps already has been—lost. There are too many Burger Kings and Kentucky Fried Chicken entrepreneurs; too much fast food and fast education that manages somehow to bypass the Three R's on its way to its chosen goal of social engineering.

The best one can say is that a venerable tradition has not been wholly lost—that there remains at least a foundation upon which to rebuild.

Conclusion

Not in Memoriam,

But in Affirmation

M. E. BRADFORD

FOR ALMOST TWO CENTURIES, and perhaps for even longer, Southerners have found a predictable source of diversion in watching the curious outsiders or visitors who are busily watching them. As we all know, there is sometimes a bit of irritation which gives a special edge to the sport. In such cases, the tenor of the exercise is forensic and, at least partially, unpleasant. But there are other occasions when we behold with wonder the uncalculating surprise taken from our conduct by "foreign" observers who have no axe to grind. I have a friend from Michigan, a fellow academic, with advanced degrees in French history and a wide experience not only of the American scene but also of Europe and the Middle East. We see one another most frequently at scholarly conferences, though our acquaintance is of some years' standing and embodies a broad scope of mutual interests and attitudes, including consulting exchanges and common projects. Moreover, we share many of the same associates and have established a pattern of ease and candor in our conversation.

Therefore I accepted as genuine and instructive my friend's reaction to an impromptu party following an exhaustive program of weighty papers on political philosophy. Most of the participants in the evening's celebration were Southern scholars, some of them well acquainted and some new to many of the group. They were of both sexes and of three generations. The common denominator of our discourse was the business of the day. Yet we spoke of much else besides: of friends and mentors and the rumors of both—their fortunes and misfortunes, their origins and our own; of illustrative stories, many of them drawn from outside the narrow confines of the academy; of adversaries, ancient and modern; of our delight in the progress of one another's work, and reports of our personal lives; and most particularly in the rehearsal of common bonds antecedent to our professional identities, visible as much in the manner of our speaking as in its content—in idiom, in humor, in certain hyperbolic gestures, verging on swagger, panache, and familiarity. The round robin of the talk was intense and friendly, serious and droll, carried on as if all present feared that it would be some time before they would be together again and were determined to hear and say it all.

For the young historian from Michigan, the dynamic of the gathering was a cause for unmixed astonishment. In the early hours of the morning, as he was leaving, he confided in both pleasure and exhaustion, "I can't believe that this is a group of intellectuals. Professors that I know do not behave in this way, even when among close friends." And he added to this observation an acknowledgment that the festivities had been more like a family reunion than the usual polite and professional alcoholic post-mortem to a long day's session. What had struck my friend was, of course, the datum of the papers gathered in this volume: that the social identity of Southerners is antecedent to and the basis of the other components of their selfhood as economic and political, academic and religious men and women.

In accounting for the traditional Southerner's attitudes toward state and society, it is useful to draw some of our terms from English intellectual history. Often I tell my students that their forebears were both Whig and Tory—or rather, a synthesis of the two, being Whig when they sought to chain the Leviathan and Tory when they followed the authority which declares that some will have five talents, some three, and some only one. There is of course a paradox involved in speaking of a corporate bond linking together a people who are, as we read elsewhere in these pages, so proverbially individualistic, so jealous of their personal dignity, and so unwilling to endure affront. But it is a paradox at the heart of the Southern personality, and of the experience of the region's inhabitants of life within the kind of regime indentified by Michael Oakeshott as a *societas*: a nomocratic order in which members "are not partners or colleagues in an enterprise with a common purpose to pursue or a common interest to promote or protect," but are instead "related . . . in terms of a practice"—a common *way*.

As we all know, Southerners, or at least white Southerners, prefer that their lives be very little regulated by the power of a national government. With us, in the formula of Jefferson's First Inaugural, the milder the restraint imposed by that remote authority, the greater our devotion to its preservation. We regard other opinions of the utility of the energetic, positive state as "theoretic and visionary," discounting them *because of* the prior and permanent allegiance which we have given to an entire mesh and network of usually nonjuridical social connections. True, at the level of local and state administration, the *mores majorum* impinge very closely upon the official structures of power. Nothing revolutionary is ordinarily proposed in such a context, and government tends to conserve the regime. Prescriptive law and custom reflect the aforementioned "way" or "practice." And the *Gemeinschaft*, the corporate spirit of the *societas*, swallows the state—not, as in the standard modern practice, the other way around.

To rephrase the matter, the social identity of Southerners does not rest upon a theory concerning the future of their homeland, its goal or meaning as a composite entity. The bond between us is of another, ancient variety. It is in contrast to that kind of connection which Oakeshott marks as the predicate of the conventional modern state, an "enterprise association," whose nature is *not* nomocratic, that is, characterized by a civil practice; but *teleocratic*, that is, defined by an end. In a politicized world, where patriotism attaches to the state rather than to the society, the teleocratic combination results in a civil theology, a polity sustained by big ideas. In its most ambitious form it is a *universitas*, which tends to be all-absorbing of those well-marshaled citizens whose lives it contains. Only with grave difficulty does it coexist with the separable and distinctive components of the *societas* which (in most cases) it replaced; for members of the *societas* are persons, not instruments. But the teleocratic apology for these outrages has always had a certain plausibility, with (in the words of Robert Nisbet) tyranny "concealed under the humane purposes which have brought it into existence."

Because for Southerners everything is social—personal without being too personal—it is no accident that they are distrustful of most types of professionalism, especially the "professional politician." They do not care for transactions conducted in a "strictly business" fashion and prefer at least a civil pretense that there are legitimate personal reasons, based on acquaintance, attitude, and amity, for any commercial exchange. The species of identity that proceeds from a shared enthusiasm for an abstraction or a "target" they recognize as tenuous—as in the operations of a mob. Therefore Southern politics, and also Southern political economy, presuppose the importance of who you are, not what you know, and seek instinctively to minimize the impact on private business of teleocratic positive law. Both are extensions of the social operation, a dynamic of voluntary associations which, according to Nisbet and Oakeshott, the state as *societas* exists to protect. These intermediate institutions which are the repositories of value as negotiated or "discovered" over a long course of history (not metaphysically derived in argument from definition) are: church, union, guild or professional association, neighborhood or place, ethnic identity, political party, club, and (most basic of all) family. Their status in a traditional society is (or is almost) providential, and the essence of their law is private or unwritten. In all of the relationships which they sustain, *being* is prior to *meaning*. They make possible the *communitas communitatum* which the Southern Fathers of the Republic hoped to secure through the American Revolution and the subsequent agreement among the states which we call the Constitution. Southerners here and now, insofar as they recall their upbringing, will agree with Nisbet that, for the sake of our posterity, "what is required . . . is the establishment of a scene in which there is a profound incentive to form, and live in and by, associations or groups which are distinct from political government." The great advantage for the South is that not all of this labor need be done "from scratch."

It is well that we should remember, when asked about the South, that even in war, during its brief experience of political independence, the Southern Confederacy behaved more like a society than like a state. In the field the Confederate Army was an extension of the region's social character, not the embodiment of a separate and antiseptic military "profession" or martial juggernaut. Under generals who were more patriarchs than imitations of Napoleon or Frederick the Great, it resembled in spirit a collection of Scottish Highland clans. When I think of the regional *Gemeinschaft*, I think always of the brigades of Leonidas Polk, Nathan Bedford Forrest, and Sterling "Pap" Price. And of Lee in the Wilderness that day when his men refused to let him assume a position in the line of fire and tugged at the bridle of Traveler until they had turned him aside.

As the expression of a vital and long-lasting bond, a corporate identity assumed by those who have contributed to it, what then is the composite character of *Why the South Will Survive*? For one thing, the essays gathered here take for granted the present reality of the regime of the South, the present relevance of certain cultural parameters which, as Richard Beale Davis has recently demonstrated, go as far back as the original settlement of the region. Except as they bear upon the definition of a still distinctive South as a "going operation," there is very little concern in these essays with the rehearsal of old quarrels or the probing of ancient wounds. To be sure, I find an extraordinary piety for the South as a product of common history, a home place, and a "way" (i.e., a manner of dealing with the inevitable problems of life). Yet this collection says far less of agriculture than I'll Take My Stand or any of the other classic documents of Southern political economy. Nonetheless, the participants in this declaration seem to agree that, despite the great surface changes that are occurring (or have occurred) in our midst, the personal life of Southerners in days to come may not change very much at all! At least if we remember that our social identity, as opposed to our political or economic role, is what finally marks us; that the other components of personal identity derive from that basic social self.

In comparison to the authors of I'll Take My Stand, we are in a number of respects less well agreed. Though we can accept with relish a description of the positive qualities of urban life, on the future of the Southern city there is little of consensus among us. Some (myself included) still have our doubts about the impact of rampant commercial and industrial development of the last sixty years and about what more of the same may produce if allowed to continue unchecked. Senator Horton speaks directly for such uneasiness, as does Mr. Anderson. Others reason to the same effect, though more obliquely. It is a self-evident proposition that what has failed in Detroit or Los Angeles is not to be attempted in Waco or Raleigh-Durham. The pity of it is that we are caught up in a whirlwind and will not accept such truth until we can no longer afford to do otherwise. The spirited individualism of ordinary Southerners analyzed in Professor Reed's contribution may not be expected to survive indefinitely in the context of Atlanta, Memphis, or Houston, most particularly if they all move into apartment complexes, join national labor unions, forget to visit their kinfolks, and attend worship services only by watching them on television. Anomie and antinomy are definitive of life as experienced in our Southern cities; so are divorce and apostasy. The intermediate institutions described so eloquently by Nisbet will be forced to carry a terrible weight, at least for the next two decades, if the South is to survive in character. After that, adjustments will be possible, as the entire American civilization becomes less and less mobile, more and more differentiated into its component parts, less concentrated and more dependent for its prosperity upon the bounty of our agriculture.

Another area of disagreement is obviously that of race. There is some evidence here of relief that it is no longer necessary to discuss the South exclusively in terms of its racial practices and problems. Yet many of us concur with the opinion of Charles Roland in his recent study of the contemporary South, *The Improbable Era,* that race "still matters," and is likely to continue to do so for Southerners black and white. That is, so long as family feeling and a sense of history continue to influence our thought and conduct. Southerners are now aware that their problems with race have not proceeded simply from their political institutions, their resistance to the nostrums of official egalitarianism, their distrust of omnicompetent government. Other Americans who deplore our history and recommend their institutions and their view of equality to our favor clearly do no better in creating racial peace than do we—if indeed they do as well. The guilt of the next generation of white Southerners is more likely to be the guilt of Esau at betrayal and forfeiture of the patrimony than guilt about the Negro. It is mere sanctimony or arrant hypocrisy to pretend, despite the changes of recent decades and the kind of pro forma responses which Southerners now make (say, when questioned by a pollster), that the fact of racial difference will cease to require of us the best of our religion, our judgment, and our manners as we negotiate precisely *how much* and *how little* race will matter within the nexus of a shared way of life. The political balance of power within the nation at large is shifting rapidly in our direction. Soon it should be possible to return the discussion of such delicate considerations to their proper sphere, within the *societas,* and then to make decisions that work toward a reasonable accommodation.

A few curious features of this book also require brief comment. *I'll Take My Stand* was chiefly the handiwork of Tennesseans and Kentuckians. In this collection appear voices from all across the South: from Virginia and Alabama and Texas, and most points in between. But the largest contingent represents the Carolinas. That so many people educated at Chapel Hill should share in such a book seems (if I may be permitted to say so) hopeful evidence that sensible persons can recover from any kind of education—at least if the early formation of their moral nature has been sound and thoroughgoing. Or else it is evidence of some great change at the University of North Carolina. Yet, as were the Vanderbilt Agrarians, most of the participants in this statement are academics; only six represent opinion from "without the pale." Among us are novelists and literary critics, poets and social scientists, historians and political philosophers, who, when listed thus, sound like the mix of special skills found in the assortment of our predecessors. But despite the similarity, there is also a difference in tone separating their book from ours. For one thing, the overall effect of the 1980 symposium is more discursive and deliberate, more under the influence of recent developments in the history of social thought and cultural analysis. The variety of interests reflected in the entire set of papers is also very broad; though emphasizing specific areas of Southern life, they answer many concerns not addressed in the 1930 manifesto. Judge Sentelle and others have quite properly focused on the folk culture of the South. Much more is said about religion than in *I'll Take My Stand*—it is a theme in several essays, and the central subject of three. Yet the emphasis is on the cultural effects of Southern religion, not upon the refinements of doctrine or sectarian disputation. For fifty years have left the South even more isolated in this respect than it was before.

However, once all of these distinctions are made and disagreements acknowledged, what finally surprises the retrospective commentator upon a book assembled from such various and previously unacquainted hands is not difference, but unity. And with that cohesion also a resemblance to our model and prototype. I suspect, to take only three instances, that we can all concur with Professor Brooks's emphasis on the importance of the anti-millenarian bias of the Southern churches, with Dr. Francis on the potential value of that prudent and realistic heritage to the future of American foreign policy, and with Mr. Garrett about the continued vigor of the region's literary performance—an achievement still ignored or misunderstood by the publishers and critical opinion-makers of the Northeast. But such is only a sample, to which I could readily attach additional proofs of near consensus drawn from the comments of Professors Havard or Montgomery, Rogers, Hobson, or Wilson. Even more striking is the evidence provided in these essays of the patria's continuing hold upon its own. After innumerable "epitaphs for Dixie" and endless predictions that regional self-consciousness would disappear with racial "reform," no such book was supposed to be possible. Nor any talk of the region as "not quite a nation within a nation, but the next thing to it." (Except, of course, on election day, when "reactionary" returns from "down there" might continue to irritate the national press.) There is clearly some reality behind such a witness so readily assembled. To share in its expression has given all of us a remarkable satisfaction.

But enough of afterthoughts. Before we undertook to frame this statement, many of us acknowledged to one another that we felt no small trepidation about our chosen enterprise. For, as we knew, we faced, twice over, the danger of presumption: first, a presumption shared with our preceptors, one implicit in any attempt to speak for the South at large; and second, the presumption of measuring ourselves against what they achieved. We foresaw that we would be belabored with the tautology that no group speaks for the South, that we would go against a pious preference for *I'll Take My Stand* as a work forever sufficient to the purpose which it has served, and that we could rightly expect to encounter that species of condescension which attaches to every conscious act of emulation. It is not enough to say that we do *as*, not *what*, the Agrarians did. Collective self-examination of the inherited things must have a present purpose, an end greater than the luxury of seeing ourselves more closely than others are wont to see us. Yet despite such trepidation, we have attempted to heed the admonition of John Crowe Ransom which concludes the "Statement of Principles" in the preface to *I'll Take My Stand*: "If a community, or a section, or a race, or an age, is groaning under industrialism, and well aware that it is an evil dispensation, it must find the way to throw it off. To think that this cannot be done is pusillanimous. And if the whole community, section, race, or age thinks it cannot be done, then it has simply lost its political genius and doomed itself to impotence." Though we might not now agree that the enemy of the regime of the South may be described as simply "industrialism," the perils which it faces are even more demonstrable than a half-century ago. In that belief, we Southerners have come together to make a statement of our own—in that belief, and despite our incidental differences.

In most respects, this group possesses two common denominators: piety toward certain qualities of life and habits of mind which have come down to us from the historic experience of the South as a distinctive culture, and a shared regard for the Twelve Southerners of 1930 and the stand they so boldly took. That a book such as we have made would someday appear was the announced expectation of four of the Agrarians during a "reunion" held in Dallas in the spring of 1968. Recently I reviewed the transcript of their conversations and found there a unanimous encouragement that the work be carried on and the teaching reapplied. John Crowe Ransom, Allen Tate, Robert Penn Warren, and Andrew Lytle were present, as well as the widow of Frank Owsley, Mrs. Harriet Owsley. Also attending was Professor T. D. Young, bearing a message from Donald Davidson, for whose sake the conference had been arranged. Yet, surprisingly, Davidson's absence (he died the following week) did little to soften the conversation into the predictable mixture of nostalgia and rumination. The old dynamic of the group reappeared before the eyes of their hosts, and the declension of our times was identified as a confirmation of their prophecies as younger men. Once again, though now eighty, Ransom spoke for his friends, and the rumor of his withdrawal from the cause of the South was utterly belied. As the discussion focused on what might now be done for their country, for the patria, Ransom queried, "Well now, what about this? Would it be possible . . . to have a new proclamation: there would be a lot of people who would be sympathetic, and they would realize that the time is more crucial now than it was when *I'll Take My Stand* came out. . . . We couldn't scare them in 1930, but I believe now that it's possible. . . . [The young people should not be left] without a doctrine." We could not have a more emphatic laying on of hands.

What, then, shall be our testimony? It is obvious that fifty years of policy and practice contrary to the Agrarian injunction has proven the impossibility of culture "poured in from the top." And though modern American education is as helpless in the role of guardian for civilized values as John Gould Fletcher and his friends foresaw, recent scholarship has provided a rhetoric, a historic and dialectical basis for the analysis that in the original manifesto often rested on custom, instinct, and acute conjecture. The American civil theology is now revealed as the absurdity which once only the South knew it to be. The politics of ends as opposed to means has led to riot and ruin. Megalopolitan industrial centers are clearly on their way to being moribund; nor is it impossible for us to imagine our entire commercial system as the sort of elaborate concrete desert envisaged in Walker Percy's *Love in the Ruins*. Neither can we believe that any new display of what our fathers called "energetic government," performed in the name of some abstract theory of individual human rights, is ever likely to give to the spirit of man the kind of guarantee secured by the old corporate identity of the South as extended family: as I said earlier, the kind of identity summarized for me by the Confederate Army in the field. I have borrowed from Michael Oakeshott the distinction between the nomocratic regime and the teleocratic. Ours is of the former kind; at whatever cost, we must be determined to keep it so. For the alternative is barbarism, though called by some other high-sounding euphemistic names.

To maintain that the South still embodies an obdurate particularity worthy of defense and preservation does not seem to us to be separatism. The New South battle cry, that "sectionalism is unpatriotic," fades into insignificance for those who recognize that only below the old surveyor's line does a great deal of the original American character survive. Those who understand aright the connection between the American Revolution and the War Between the States, Mr. Lincoln's refounding of the Republic, the Gilded Age, Manifest Destiny, and the nation's imperial role in the twentieth century will insist that nothing can be more patriotic than for the South to be itself. This proposition has grown in plausibility since the race problem has ceased to be the peculiar responsibility of our region. And because so many of our countrymen from other sections are deciding every day to come and live among us: making that decision not in the hope of reforming us, but in the expectation that they will reform themselves, even though they are not quite sure how that may be done.

This latest migration out of Zion might well offer an opportunity to give the Yankees what-for for having ruined the country. Such exercises are delightful. But, out of politeness, we have usually confined that teaching to implication and aside. Since they now are somewhat better prepared to listen to us than was heretofore the case, it is enough that we have not imitated the errors of recent collections of this kind with truckling and embarrassment at this or that local weakness from which we wish to be dissociated even before we begin. Our posture has been to take the offensive, and to leave to others the rituals of remorse in which they are more skilled. The measure of any regime, of any economic, social, or political system is its human product. This is an axiom, call it Agrarian or whatever you will. That industrial civilization as we have known it and energetic government *cannot* produce the complete man taken as norm by the Nashville circle is no longer a proposition subject to intelligent dispute. What we were told would be progress has left a vacuum in which solipsism and deracination, Marxism and related nostrums have moved at will. The Gross National Product at its best cannot negate this truth, nor may religion be expected to flourish under such circumstances. What has survived of the South that traced its lineage to the England of the seventeenth and eighteenth centuries is still visible and functioning because agriculture has been the "model," the prototype for all other vocations in which the Southerner joined the public and private things. Stewardship is still an intelligible conception for the host of Southerners who live in clusters surrounding our great cities and who do a work very different from that performed by their ancestors. Real property is yet preferred over other kinds, and liberty is understood by them as being dependent upon their participation in the corporate life, the

intermediate institutions described above. As for equality, Southerners have always known that it was the enemy of moral liberty,
unless restricted in its meaning to signify nothing more than a guarantee against favoritism by those in power toward the members
of their faction. We Southerners are still a people of the law. But
law cannot make men equal, either in opportunity or in condition;
though within the limited sphere of its authority, it may be the same
for whoever comes before it. To offer either more or less is to invite
the reign of envy. As Richard Weaver insisted, a high degree of im-
munity to that besetting modern virus is a major part of the explanation of the survival of the regime. Class struggle we neither have
nor want.

What then should be our counsel to our fellow Southerners, insisting upon all that we have said, yet admitting at the same time
that the South which we defend is a region greatly changed from
what it was in 1930—changed in appearance and in situation, if not
in spirit? First, it is important that we consciously recognize what
our practice specifies that we believe: that a culture is made up of a
set of habits or modes of conduct, "of chairs and tables, songs and
tales," and also of familiar sights and sounds and smells, and finally
of manners. It is a way of life, and not a goal for life, which requires a
deference prior to all analysis. It exists in South Carolina and Tennessee and Texas—not in covenant and eschatology. And also in
speech and in serious literature where the familiar word is given
lasting form. All of these attitudes rest, of course, upon a sound on-
tology, a reluctance to do violence against the given things; upon the
creed of memory, and upon the old Revelation for which, as Professor Landess has recalled to us, our fathers sought no updated re-
placement. Community is grown, not made. To repeat, community
is something anterior, first submitted to and only then examined by
those whose sense of personal worth and joy in life depend upon its
survival. To be sure, all members of a community should feel that
they have a stake in its continuation if their loyalty is to be presumed, but such members must also realize that the whole of that
corporate entity cannot be expected to risk dissolution in order to
gratify the private expectations of any of its component parts.

Of specific recommendations for the future of the South and of
prognostics, there is a sufficiency in the preceding essays. My own
suggestion, which has informed much of my adult life, is that we
cultivate the arts of memory, and thus hope to preserve to our posterity the bond which has heretofore (and I borrow from Burke)
linked together among us "the dead, the living, and the yet unborn."

For the sake of memory let us preserve the iconic things—buildings, monuments, gardens, rites, celebrations, and stories—which have defined us for over three hundred years as a people apart, and which carry in themselves the seeds of restoration as a context for the tradition. Objections to these reminders of an earlier South or to an attention to its history must be resisted, at every turn and with every resource. Those who would destroy the icons and erase that memory are not Southerners as we define the species here, but instead serve chiefly to recall to us why we have never agreed to be "absorbed" by the deracinated abstractions of the Union at large. The Romans taught their sons to look backward in order to prepare for the morrow. Roman literature kept alive the rumor of the Republic and the authority of its example for centuries after the elevation of Augustus. If our friends tell us that these days are dark, then we should recite something like the hopeful formula of Mr. Davidson in his later years, one that he repeated to me many times over: that in order to get better, it must first get a good deal worse. With these priorities observed, our descendants may know that "we have not loosely, through silence, permitted things to pass away as in a dream."

Afterword

A Semi-Centennial

ANDREW LYTLE

FIFTY YEARS, half a century, does not come within the spiral of history. Although the years are fifty, it is not the years which mark it. Most of life passes as do the seasons; but a few events, public and private, remain. Things that count never seem ended. You do not look back; you look at—a kind of perpetual present tense. During the last half-century *I'll Take My Stand* has seldom been out of print. The royalties have been small, the publishers generally uninterested; yet it will not die. It is contemporaneous, not a historical document. Not yet. No better proof can be evinced than these essayists who celebrate its semi-centennial and make their statements—rather, their professions of faith (some of them)—about the South, what theatens it, what distinguishes it from the other regions of the country.

It gives me the occasion to consider how I think about it now. First of all, it seems obvious that the Agrarians were better prophets than they knew. Certainly we failed to get the kind of attention necessary to delay or modify the evils of Industrialism. But we did not think of ourselves as prophets. After the stock market crash of 1929 and the Depression, our hopes were raised for a time that we might be listened to. We were trying to stop something we felt boded no good for our kind of life, which once had been (and still was, to an extent) the dominant kind of life for the entire country.

Family and neighborhood made the world we inhabited. Travel through the countryside today and you will find it empty. People dwell there, but as individuals, except in certain stubborn and traditional pockets. They do not compose a community. Travel to the towns and small cities and they all look stamped out of plastic.

They differ mainly in size. The outskirts hold flat buildings of assembly plants owned from afar; more sinisterly, factories dealing in chemical poisons pollute the countryside. People as well as the towns are beginning to have an anonymous look. Underneath, not quite covered but crowded out of any meaning, like General Lee's house in Richmond, relics of the past stand. They will stand for a while, until the ubiquitous bulldozer or that flinging ball pushes them into some trash heap. I am mindful of the restoration in places like Charleston, Savannah, and New Orleans and elsewhere, but the life which built these dwellings and public buildings has not been restored.

So the Agrarians failed. We failed at least to make any practical impact upon the amoeba-like growth of the machine and its technology. Only recently has it come to me why this is so. No man can know why, but I will venture this: none is prepared for the violent revolution which changes the nature of the familiar. I feel that this is why the communities threatened with extinction only sympathized with the book's protest. They could not believe that *their* way of living would disappear. Well, it has.

I can wish now that *I'll Take My Stand* and the writings that followed had made it clearer that, in defending what was left of Southern life, we were defending our common European inheritance. Maybe the time was not right for that kind of admonition. I did follow Red Warren and Allen Tate in wanting the title of the book to be "Tracts against Communism," but this now seems inadequate. It was too political, as in other times were states' rights and the divine rights of kings. Rights are properties, not the thing itself. States exercise sovereign powers, not rights. It was a tactical error of supreme importance that Southern rights supplanted sovereignty. Nor do Christian kings possess divine rights. They are the secular agents of God.

It takes but one bad idea to ruin a man or a state. The idea that mankind can control nature, and that nature concerns only matter and energy, has lost us belief in the divine order of the universe. Materialism with all its accompanying isms is a sorry substitute. To put it in religious terms, we have lost the covenant with God; we perforce must practice magic. What is magic but the pretense and effort to control nature toward some private end. That end is inevitably power.

I've said it elsewhere, but I'll repeat: The opposite of love is not hatred. It is the addiction to power. Hatred is the eclipse of love, but under proper conditions love can be redeemed. But when the will fails, power can overwhelm love's beneficent properties. Magic in human intercourse manifests itself as lust, abusing and casting aside its object. This is a part of the universal human condition, and the victims can be rescued. But the magical incantation over nature is more indirect as to its effects. Of course, an office must have the power to execute its functions. It is the violation of this power that should concern us, for magic can seem to possess the ultimate secrets of knowledge. It is one thing when an Indian shaman, failing in his incantations to bring rain, blames his failure on the lechery of the young women (never the young men) and points to the flattened bean patches as evidence. If the drought persists, such an excuse fails him, and the tribe puts him to death. But what can we do when our shamans have tampered with alchemical discoveries and released the cataclysmic genii from the jug? The side effects of this malevolent power we cannot neutralize, not even by burying them in the ground. They reappear in mysterious diseases, miscarriages and malformed children, and in the foods of life. They even threaten life itself with sterility.

Because of the loss of the covenant with God, those who rule us at home and in foreign affairs are at a loss as to what to do. These scientists, these economists, these politicians make one incantation after another, but none can agree. None can agree, for they all accept that the trouble is only a matter of managing the machine of state. We have forgot that we are made in the image of God, and schoolchildren are forbidden to pray together.

Those who rule us, wherever they come from, are the inheritors of that power which destroyed the Confederacy and with it the idea of the federal republic, which at least gave lip service to the divine in Deism. I don't see how we can be too hopeful of a Christian regeneration of any institution. Magic obfuscates any enlightenment of present or future ways, but there is solace in the fact that these essayists exhibit belief in the persistence of what we think of as Southern.

We might take further hope from another consideration. There is a north and south the world over, with distinctive characteristics. Provence is different from Normandy. The south and southwest of England which had the only English king called Great is not like the Danelaw. It would be to little purpose to discover whether it is the climate which makes the people or whether the climate draws distinctive natures to flourish as the weather, the seasons, and the land determine. Certainly our geography nourished the family, without which no Christian state can stand. After the physical places which

fix a people in its customs and belief are gone, can the family function as it did when it belonged to a community of families? We
know the answer to this question. The family is the most ancient of
institutions.

In mythology and history old families carry the drama of human
needs, as they watch with jealous interest the safety of the res pub-
lica, even when they undermine its health. Of course, no one family
is older than another, but the families who think of themselves as
old nourish their history, their pride, their fortunes, all qualities
which they feel set them apart and promise longevity. To them the
once-familiar debate between inheritance and environment is an academic question, brought up no doubt by those who had no family.
For them only the bloodlines hold the truth.

As proof from nature, they will point to the thoroughbred. This
prince of animals did not just happen. At the source is always an
Arab horse, and we know that in battle the Arabs carried in a sad-
dlebag the horse's bloodlines, in case of the rider's death. I had an
old cousin who, writing down parts of his descent, in a moment of
absentmindedness shifted an ancestor to the line of a Lindsay Ara-
bian. It didn't seem particularly humorous to him when he discovered his mistake, nor indeed much off the point. His interest was
merely a part of an old habit of calling a family after its farm. The
farm was not only the land; it composed all the creatures inhabiting
it, and all the things that grew. Even Brother Rabbit. This connection is no idle matter, or the sentimentality of pride. It is finally
metaphysical. The identification of man through family with physical nature measures the state of religious belief. This induces a respect for and concord with all of God's creation, and a more practical
knowledge of what to expect from the world. It teaches that you
often eat your meat with sorrow and that you can lose in vital ways
all that is dear. This is the supreme historical admonition we should
accept from the downfall of the Confederacy. Everywhere else in
this nation's "progress" there has been a succession of triumphs, until now. I would hazard the guess, when the true crisis comes, as it
will, that a Southern-born man will step forward and meet it. This
because he has known defeat of his society, because he has eaten his
bread in sorrow—in effect, because he knows what the world is,
that it is not all teatty.

This is not said in pride but out of common sense, which depends
upon the hard learning from experience. Let me extend it and say it
will be someone or many from a republic of families as he or they
oppose the abstract state, usually referred to as the government.

This kind of individual will know himself because of his love for the family. This is not to say that being a member of a family is one long love feast, but it does involve a freedom of intercourse among its members, a hierarchy of order, and the will to defend it or any part of it when threatened. Today the abstract state is totalitarian; that is, the power state, Calhoun's rule of the numerical majority, always controlled by a minority with partial and selfish interests. The Agrarians called it industrial, as did recently the news media in denominating the summit conference of the Western states as the "industrial nations." But whatever we call it, it opposes power to charity, the rule of man to the covenant with God. To repeat, its processes move by the incantations of magic; whereas the family, because of its love for its members and its surroundings, is instinctively religious. It knows that in great stress it must pray; that to bind together, to harmonize the opposites of public and private, it must cherish and sustain ceremony, ritual, the formal conventions which fix the eternal truths in poetic language. (By "poetic" I mean the only language which can translate the eternal mysteries into a simple understanding.)

Manners are the means of discipline and intercourse between members of the family and strangers. Good manners are not only charitable; they also protect us from the world's intrusion, and the world from us. Because of the family's fixity to place and loyalty to kin, it is harder for an absent power, either domestic or foreign, to traduce or manipulate it against its true interests. The proletariat or any group dependent upon wages and social security alone is more easily threatened. But the family has its weaknesses, too. Its innate conservatism and its antipathy to change make it acutely vulnerable to dramatic innovation. This can be from a failure of vision, a rigidity of habit and mores, and too often from an isolation from that which will undo it.

The South, particularly the Old West of Tennessee and Kentucky, experienced an influx of Scottish and Scotch-Irish before and after the annihilation of the Highland clans by the Duke of Cumberland, that archetypal Sherman. This bloc of people brought with them an adherence to the clannish feeling of family, as well as its inboned history of defeat. Their presence gave a distinctive quality to our sense of behavior of the region. The Scotch-Irish were said to keep the Sabbath and everything they laid their hands on. I don't know what bureaucrat so defined them, but the very understanding of themselves was through the family and clan. Clan means children. The chief or captain, as he was earlier called, was kin to everybody under his authority; this is the rule of blood. It had and has its blood feuds and other sins of pride, but I propose it to be more durable than the rule of purse or sword. Even now, when the clan is a sentiment only, our particular sense of family still derives from it. It is the lasting inheritance of the tribe. When it ceases to rule, the state changes its nature, and this usually means into a rule of irresponsible power. During and after its imperial days Athens strained the tribal democracy beyond its capacity. Power to rule others supplanted the will to rule themselves, and brought the Peloponnesian War and ruin.

Although history reveals to the present rulers how the past rulers lost a war or a state, few seem able to learn anything from history. And yet for four hundred years or longer the West has gradually come to look to history for its truths; that is, it has looked to man for the judgment of mankind. It is reported that Hitler said, "If you lie enough, it becomes the truth." Where does this leave history as man's guide? Or where does it leave us all in our present plight, if we do not by some miracle renew the covenant with God?

Contributors

CLYDE N. WILSON is professor of history at the University of South Carolina and editor of the Papers of John C. Calhoun.

JOHN SHELTON REED is professor of sociology at the University of North Carolina at Chapel Hill. He is the author of *The Enduring South: Subcultural Persistence in Mass Society* and other works.

WILLIAM C. HAVARD is chairman of the department of political science at Vanderbilt University and a recent president of the Southern Political Science Association. He has written and edited a number of works, including *The Changing Politics of the South*.

FRED HOBSON is associate professor of English at the University of Alabama. He is the author of *Serpent in Eden: H. L. Mencken and the South* and other works.

HAMILTON C. HORTON, JR., an attorney, has been the leader of his party in the North Carolina General Assembly and has held other public offices.

DON ANDERSON, formerly a member of the staff of the United States House of Representatives, is executive director of the National Association for the Southern Poor, Norfolk.

GEORGE C. ROGERS, JR., is Yates Snowden Distinguished Professor of History at the University of South Carolina, and is the author of numerous works on the history of his state.

SAMUEL T. FRANCIS is a legislative assistant for national security to Senator John P. East of North Carolina.

THOMAS FLEMING has been a professor of classics and headmaster of a private academy in South Carolina, and is the publisher of *Southern Partisan* magazine.

GEORGE GARRETT is a widely heralded poet, novelist, and teacher.

DAVID B. SENTELLE, of Matthews, North Carolina, is an attorney. He has been a district attorney and judge.

THOMAS H. LANDESS is chairman of the department of English at the University of Dallas. He is the author of a study of Julia Peterkin and other works.

MARION MONTGOMERY, professor of English at the University of Georgia, has published novels, poetry, and critical studies.

CLEANTH BROOKS, Gray Professor of Rhetoric Emeritus at Yale University, is a distinguished literary scholar and critic. He contributed an essay on religion to *Who Owns America?*

M. E. BRADFORD is professor of English at the University of Dallas. He is the author of *A Better Guide Than Reason: Studies in the American Revolution* and of numerous other works in and on the Agrarian tradition.

ANDREW LYTLE, who has provided an afterword to the statements of the Fifteen Southerners, is a distinguished novelist and editor emeritus of the *Sewanee Review*. He was a contributor to the Agrarian symposia *I'll Take My Stand: The South and the Agrarian Tradition* (1930) and *Who Owns America? A New Declaration of Independence* (1936).

CPSIA information can be obtained
at www.ICGtesting.com
Printed in the USA
FFOW03n1243161215
19571FF